Student Knowledge & Skills

	Core Subjects	21st Century Themes	Learning and Innovation Skills	Information & Technology	
Early Stage	Student work primarily demonstrates rote factual knowledge in core academic subjects.	Themes like civic literacy, financial literacy, entrepreneurial literacy, health literacy and environmental literacy are occasionally represented in student work, most often in the form of one-time special projects.	Up to 25% of student work in core academic subjects may display higher order thinking skills like critical thinking and problem solving.	Up to 25% of student core academic subjects display information literacy, media literacy and ICT literacy.	academic subjects may display self-direction, flexibility, adaptability, cross-cultural awareness, responsibility, productivity and accountability.

Transitional Stage

Student work demonstrates mastery of core academic subject knowledge.

Between 25-75% of student work demonstrates higher order thinking skills like critical thinking and problem solving in the context of core academic subjects.

Understanding of at least one of the following 21st century themes is evidenced in K-12 student work: civic literacy, financial literacy, health literacy and/or environmental literacy.

21st Century

All student work demonstrates mastery and understanding of core academic disciplinary knowledge.

Additionally, over 75% of student work demonstrates:

- Mastery and understanding of civic literacy, financial literacy, global awareness, health literacy and environmental literacy.

- The ability to think critically, problem solve, create, innovate, communicate and collaborate.

- Information, media and technology literacy.

- Self-direction, flexibility, adaptability, cross-cultural awareness, responsibility, productivity and accountability.

- The ability to "learn how to learn" and application of this ability to self-monitor and improve learning progress across all subjects.

Students are active collaborators in the teaching and learning process (e.g., students act as co-creators of knowledge along with other students, teachers and education leaders; students help identify, craft and complete meaningful capstone projects and other inquiry-based learning experiences).

Every student creates and manages his/her progress in an age-appropriate personal learning plan that includes his/her goals for content knowledge and skill acquisition inside school (classes and class work) and outside school (afterschool, employment, extracurricular).

Education Support Systems

	Standards	Curricula	Instruction
Early Stage	Up to 25% of core academic content standards integrate 21st century skills.	Curricula design processes focus primarily on core academic content knowledge. Up to 25% of core academic content curricula explicitly integrate 21st century skills.	Most instructional strategies are teacher led and focused exclusively on a subject-matter based approach (e.g., lectures, presentation of facts). Learning activities tend to be the same for all students.
Transitional Stage	Between 25-75% of academic content standards integrate 21st century skills.	Between 25-75% of core academic content curricula explicitly integrate 21st century skills along with global awareness, civic literacy, financial literacy, health literacy and environmental literacy. Curricula design processes occasionally follow backwards-design principles (e.g., Understanding by Design) that identify 21st century skills as key outcomes.	Between 25-75% of instructional strategies utilize a student-centered approach to teaching and learning core academic subjects and 21st century skills (e.g., differentiated instruction, inquiry-based learning). Some educators develop and use lesson plans with outcomes for both core subject content mastery and 21st century skills development (e.g., a single unit may be developed with an increased emphasis on critical thinking and problem solving).
21st Century	Standards in all academic content areas integrate 21st century skills in age- and subject-appropriate ways that are observable and measurable. All academic content standards communicate the "big ideas" that should frame the teaching and learning of core academic subject knowledge and enable deep mastery (avoiding the "mile wide, inch deep" problem). All academic content standards incorporate the appropriate use of technology tools. All academic content standards operate as part of an aligned system of curriculum, assessments and professional development.	Over 75% of core academic content curricula explicitly integrate 21st century skills. All curricula design teams utilize best practices for backwards-design (e.g., Understanding by Design) that identify 21st century skills as key outcomes. Curricula processes and decisions are regularly reviewed and/or redesigned to enable deep academic content knowledge and 21st century skills mastery. Curricula materials in every grade and subject provide clear guidance to practitioners on how to "unpack the standards" and teach for understanding, with a purposeful focus on 21st century skills (e.g., 21st century skills curricula mapping has been completed and implemented; curricula-embedded 21st century skills assessments are common.)	Educators develop and teach units and lessons that are designed to enhance deep mastery of core subject knowledge and 21st century skills (e.g., lessons are rigorous and relevant to student experiences, and call for authentic application of knowledge and understanding). Educators use developmentally appropriate practices to differentiate instruction and optimize a student's ability to master 21st century skills (e.g., feedback on 21st century skills mastery is timely and geared toward individual learning styles). Instructional practice actively engages students in the planning and implementation of teaching and learning activities. Educators construct lessons that enable a student's progression from teacher-led to self-directed learning.

Education Support Systems

	Assessments	Learning Environments	Professional Development
Early Stage	Up to 25% of student work is assessed at the classroom level for mastery of 21st century skills.	Up to 25% of decisions surrounding learning environments include considerations for supporting student mastery of 21st century skills (e.g., parents and students can access school records, assignments and performance information online).	Professional development primarily focuses on improving educator capacity to teach core academic content. Up to 25% of professional development opportunities are available regardless of time or place (e.g., there is easy access to self-paced, technology-enabled professional development environments). Some professional development opportunities focus on 21st century skills and/or themes like global competence or civic literacy.
Transitional Stage	Between 25-75% of student work is assessed at the classroom level for mastery of 21st century skills. Capstone projects and portfolios are used in select circumstances to assess student performance (e.g., portfolio-based assessments exist primarily in gifted programs or limited scale pilot projects).	Between 25-75% of decisions surrounding learning environments include considerations for supporting student mastery of 21st century skills (e.g., physical spaces and online tools enable collaboration).	Between 25-75% of professional development focuses on improving educator capacity to teach core academic content in ways that enhance 21st century skills (e.g., training opportunities cover the teaching of global competence in the context of core academic subjects, designing project-based and inquiry-based units, or the development of 21st century skills rubrics for classroom use). Between 25-75% of professional development opportunities are available regardless of time or place (e.g., easy access to technology-enabled professional development environments). Professional development opportunities are customized and personalized. Best practices around the integration of 21st century skills are available and showcased.
21st Century	Student progress in mastering core subjects and 21st century skills is measured over time through a comprehensive, balanced assessment approach (e.g., formative, benchmark, summative and/or large-scale assessments). Over 75% of student work is evaluated at the classroom level for mastery of 21st century skills. A variety of classroom-based assessment strategies are commonly used for all students, including portfolios, capstone projects, performance-based assessments and curricula-embedded assessments, among others (e.g., these are widely used across all student populations). Students are active participants in recording and understanding their classroom performance and use this understanding to guide and refine their work. Education leaders, educators, students and parents have access to a wide range of 21st century skills assessment data to inform and improve 21st century skills mastery in real time. All assessment data is generated, shared and used as part of a transparent and aligned system of measurement that supports improvements in student learning (e.g., classroom, district, state and national data can be combined and/or disaggregated as needed to inform improvement at all levels of the teaching and learning process: individual students, student sub-populations, programs, professional development, curriculum, etc.).	Over 75% of learning environments support the teaching and learning of 21st century skills by: • Providing physical and technology structures that are flexible and adaptable, enable collaborative group work and encourage engagement with the surrounding community. • Offering flexible units of time that enable interdisciplinary project-based teaching and learning. • Designing environments in response to best understanding of developmentally appropriate practices for supporting the whole child (e.g., school time of day, length of instructional blocks, sequence of learning activities throughout a school year, physical and emotional safety, full engagement with school and community, etc.). • Providing appropriate technology infrastructure and tools that support student acquisition of 21st century skills. • Providing every student with a personal learning plan that articulates the school's role in supporting student mastery of core academic content and 21st century skills.	Over 75% of professional development focuses on improving educator capacity to teach core academic content for understanding, in ways that enhance 21st century skills mastery (e.g., training opportunities support educators in developing 21st century skills assessments for classroom use, supporting teacher leaders in 21st century skills integration, developing capstone projects and/or integrating inquiry-based strategies into practice). Professional development is job-embedded, customized, collaborative and technology-infused; it is both formatively and summatively assessed; it is available regardless of time or place. All educators have access to and use capacity-building learning communities, professional coaches, technology infrastructure and instructional tools that enhance student mastery of 21st century skills. Teaching standards, teacher preparation and teacher certification processes integrate 21st century skills.

	Administrators and Teacher Leaders	**Educators**
Early Stage	Education leaders promote core academic content mastery as the primary vision for student achievement. Some education leaders express support for strategic planning around 21st century skills. Education leaders have identified high priority issues related to equitable education opportunity and have established measurable goals for the district (e.g., access to quality teachers and schools, access to technology, IDEA, etc.).	Educators act primarily as providers of core academic subject content (e.g., facts are shared in a one-way, teacher-to-student transmission). Instructional strategies are focused on subject matter mastery. Technology use is occasionally integrated into lessons.
Transitional Stage	Education leaders promote deep content mastery along with some 21st century skills as the vision for student achievement. Education leaders initiate occasional, small-scale pilot projects that purposefully focus on 21st century skills in the context of core academic subjects. Education leaders actively address high-priority equity issues and monitor progress around them (e.g., access to quality teachers, access to technology, IDEA, etc.).	Between 25-75% of educators employ instructional strategies that purposefully develop mastery of 21st century skills in the context of core subjects. Educators facilitate student acquisition of core subject knowledge and applied 21st century skills using a range of methods including direct instruction, collaborative projects and technology-infused assignments.
21st Century	Education leaders have developed consensus around a vision for student learning that includes both core academic content mastery and 21st century skills. Education leaders communicate this vision regularly among the broader community. Education leaders promote, facilitate, model and support the comprehensive integration of 21st century skills into curricula, professional development, instructional practices, accountability systems, resources, management and operations. Administrators include educator mastery of 21st century skills as a component of performance evaluations. Education leaders include student mastery of 21st century skills as a criterion for evaluating school and district performance. Education leaders hold themselves accountable for accomplishing stated yearly goals regarding equitable education opportunity. Teacher leaders are well-integrated in every school; these teacher leaders model and foster integration of teaching and learning of 21st century skills so that all educators can model skills like creativity, critical thinking and problem solving (e.g., they facilitate 21st century skills-related mentoring, peer support, induction of new practitioners, professional learning communities, professional development, etc.).	Over 75% of educators employ an appropriate and diverse range of instructional strategies from direct instruction to project-based learning that purposefully develop deep understanding of core subjects and student mastery of 21st century skills. All educators have access to and independently pursue 21st century skills-related learning communities and/or professional development opportunities. All educators use learning communities to collaboratively and systematically review student work and plan for instruction related to student mastery of 21st century skills.

Policymaking

Policymakers

Education policy making focuses primarily on policies that support student content mastery.

Up to 25% of standards, assessments, professional development and curricula are aligned and include 21st century skills.

Licensure of educators and accreditation of teacher education institutions focus on pedagogy and mastery of core subjects.

Education policy making integrates some 21st century skills (e.g., critical thinking, problem solving, technology literacy, global awareness and/or civic literacy) into policies that support student content mastery.

Between 25-75% of standards, assessments, professional development and curricula are aligned and include 21st century skills.

Licensure of educators and accreditation of teacher education institutions incentivize the integration of some 21st century skills, such as technology literacy, into programs.

Consistently set policy that supports student mastery of 21st century skills.

Ensure appropriate funding to support and monitor progress on the comprehensive integration of 21st century skills across the education system.

Create tangible incentives for educators to lead, teach and assess 21st century skills.

Act as advocates at the local, state and federal levels for an evidence-based accountability system that strengthens student mastery of 21st century skills.

Ensure that all standards, assessments, professional development and curricula are aligned, and include 21st century skills.

Ensure that state policies are aligned with districts and schools to ensure 21st century skills integration and implementation.

Develop criterion for licensure of educators and accreditation of teacher education institutions that includes the comprehensive integration of 21st century skills.

Invest in assessments and professional development that cover student mastery of 21st century skills.

Incentivize/utilize educational cooperatives (education service agencies) as major resource centers for professional development of 21st century skills.

Partnering

	Parents	Business	Community
Early Stage	Up to 25% of parents have 24/7 online access to student performance information. Parents participate annually in school-based planning discussions.	Businesses occasionally collaborate with K-12 partners to address student workforce preparedness and college readiness issues. Businesses occasionally support K-12 schools with technology programs and/or infrastructure.	Community leaders have expressed interest in establishing a regional education and workforce strategy for improving mastery of 21st century skills. Some K-12 leaders, community organizations, public agencies, libraries and museums occasionally share resources and facilities to benefit the larger community. Some educational associations and professional organizations have expressed interest in developing collaborative community work around 21st century skills.
Transitional Stage	Between 25-75% of parents have 24/7 online access to student performance information. Parents occasionally partner with the school and local community organizations to support student acquisition of 21st century skills (e.g., parents help identify and support extracurricular, afterschool and/or other opportunities that advance student mastery of 21st century skills).	Business leaders participate in an annual discussion with K-12 leaders to identify key priorities in preparing students for the 21st century workforce and higher education. Businesses occasionally support K-12 schools and students by providing relevant internships and/or mentors that enhance student mastery of 21st century skills.	Community leaders have initiated and completed a 21st century skills community scan, identified the highest priority skills and established partnerships among community groups to begin addressing these needs. Some community programs purposefully focus on 21st century skills mastery among citizens. Community leaders regularly partner with K-12 leaders to initiate innovative projects that address 21st century skills in the community. K-12 leaders, community organizations, public agencies, libraries and museums regularly share resources and facilities to benefit the larger community. Educational coalitions, associations and/or professional organizations have initiated a regional or statewide project around 21st century skills.
21st Century	Over 75% of parents have 24/7 online access to student performance information, including student progress on mastery of 21st century skills. Parents regularly partner with the school and local community organizations to support student acquisition of 21st century skills (e.g., parents serve on 21st century skills-related school committees; parent organizations initiate and support school activities that focus on 21st century skills). Parents understand the importance and relevance of the 21st century skills teaching and learning vision and act as advocates in the larger community (i.e., beyond the immediate school) to build support for the integration of 21st century skills in formal and informal learning environments (e.g., in school, at home, and through afterschool programs, internships, jobs, etc.).	Business leaders regularly engage in meaningful dialogue with education leaders, in both formal (strategic planning, vision setting) and informal (volunteering) settings around the skills needed for workplace and higher education success. Business leaders participate with schools in an annual review of K-12 and community-based educational opportunities that enhance student mastery of 21st century skills. Business leaders provide every high school student with well-mentored internships and other opportunities that strengthen 21st century skills. Business partners with schools to create innovative programs that foster 21st century skills (e.g., creating a student-run credit union).	Community leaders have developed consensus around a 21st century skills vision for the "learning systems" available to all citizens and communicate this vision across a number of available formats (traditional media, social media, community gatherings, etc.). Non-K-12 learning organizations consult annually with K-12 leaders, community organizations, public institutions (e.g. museums, libraries), businesses and others to continually refine the community's and/or region's approach to strengthening 21st century skills, not just for students but for all citizens. Community-based learning partners (museums, libraries, afterschool programs, informal learning organizations, etc.) publish an annual listing of programs specifically geared for students that are aligned with the K-12 approach to 21st century skills. Community-based approaches to 21st century skills are part of an aligned, comprehensive economic and workforce development strategy that supports the entire region. Educational coalitions, associations and/or professional organizations are active leaders and collaborators around local and regional 21st century skills-based projects.

Partnering

	Higher Education	**Vendors**
Early Stage	Up to 25% of teacher education programs have integrated 21st century skills teaching and learning into the graduation requirements for all preservice students. K-12 and higher education leaders occasionally work together to enhance student readiness for college, but rarely emphasize 21st century skills.	Vendors offer content, tools and resources that support student mastery of core subjects. Vendors provide technology-enabled resources, assessments and curriculum.
Transitional Stage	Between 25-75% of teacher education programs have integrated 21st century skills teaching and learning into the graduation requirements for all preservice students. K-12 and higher education leaders often work together to enhance student readiness for college, including some 21st century skills. Research is occasionally conducted in colleges of education around effective teaching, learning and assessment methods regarding 21st century skills mastery.	Vendors offer content, tools and resources that support student mastery of core subjects along with some 21st century skills. Vendors provide regular opportunities for K-12 leaders to provide input on 21st century skills content, tools and resources. Most vendor materials are offered in digital as well as traditional formats.
21st Century	Over 75% of teacher education programs ensure that all candidates participate in field experiences that require the integration and use of 21st century skills teaching strategies. Education leadership programs emphasize faculty development of 21st century skills. Also, education leaders learn and practice strategies for fostering continuous learning of practitioners, creating environments in which educators collaborate and develop lessons that enhance students' acquisition of 21st century skills. Faculty members possess and utilize a strong, current base of professional and pedagogical knowledge and skills including 21st century skills, themes and core subject knowledge. Faculty members conduct active research to determine successful pedagogies and other practices that enhance the teaching and learning of 21st century skills. Results are shared with policymakers and educators across the K-12 learning system. Student mastery of 21st century skills is articulated as a requirement for matriculation and college readiness.	Vendors create content, tools and resources that comprehensively integrate student mastery of core subjects and 21st century skills in ways that are observable and measurable. Vendors invest in evidence-based, technology-enabled resources, assessments and curriculum that deepen content understanding and 21st century skills mastery among students. Vendors invest in research and development that leads to improved teaching and assessing of 21st century skills. Vendors develop robust human capital and professional development tools that support 21st century skills mastery among education leaders, practitioners and other educators.

States, Districts, Schools

Early Stage

Some districts and schools have developed consensus around a vision and measurable goals for student mastery of 21st century learning.

Transitional Stage

The district's strategic planning documents reflect 21st century skills as key imperatives.

Districts and schools track measurable goals related to student mastery of 21st century skills.

States, districts and schools document and share examples of administrator, educator and student use and application of 21st century skills teaching and learning.

Current district and school policies, procedures, operations and practices have been inventoried for their effectiveness at supporting 21st century learning.

21st Century

States, districts and schools are implementing a vision for student mastery of 21st century skills (e.g., the district's strategic planning and budget reflect 21st century skills as key imperatives).

States, districts and schools monitor and track their success over time at incorporating 21st century skills across the system.

District leaders honor and publicize 21st century skills best practices in schools.

Districts rely on a balanced mix of assessment data along with other indicators to drive continuous school and district improvement around 21st century skills.

State, district and school policies support district-based continuous improvement efforts around 21st century skills.

What Are Leaders Saying about This Book and Its Authors?

"*The Leader's Guide to 21st Century Education* is a terrific resource for educators prepared to make the substantive changes essential to improving our schools. The authors recognize that providing students with 21st century skills will require educators to become deeply engaged in the collective inquiry, consensus building, collaborative efforts, action research, and shared learning essential to the process of continuous improvement. Kay and Greenhill don't provide a quick-fix program or easy answers. They instead offer something far more valuable—insights into the important questions educators must consider if they are to meet the needs of contemporary students. *The Leader's Guide to 21st Century Education* makes an important contribution to the school-improvement literature, and I *highly* recommend it."

—Rick DuFour, Educational Author and Consultant

"Ken Kay and Valerie Greenhill have provided an invaluable contribution to the education reform movement by articulating a step-by-step guide designed to assist district leaders interested in creating 21st century education school systems. With practical examples and specific guidelines delineating the practices of high performing systems, this book lays out a concrete vision and roadmap for delivering the educational outcomes that our children will need for success in 21st century work and civic life."

—Barbara Chow, Program Director, Education Program, William & Flora Hewlett Foundation

"In this book, Ken Kay and Valerie Greenhill offer an insightful, practical, and highly readable roadmap to lead our schools and districts on a journey that prepares all students for lives of purpose, service, and productive and creative work in the 21st century. Grounded in their pioneering work with leadership teams to promote 21st century skills they have crafted a book that can be read with equal benefit independently or as part of a collective effort of a leadership team that has stepped up to prepare all students to invent the future. Anyone concerned about the future of education should read this book."

—Fernando M. Reimers, Ford Foundation Professor of International Education, Harvard Graduate School of Education

"We need young people who are effective problem solvers," declare Kay and Greenhill, students who know "how to apply the knowledge they have to contexts [with which] they may not be familiar." *The Leader's Guide to 21st Century Education: 7 Steps for Schools and Districts* offers a framework for re-creating education in our schools to prepare our students for life in the 21st century. Using roadmaps, real life stories, and lessons learned, this book skillfully leads educators through such thickets as accountability, resistance to change, and the false dichotomy posed between teaching skills and teaching content. An important and welcome addition to a crucial discussion taking place in education today!"

—Daniel A. Domenech, Executive Director, American Association of School Administrators

"Kay and Greenhill have amassed a huge amount of material on 21st century teaching and learning and put it into a clear, readable, user-friendly format. This book is more than a "guide," it is the ultimate blueprint for realizing transformation in our schools. Outlining what it will take to lead, guide, nurture and implement the 4Cs (critical thinking, communication, collaboration, and creativity) through teaching and learning in our schools—it is a must-read for education leaders striving to develop 21st century learners.

I am especially pleased that school board members around the country (many of whom have been active proponents of 21st century education) will be able to leverage this valuable resource to help move their districts forward."

—Anne L. Bryant, Executive Director, NSBA

"In a rare move, unique in today's reform climate, education thought leaders Ken Kay and Valerie Greenhill offer a framework for schools that embraces critical thinking, communication, collaboration, and creativity. With *The Leader's Guide to 21st Century Education: 7 Steps for Schools and Districts*, Ken and Valerie lay out an action agenda for creating school environments where educators are decision makers and students are active learners, resulting in well-educated communities."

—Dennis Van Roekel, President, National Education Association

"This book provides the practical guide for converting aspiration into reality for any school leader determined to implement the changes that result in student learning outcomes that are truly relevant to the 21st century. Ken Kay and Valerie Greenhill have been national leaders in defining the education all students need; now they have brought their vast experience to bear on the individual school.

Changing education policy is a long and murky process. This seven-step practical guide prepares every committed educator to begin changing students' lives immediately.

While this book is about how to implement real change at the school site, it should be required reading for every legislator and policymaker who can see firsthand the impact of the policies they enact while gaining greater appreciation for what needs to be done."

—Bob Wise, President, Alliance for Excellent Education

"Ken Kay and Valerie Greenhill have more than earned the right to do a book like this. No one did more to heighten the awareness of educators and others about the new set of skills that are now called 21st century. Through the Partnership for 21st Century Skills and EdLeader21, they took big concepts, connected them to policy, and anchored them in the reality of districts and schools. This guide gives all of us the roadmap we need to create learning environments truly designed to prepare our children for jobs and opportunities we can't even imagine."

—Ronald Thorpe, President and CEO, National Board for Professional Teaching Standards

"Ken Kay and Valerie Greenhill offer exceptional advice for transforming schools for 21st century learning. Leaders at all levels will find tremendous guidance on their path toward educational success for all students. This book recognizes the essential role of professional learning communities in preparing adults and students for the 21st century. It is practical, powerful, and inspirational."

—Stephanie Hirsh, Executive Director,
LearningForward (formerly National Staff Development Council)

"Ken and Valerie have spent much of the last decade traveling the country on behalf of 21st Century Skills. This book recalls many of the ideas and examples they have encountered and collects them for the first time in a form that is both accessible and inspirational for schools and districts eager to begin the challenging work of school transformation. This book will be an important addition to the library of any educational leader who is interested in implementing 21st century skills."

—Tim Magner, Executive Director, Partnership for 21st Century Skills

"As a nation, we have an opportunity to incorporate the Common Core [State Standards] with the 21st century skills necessary for all students to succeed. Ken and Valerie have taken the last decade of their work to create a compelling framework for us all to follow. The framework and processes outlined in this book create a toolkit for leading 21st century learning in your school district and community. Their suggested processes apply the 4Cs—creativity, collaboration, communication, and critical thinking—to help you create a 21st century school district supported by a 21st century community. They urge us to use the 4 Cs to create the 4 Cs.

Following the seven steps outlined in the book will enable us to demonstrate the leadership and direction in education that this nation desperately needs."

—Jack Dale, Superintendent, Fairfax County Public Schools

"District leaders who want to prepare their students for success in the future must embrace 21st century learning. But what IS 21st century learning, how can district leaders assess where they are, where they need to go, and what they should do when they "get there?" Ken Kay and Valerie Greenhill's book provides that roadmap and more. In addition to providing a seven-step model for success, it also highlights best practices across the country, and provides opportunities for growth and reflection during the journey."

—Cathy Gassenheimer, Exec. VP, Alabama Best Practices Center; A+ Education Partnership

"We, as educators, need to align what we are doing with what the changing world is demanding. Ken Kay and Valerie Greenhill of Ed Leader21 have identified seven steps that support the creation of relevant, 21st century schools and districts. While implementation of these steps may not be linear, they provide a solid framework for shifting the paradigm. The descriptions of these steps clearly inform us of the complexity and depth required to prepare students for futures unknown, because of the changing world. Part of the "unknown" is brought into view with real examples from the trailblazers engaged in this work. Pay attention. This is an important and urgent message."

—Karen Aka, Chief Academic Officer, Academy21

"Without question, America's K-12 education sector is a topic of much concern and debate. Reforms abound as we struggle to maintain and advance America's historic global educational advantage. We must be careful to be mindful of key goals of education as we look for solutions to our challenges. Shortsighted accountability solutions that are driven by simple-minded notions of education outcomes will drive us in the wrong direction. This book helps keep us properly focused on critical thinking, communication, collaboration, and creativity. Kay and Greenhill provide ample argument for why these are important goals, but even more importantly, they provide a roadmap for education leaders to actually achieve them. Based on their years of experience in the policy and implementation arenas, they present plenty of excellent examples of how school districts across the country serving a wide range of students can achieve true 21st century outcomes.

This book is more than a must-read for school leaders and aspiring leaders, it is a shop manual for success. It needs to be dog-eared and underlined with lots of notes in the margins."

—Ron Marx, Dean, College of Education, University of Arizona

"This is not just another book about why we must reshape and redefine our 20th century education system to enable young people to excel and thrive in a 21st century world. Based on the best lessons learned from the field, this book offers a set of groundbreaking strategies to help school leaders build the kind of learning environments that are truly transformative for the 21st century. With over a decade of policy work and applied research at their fingertips, Kay and Greenhill have created an accessible and rich menu of options that can be effectively implemented by educators who wish to lead."

—Margaret Honey, President and CEO, New York Hall of Science

The Leader's Guide to 21st Century Education

7 Steps for Schools and Districts

Ken Kay

Valerie Greenhill

PEARSON

Boston   Columbus   Indianapolis   New York   San Francisco   Upper Saddle River
Amsterdam   Cape Town   Dubai   London   Madrid   Milan   Munich   Paris   Montreal   Toronto
Delhi   Mexico City   São Paulo   Sydney   Hong Kong   Seoul   Singapore   Taipei   Tokyo

Vice President, Editor in Chief: Aurora Martînez Ramos
Executive Editor: Linda Ashe Bishop
Senior Acquisitions Editor: Kelly Villella Canton
Editorial Assistant: Annalea Manalili
Senior Marketing Manager: Christine Gatchell
Project Manager: Karen Mason
Manufacturing Buyer: Megan Cochran
Text Designer: Element LLC
Manager, Rights and Permissions: Robert Tonner
Manager, Cover Visual Research & Permissions: Diane Lorenzo
Cover Designer: Jenny Hart
Cover Art: Provided courtesy of EdLeader21
Full-Service Project Management and Composition: Element LLC
Text Design and Illustrations: Element LLC
Printer/Binder: Edwards Brothers Malloy
Interior Photos: Author photos: Britta VanVranken;
   interior photo (of butterfly): © Gregg Williams/Fotolia

Credits and acknowledgments borrowed from other sources and reproduced, with permission, in this textbook appear on appropriate page within text.

Many of the designations by manufacturers and sellers to distinguish their products are claimed as trademarks. Where those designations appear in this book, and the publisher was aware of a trademark claim, the designations have been printed in initial caps or all caps.

Between the time website information is gathered and then published, it is not unusual for some sites to have closed. Also, the transcription of URLs can result in typographical errors. The publisher would appreciate notification where these errors occur so that they may be corrected in subsequent editions.

Library of Congress Cataloging-in-Publication Data
Kay, Ken, author.
   The leader's guide to 21st century education: 7 steps for schools and districts/Ken Kay, Valerie Greenhill.
        pages cm
   ISBN 978-0-13-211759-3 (alk. paper)
  1. School management and organization—United States.   2. Educational leadership—United States.   I. Greenhill, Valerie, author. II. Title.
   LB2801.A2K39 2013
   371.20973—dc23
                                                                 2012015751

     7 8 9 10   V036   15 14

www.allynbaconmerrill.com

ISBN 10:   0-13-211759-2
ISBN 13: 978-0-13-211759-3

This book is dedicated to
all educators who have the courage to lead us
to a new model of education worthy of our 21st century students.

A Note from the Publisher

CourseSmart eBook and other eBook Options Available

CourseSmart is an exciting choice for purchasing this book. As an alternative to purchasing the printed book, you may purchase an electronic version of the same content via CourseSmart for a PC or Mac and for Android devices, or an iPad, iPhone, and iPod Touch with CourseSmart Apps. With a CourseSmart eBook, you can read the text, search through it, make notes online, and bookmark important passages for later review. For more information or to purchase access to the CourseSmart eBook for this text, visit **http://www.coursesmart.com**.

Look for availability of alternative eBook platforms and accessibility for a variety of devices on **www.mypearsonstore.com** by inserting the ISBN of this text and searching for access codes that will allow you to choose your most convenient online usage.

About the Authors

Ken Kay is the Chief Executive Officer of EdLeader21.

Ken has been the leading voice for 21st century education for the past decade. He co-founded the Partnership for 21st Century Skills in 2002 and served as its President for eight years.

As executive director of the CEO Forum on Education and Technology, he led the development of the StaR Chart (School Technology & Readiness Guide), used by schools across the country to make better use of technology in K–12 classrooms.

Ken spent 28 years in Washington, DC, where he gained a national reputation as a coalition builder on competitiveness issues in education and industry—particularly policies and practices that support innovation and technology leadership. He founded a landmark coalition of U.S. universities and high-tech companies focused on research and development issues. He also was the founding Executive Director of the premier CEO advocacy group in the U.S. computer industry.

Ken is a graduate of Oberlin College and the University of Denver, College of Law. He and his wife, Karen, have three adult children, a daughter-in-law, and a grandson, Ollie. They live in the desert outside Tucson, Arizona, with their golden retriever, Bisbee.

Valerie Greenhill is the Chief Learning Officer of EdLeader21.

Valerie leads EdLeader21's capacity building work. She is currently focused on supporting district leaders in their efforts to integrate the 4Cs—critical thinking, communication, collaboration, and creativity—into assessment and curricula systems. She leads member work in key national initiatives such as the PISA-Based Test for Schools pilot, 21st Century District Criteria, and 4Cs Rubrics.

From 2004–2010, Valerie served as the Director of Strategic Initiatives for P21 (Partnership for 21st Century Skills), where she established and led work to integrate career and college readiness skills into standards, assessments, curricula, instruction, and professional development. She focused extensively on the assessment of 21st century skills, developing numerous tools and resources to advance the organization's goals.

Valerie earned an M.Ed. in educational media and computers from Arizona State University and a master's in English from the University of Arizona. She is an honors graduate of Vassar College.

Valerie was raised in Tishomingo, Oklahoma and has made Tucson, Arizona her home since 1993; She is active in her community, currently serving as Board President of the Children's Museum Tucson.

She lives with her husband, two daughters, and a very cool but high-maintenance Tibetan Terrier.

Acknowledgments

The number of colleagues and friends who contributed to this book is astounding. We are so grateful for your time, support, and encouragement. Thank you to:

- Our EdLeader21 team—Alyson Nielson, without you we could not have written this book, period; Mary Buckley, your tireless copyediting, proofing, and logistics kept us sane (and more accurate); Melissa Briones, your support of the entire team makes everything run more smoothly.
- The many advisors whose strategic advice helped establish the focus for EdLeader21 and, therefore, this book—Terry Crane, Karen Bruett, Bob Pearlman, and Mark Strickland; we'd also like to thank John Kenny—your support in the early stages of this work was crucial to our success.
- The education leaders who have joined EdLeader21 and are implementing 21st century education in your schools and districts. Your dedication to your students is inspiring.
- The teachers, principals, and administrators who have been so generous with their time; thank you for allowing us to learn from you and highlight your best practices in this book.
- Our colleagues in the field of education whose research, experience, and views inform our own throughout this book.
- All of the people and organizations that have supported the Partnership for 21st Century Skills—you helped get the 21st century education movement started and you continue to build its momentum. We are grateful for your leadership and for the P21 staff's diligent work.
- Kelly Villela Canton, our editor at Pearson, who guided us toward the seven steps focus that became this book; thanks also to the rest of the Pearson team—Nancy Forsyth, Aurora Martinez, Linda Bishop, Karen Mason, Annalea Mannalili, Krista Clark, Christine Gatchell—who helped shape, produce, and publish the manuscript; and to the team at Element LLC—managed by Katie Wilbur—who physically took our manuscript and transformed it into the formatted pages.
- The many organizations who have provided valuable support: the William and Flora Hewlett Foundation, Pearson Foundation, KnowledgeWorks, EF Education First, and Houghton Mifflin Harcourt. We'd like to especially acknowledge Barbara Chow, Kathy Hurley, Mark Nieker, Matt Williams, Kate Berseth, and Laura Murray for your unwavering support and sage counsel.
- Those of you who are reading this book and considering joining us on our collective 21st century education journey.

Thank you all for being part of our work on 21st century education.

—Ken and Valerie

One Important and Final Thank You

To my wife, Karen: Karen, without your incredible devotion and commitment to me, 21st century skills, and this book, the last decade would not have been possible. Thanks for always bringing three more Cs into my life: cheer, compassion, and clarity. To my kids and grandson: Bergen, Braden, Jeff, Sarah, and Ollie, you are the 21st century and it is in good hands—thanks for providing me the inspiration to keep going. To Oma: Mom, you inspired all of us. To my collaborator and colleague, Val—thanks for our years of work together. You have really taught me the value of collaboration, critical thinking, communication, and creativity. We have lived it.

—Ken

To Andrew Greenhill, my husband—I appreciate you being such an insightful, enthusiastic sounding board during this process, for making all the extra lunches for our girls and for your good humor about the months and months of book clutter, both in the house and in my head. To my daughters, Sophia and Dylan Greenhill–thank you for reminding me every day that these ideas are right and important and worth the effort. Ken, thank you for an incredible decade of partnership infused with the 4Cs! To my parents, Floy and Lewis Parkhill—I am profoundly grateful that you have always been my wisest and most valuable teachers.

—Valerie

Brief Contents

Contents

Preface

Appropriately enough, our 21st century education journeys began in 2000. At a meeting of education and business leaders in Chicago preparing for a meeting with the *Chicago Tribune* editorial board on education technology, our friend Karen Bruett, the head of education marketing for Dell, said, "I know what you ought to do next. You should develop a new national coalition on the question, 'What skills do young people need to succeed in the new global economy?'"

That simple challenge sent us off on our 21st century education journeys, and we haven't stopped. We helped found The Partnership for 21st Century Skills (P21), the coalition that established the well-known "Framework for 21st Century Learning" (also known as "the rainbow").

For each of us, this has been an exciting journey. The opportunity to participate in a profound dialogue about fundamental transformations in K–12 education has been an inspirational challenge. After almost a decade of working with policymakers at the state and federal levels, however, we began to notice that more and more local education leaders were asking us how best to implement 21st century skills in their schools and districts. We became more and more interested in working with superintendents, principals, school board members, and local business leaders who were asking us to help them implement their visions for 21st century education. Nationally, it seemed as if we no longer needed to debate the need for a new model of education in the 21st century; the real question was: How do we make it happen?

The idea for this book arose from that shift. As we began working with school and district leaders, we wanted to share their experiences and to offer our insights into what we were seeing and hearing. Our goal with the book is to offer an implementation-oriented resource for education leaders at all stages of 21st century education implementation—whether early or advanced.

One thing that stands out clearly for us is this: No school or district is doing real 21st century education work today without a strong leader. Individual teachers or programs can produce inspirational results, but without the support of teacher-leaders, principals, and superintendents, the work does not sustain itself. So we have written this book for teacher-leaders who are trying to get their principal or superintendent "on board"; we have also written this book with the superintendent and principal in mind, so they can share this book with their senior team members, principals, teacher-leaders, and leaders in colleges of education.

Overview of the Book: 7 Steps and 4Cs

The structure of this book is simple. Steps 1–7 align with our implementation model, the 7 Steps. We hope the seven steps will be helpful to you, whether you're getting started or already well on your way toward implementation.

In more than a decade of working on various aspects of 21st century education, we've seen many models of implementation. Most often, the effort began as the result of a strong superintendent. But we have also seen a dynamic principal, teacher, or tech director initiate the work. In some cases, the effort was started by a member of the school board. There really has been no "cookie-cutter" approach for undertaking 21st century education initiatives.

For this reason, we do not highlight a single district or school to serve as the primary model. Rather, we have identified seven common steps that we have observed in a number of schools and districts throughout the country. We hope these steps, along with the varied examples we offer, will provide a mosaic-like picture to help you launch or advance your 21st century education work. The seven steps are detailed in the figure below:

THE 7 STEPS FOR EDUCATION LEADERS

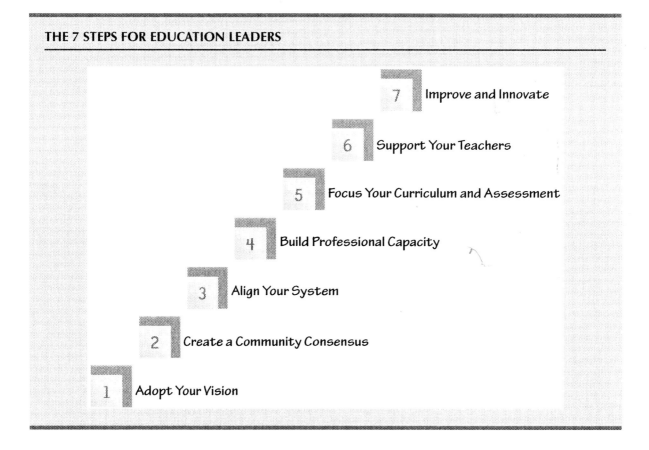

7 Improve and Innovate

6 Support Your Teachers

5 Focus Your Curriculum and Assessment

4 Build Professional Capacity

3 Align Your System

2 Create a Community Consensus

1 Adopt Your Vision

In addition to the seven steps, the other organizing principle for this book is the "4Cs." When P21 developed the "Framework for 21st Century Learning," 18 different skills were defined. Since then, more than 16 states have adopted this framework and agreed to build 21st century outcomes into their standards, professional development, and assessments. However, given the Framework's breadth, educators and policy makers were often challenged with where to begin. To solve this challenge, P21 reached out to the education community and the public and identified four skills that were deemed to be the highest priorities for educators: the 4Cs—critical thinking, communication, collaboration, and creativity.

As you will see in Steps 1 and 2, we encourage every school and district leader to develop your own unique model. But we strongly recommend that you use the 4Cs as a starting point. Throughout the book we use the term "4Cs" as a placeholder term for whatever specific vision your school or district has adopted.

In the book, we will help you identify which of the 4Cs you can use as organizing principles for each of the seven steps. This book is designed, in fact, to help you use the seven steps and the 4Cs to drive system-wide transformation.

STEP 1: Adopt Your Vision

It might seem counterintuitive in the current environment, but this is actually a great time to be demonstrating leadership in education. Spirits are low, budgets are down, and 20th century forms of accountability are demoralizing. But this is exactly the time for strong leaders to step forward and offer a compelling vision.

In Step 1, we urge you to develop your own personal vision of 21st century education. This will require you to come to some personal closure on just what knowledge and skills young people graduating from your school or district need to have.

It will be important for you to read and assimilate materials on what it takes for a young person to be an effective citizen in the 21st century, as well as materials on the new global economy. Educating yourself on what employers believe are the key skills of a 21st century workforce will also be helpful.

In Step 1, we ask you to consider eight perspectives on transformation in society and which of these are the most compelling in your personal vision for education. We will also help you determine the role you want the 4Cs—critical thinking, communication, collaboration, and creativity—to play in your school or district. How important are the student outcomes of critical thinking, collaboration, communication, and creativity to your notion of 21st century model of education? How intentional and purposeful do you want your school or district to be about these outcomes? We will also have you consider what skills beyond the 4Cs you personally believe need to be prioritized (for example, global competence or self-direction).

This background will allow you to make some decisions for yourself: What is the change you want to be leading? Is your school or district currently intentional or purposeful enough about the outcomes you believe are important? This process will allow you to come to closure on your own personal vision for your 21st century school or district. This is the starting point for your 21st century journey.

At the end of Step 1, we also discuss the degree to which the 4Cs are not simply relevant as student outcomes. They are also the skills around which you can and should build your leadership agenda.

STEP 2: Create a Community Consensus

In Step 2, we ask you to focus on working with others to co-create a vision for your school or district. We will focus a great deal on your communication and collaboration skills as a leader. We will give you some concrete tools to use in effectively communicating your vision for 21st century education. We will also help you focus on some key messages you can use to support your initiative as well as some criticisms you might hear. We offer some suggestions on how to respond to criticisms.

In Step 2, we will also focus on how you can model your collaboration skills. We offer suggestions on how to find "early adopters" and generate broad support for your initiative. We give you specific suggestions on where you are likely to find support for your proposal, and we describe a number of resources (which are included in

Appendices 7–10) to help you in your outreach to your students, business leaders, and community groups.

Step 2 is essential. You've taken your own personal vision of 21st century education, and you've now co-created it with your community. You and the key stakeholders in your community now have a shared vision of your school or district's strategic direction for 21st century education.

STEP 3: Align Your System

If Steps 1 and 2 are done well, you have built a powerful consensus on the direction for your 21st century education work. This can establish a sense of clarity about what needs to happen next, but it might also make you painfully aware that your current system is out of alignment. You might realize that the current structures of teaching and learning do not support the outcomes you have just embraced.

In this context, engaging in self-assessment so you are aware of where all of the parts of your system currently stand relative to your vision, is most useful. P21 created the MILE Guide for this purpose. In this chapter, we will help you use the MILE Guide to conduct a self-assessment. We will also have you develop an alignment strategy so that your vision for 21st century educational outcomes can be implemented more efficiently.

STEP 4: Build Professional Capacity

Up until this point, you have spent a lot of time thinking, planning, and building consensus. Now you need to think about resources—reallocating resources or finding new ones in a tough economic climate.

One primary investment must be to provide effective professional learning for teachers. Steve Paine, former Commissioner of Education in West Virginia, has said that 80 percent of his overall efforts on 21st century education have focused on building teacher capacity. That percentage sounds about right to us.

Step 4 discusses how to use the 4Cs in two important ways to improve professional development for teachers. First, we suggest using the 4Cs as the primary design guidelines for professional development. Just imagine how different and powerful PD would be if it challenged teachers to:

- Think critically;
- Collaborate and communicate effectively;
- Be creative and innovative in their teaching.

We also stress the importance of the 4Cs as the content focus for professional development. We provide strong examples of schools and districts that have prioritized the teaching and assessing of critical thinking skills. This kind of approach to professional development is the focus of Step 4.

STEP 5: Focus Your Curriculum and Assessment

This step is perhaps the most challenging for a number of key reasons. For one, the lack of "plug and play" assessments makes it hard to offer easy solutions for key stakeholders like school boards, teachers, and parents. However, leading districts are creating innovative practices every year, and they are breaking new ground in embedding 21st century education into curriculum and assessment systems. The hard work of reshaping curriculum and assessment is an important part of the 21st century journey.

In Step 5, we will help you think about what direction you need to take both your curricula and your assessments. How can curricula and assessments focus on content *and* the 4Cs? This step encourages you to:

- Evaluate the level of 4Cs integration in current curricula and make necessary design changes.
- Ensure that the 4Cs are being measured in student performances and that these assessments inform teaching and learning in the classroom, school, and district.

STEP 6: Support Your Teachers

The work of 21st century education cannot happen without the commitment of teachers, and teachers need support to make it happen. Education leaders must be clear about what kinds of support classroom teachers and other educators need. This step encourages you to consider questions such as:

- Do we have effective professional learning communities in place?
- Do we have learning environments that truly support educators in this work?
- Do teachers have the flexibility they need to engage students in project-based learning and multidisciplinary content?
- Are educators given timely, constructive feedback about the work they are doing?

In Step 6, we encourage you to acknowledge, support, and share excellent teacher practices. We also challenge you to identify and remove barriers that inhibit effective teaching and learning, such as lack of mentoring for new educators, inflexible scheduling, and/or inadequate physical/technical infrastructure. Teachers are critical partners in your work, and their needs deserve your utmost attention.

STEP 7: Improve and Innovate

You might be happy to get to Step 7, but in the 21st century, your work is never done. It is simply an opportunity to reflect, revise, and improve. But the final step of our model is absolutely critical because it goes to the overall culture that you have created for your school or district.

In Step 7, we help you understand a continuous improvement culture and we challenge you to bring this approach to your schools and districts. We ask the following questions:

- Do you have a culture that supports continuous improvement of students, teachers, and leaders?
- Do your professional learning communities embrace continuous improvement of the 4Cs in their work?
- Has your leadership team identified organization processes, such as human resources policies, where the 4Cs can be embedded in the work of the district?

In Step 7, we encourage you to understand and model a spirit of continuous improvement. We ask you to reflect on whether you have created a new 21st century continuous improvement culture that truly aligns with the new outcomes that you have established.

This is a good note on which to end the cycle because it makes clear that this work is never done. It is a work in progress, as it should be. You are training your young people for a world of continuous improvement, and they should see that culture modeled for them within their own school and district.

The more we reflect on this work, the more confident we are that the seven steps outlined in this book will truly support your goals for change. Starting with a leader's vision; refining that vision with the stakeholder community; aligning professional development, curriculum, and assessments to the 21st century outcomes; strongly supporting teachers in their work in every way we can; and then continuously improving the process—this is a clear and compelling way to think about your 21st century journey.

Features of this Book

While ours is not the first or only book about improving education, it is unique in its focus on 21st century education implementation for leaders. It is designed to help education leaders initiate and lead a 21st century school or district. While we spend a little time on why we need 21st century skills and what they are, we encourage you to use this information in the context of framing the goals and vision for your school or district. The primary focus of this book is how to implement the vision in your school or district. Specifically, we share our seven-step model that begins with a broad vision about student outcomes and moves through the necessary strategies (PD, curricula, assessment) to ensure all students are benefiting from the transformation. Throughout the book, we also try to connect the positive work we are witnessing around the country with an overall vision for 21st century education. We talk about how strategies such as Understanding by Design (UBD) and professional learning communities (PLCs) are being used around the country in ways that support 21st century education.

Each chapter in the book covers one of the steps in our 7 Step model. In each Step, we share:

- A 4Cs Focus, providing a high level snapshot of how each of the 4Cs (critical thinking, communication, collaboration, creativity) intersects with the topic of the chapter.
- Examples from districts around the country that are working on that step.
- Final thoughts that summarize key reflection points about the step.

This book also contains appendices in which we have compiled several one-of-a-kind implementation tools (that have not been aggregated previously):

- Resource guides on the most important 21st century outcomes are provided in Appendices 3–6.
- Outreach tools for students, business leaders, and civic groups are highlighted in Step 2 and included in Appendices 7–10.
- The P21 MILE Guide is highlighted in Step 3 and included as an insert in the front of this book.
- Examples of a project task, rubric, and protocol that support 4Cs work in curriculum and continuous improvement are included in Appendices 11–13.

EdLeader21

Another part of our 21st century education journey began a few years ago when we decided to launch EdLeader21, a professional learning community for leaders who are pursuing 21st century education initiatives. We are fortunate to be working with hundreds of committed educators who want to share and learn from each other in the service of students. Currently, we are:

- Building a master set of rubrics for each of the 4Cs.
- Defining the criteria for a 21st century school or district.
- Piloting innovative assessments to help our districts measure the 4Cs.

Within EdLeader21, we are also providing professional development for leaders and teachers, including webinars with 21st century education experts. We have worked with our members to co-create implementation resources for 21st century schools and districts, many of which are included in Appendices 1–13. Our face-to-face member meetings allow us to share lessons learned and support the work being done by colleagues across the county. And we have provided a social network for hundreds of education leaders to stay connected and work together on issues and projects of common interest.

We hope you will consider joining our professional learning community. Please visit us on our website at www.edleader21.com, request more information, and request a virtual tour of our community website. We'd love to have you join us in this ongoing collaboration focused on 21st century education.

Let's Get Started

There is no more important endeavor today than ensuring all students are successful in life, work, and citizenship in the 21st century and transforming our schools and districts to support such a vision. This will not occur without generations of education leaders committed to that change and prepared to work together to implement it. We hold a deep and abiding admiration for the education leaders who have been working so diligently for years on 21st century education initiatives. We offer this book to support their work and, we hope, to inspire a new generation of education leaders who will continue the necessary and honorable work of improving U.S. education systems for all our children.

Thank you for joining us. Now let's get started.

Adopt Your Vision

Step 1 is all about the 4Cs:

- Critical thinking
- Communication
- Collaboration
- Creativity

We recommend that you use these four skills as the starting point for your vision for your school or district. While you might want to add an additional outcome or two, most leaders we have worked with have used the 4Cs as the starting point for their vision. While you will use a lot of critical thinking skills in this step to reflect deeply on where you want to lead your school or district, Step 1 is about using all of the 4Cs as the foundation of your vision.

Introduction

Education leaders today are constantly besieged with an onslaught of day-to-day crises and challenges. Most leaders we know don't have much time for vision. However, it is much easier to lead if you have a simple, centered sense of what you really want for your students.

Consider, for example, your own answers to the questions we have been asking education leaders for more than a decade: "How is your district/school preparing its children for the demands of the 21st century?" and "Have you adopted a 21st century model of education? If not, do you need to?"

Ken recently visited his old school district in New York, and in the front lobby, a question was prominently displayed: "What will our students need to know and do in 2025?" They chose 2025 because it would be the year of graduation for the incoming kindergarten class. Many schools and districts have been asking this question to generate robust discussions by school boards and stakeholder groups. We know you will want to engage in these dialogues and we have some constructive suggestions on how to do that in Step 2. But in this first step, we ask you to start by spending time on reflecting inwardly. Every stage in this journey rests on the foundation that is your *personal* vision for 21st century education. A deep, well-thought-out conviction about your vision serves as the most important anchor for you, your school, or your district.

If your school or district does not have a coherent vision for its role in 21st century education, you are likely to lead your team in a myriad of disconnected directions—jumping from tactic to tactic—making it very difficult to achieve the most important outcome: 21st century readiness for every student.

On the other hand, if you begin with a solid understanding of your personal vision, you have the ability to work together with your fellow educators and stakeholders on the school or district vision. You can work with your board, your students, your teachers, your leadership team, and your community to build a collective vision that you can all embrace.

Step 1 will help you define your vision of 21st century students and the education they need to get there. In our experience, there are two lessons learned in this process. First, there is no single vision for 21st century student success that is the same in every school or district. Second, **lasting success always comes down to leaders like you**. For the vision to make an actual difference in students' lives, it must come from and be embraced by the leaders of the school and district. A vision that is born of genuine, authentic, passionate leadership is never simple, never cookie-cutter, and never easy. But it is necessary.

So we offer this step as you begin your journey to becoming an effective 21st century education leader for your school or district. When your personal motivation about the work is clear to you, energizing your community of fellow educators will become a much more straightforward exercise. As Superintendent Jim Merrill of Virginia Beach, told us in 2010, "I have finally found the thing in education that truly motivates me and it's this 21st century education initiative. This is why I am supposed to be a leader in this field" (Merrill, 2011). After reading Step 1, it is our hope that you will embrace a vision that works for you (and be as enthusiastic about it as Superintendent Merrill).

In order to help you in that process, we will share a number of perspectives to help you determine what changes in society are most relevant to you and your students, school, and district; we'll also offer some advice on where to start and how to expand your vision where necessary.

Perspectives on 21st Century Life

With every 21st century education initiative, the starting point for the conversation boils down to one word: "change." You are asking your school or district to change, so it will help you to clarify for yourself, and then your constituencies, what changes in society are really driving the need to change education. In this section, we will highlight some of the most significant shifts affecting society generally and educators specifically. We believe your vision for 21st century education will be better-rounded and more thoughtfully constructed if you consider what these shifts mean to you and your community and, therefore, what role they play in your vision for student success.

We have highlighted eight perspectives on societal change that we believe are profound, but we don't expect every one of these to resonate with you. We encourage you to select the perspectives that are the most compelling to you. This will permit you to offer a rationale for your vision that is rooted in your own personal sense of purpose and direction.

Perspective #1: The Workforce

Workforce skills and demands have changed dramatically in the past 40 years. Our system of education was built for an economy that no longer exists. Your vision for education will inevitably draw upon the issue of workforce and career preparedness in the digital economy.

Levy and Murnane, noted economists who focus on the workforce, have done groundbreaking research that shows where the job declines and inclines of the past 40 to 50 years have been (Autor, Levy, and Murnane 1279–334) (see Figure 1.1). The chart shows that there have been steady declines in routine work. This is because the more routine a task, the easier it is to digitize it. Once the work can be digitized, the work can be automated or it can be "off-shored."

routine - old digitized non-routine

On the other hand, as Figure 1.1 shows, jobs that involve non-routine analytic and interactive communication skills are increasing rapidly in the 21st century. These are jobs that require critical thinking and interaction with people—things that are not easily replicable. Jobs that focus on the special needs of students, patients, clients, and customers are not likely to be digitized, automated, or off-shored. The perspectives of labor economists like Levy and Murnane provide a useful backdrop for thinking about our current model of education and whether it is adequately aligned with the needs of the modern economy.

Fifty years ago, our K–12 system was largely focused on the routine. Memorization and "following instructions" were the order of the day, and they fit nicely into jobs that were routine manufacturing jobs in hierarchical organizations. Those approaches are also well suited for people who would end up in a single career or in just a few jobs in their lifetime. Today's young people will be competing for jobs that require non-routine complex thinking and interactive communication skills. Our education model has not kept pace with these changes. In this context, Levy and Murnane's work provides a helpful way to describe the transformation that is needed in all

21st century require non-routine

FIGURE 1.1   How the Demand for Skills Has Changed

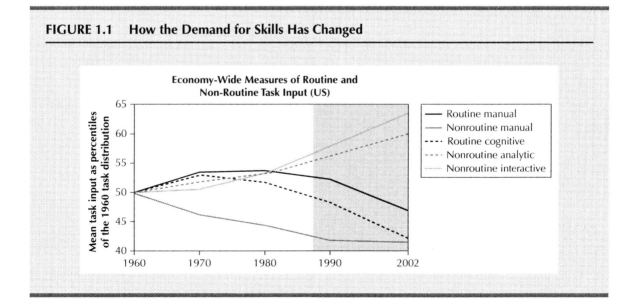

educational systems—changing from a model that currently prepares people for routine work to a model that will prepare people for analytic and interactive work. Perhaps this is a helpful way for you to frame the challenge of preparing our young people for 21st century life and work.

In addition to Levy and Murnane's work, an important initiative in the early '90s laid the foundation for how we now think about preparing our young people for 21st century careers. The Labor Secretary's Commission on Achieving Necessary Skills (SCANS) was formed in 1990 and sought to define the skills required for success in the modern, high-technology economy. The commission's report, "Skills and Tasks for Jobs: A SCANS Report for America 2000," highlighted many competencies now commonly referred to as 21st century skills—problem solving, creativity, information analysis— and continues to be a valuable source of information for individuals and organizations involved in education and workforce development.

About a decade later, the Partnership for 21st Century Skills (P21) built upon this work in its seminal report, "Learning in the 21st Century." The report outlined a framework for 21st century learning that defines the full range of knowledge and skills required for success in college, life and career.

Another publication that helped educators understand the corporate perspective on workforce readiness was "Are They Really Ready to Work?" This report shed light on corporate human resource managers' perspectives on the knowledge and skills of recent graduates. When employers were asked to rank the content and skills that were most valuable among high school graduate hires, the response was illuminating. These executives overwhelmingly prioritized the following skills: work ethic, collaboration, good communication, social responsibility, critical thinking, and problem solving.

When the HR managers were asked to identify the weaknesses among recent hires that were high school graduates, the executives cited the following deficiencies: written communication, leadership, work ethic, critical thinking, problem solving, and self-direction. And when they were asked to identify the competencies that would grow in importance in hiring decisions in the next five years, critical thinking, health and wellness, collaboration, innovation, and personal/financial responsibility topped the list.

These perspectives were reinforced by the 2010 Critical Skills Survey conducted by the American Management Association (AMA). The AMA asked 2,100 small, medium and large businesses their views about the importance of critical thinking, communication, collaboration, and creativity in their organizations. They asked if their organization measured those skills and competencies during annual performance reviews. More than 70 percent said they measured critical thinking, communication, and collaboration skills. More than 50 percent said they measured creativity skills.

This is a good point upon which to reflect. Do you assess your students on these skills? Should you? Do you assess your teachers on these skills? Should you? Do you assess your administrative team on these skills? Should you?

The AMA also asked businesses whether they made an effort to assess these skills when hiring new employees ("AMA Critical Skills Survey 2010"). More than 75 percent of the HR managers said they made an effort to assess the critical thinking and communication skills of potential employees. More than 60 percent said they made an effort to assess the collaboration and creativity skills of potential employees.

This is cause for another set of reflections:

- Do your students know that they will be assessed on these skills in the workforce?
- Do your teachers know that these are critical skills in the workplace?

Nearly 75 percent of the respondents to the AMA survey said that these skills will be of even more importance in the next three to five years. More than 90 percent of the respondents said that these skills were critical to the growth of their organization. About 80 percent of the respondents said that if students mastered the basic core subjects as well as critical thinking, communication, collaboration, and creativity skills, they would be ready for the challenges of the 21st century economy.

Such data provide you with another way to describe the educational transformation needed in your community. The workforce of the 1950s did not require critical thinking, communication, collaboration, and creativity skills. They were not a young person's ticket up the economic ladder. Educational institutions were not purposefully and intentionally focused on these outcomes for all students. As the demands of the workforce have shifted, the underpinnings of the educational model have not.

If your school or district is a typical one, the gaps between the knowledge and skills required for success in college, life, and career and the knowledge and skills your graduates are learning are significant ones. As you refine your personal vision, be sure to consider where your students really need to be and whether the system is helping them get there. Use your own creativity and critical thinking skills to use the reports and resources that help you define the direction(s) you want to take.

Before moving to the next perspective, please consider the questions in Reflection Box 1.1.

1.1 REFLECTIONS ON THE WORKFORCE

Here are some questions we think you might find helpful to contemplate:

- Do you think your school's or district's model of education has sufficiently changed so that students are now prepared for more complex and interactive jobs? Is your school or district providing *every* student with complex thinking and communication skills?
- Does the frame of "routine thinking" versus "complex thinking" offer a helpful way for you to think about the transformation you want to lead in your school or district?
- Do you share the view that if your students mastered core subjects and critical thinking, communication, collaboration, and creativity, they would be ready for the challenges of the 21st century economy?
- Do you have a sense of what business leaders in your own community think of your graduates? Do you have a sense of what business leaders and parents in business think are the key capabilities that young people must possess?

Perspective #2: The Flat World

The data about the workforce as noted by Levy and Murnane, SCANS, and P21 are all incredibly helpful as framing material. But the ideas embedded in all this work came into full public consciousness when Thomas Friedman's groundbreaking book *The World Is Flat* was published in 2005. Put in the context of the emerging global economy, suddenly all the workforce-related research of the 1990s had a new sense of urgency.

Friedman presented a new global landscape that was being reshaped by information and technology and networks. He explained how governments, organizations, and hierarchies of all kinds were being "flattened" by these new tools. Individuals were being empowered by having information, vast resources, and powerful networks at their fingertips. This enabled them to operate with more leverage then they did in traditional hierarchical structures.

Many educators wished *The World Is Flat* had gone into greater detail about the role of schooling in a flat world. That topic has been covered in Friedman's more recent work, *That Used to Be Us*, written with his colleague Michael Mandelbaum. The book makes a powerful case for the term "Flat World 2.0," which is relevant for all of us working in education today:

> … Flat World 2.0 is everything Flat World 1.0 was, but with so many more people able to connect to the Flat World platform, so many more people able to connect with others who are also connected, and so many more people now empowered to find other people of like minds to collaborate with—whether to support a politician, follow a rock group, invent a product, or launch a revolution—based on shared values, interests, and ideals. (Friedman and Mandelbaum 60)

Equally important, Friedman and Mandelbaum make a very explicit connection between the concept of the flat world and education; they help create a context for change in education and suggest some potential directions for improved approaches to education. The flat world has implications for every organization and every person in it. Individuals have access to more and more information about their organizations, but with that information comes the responsibility to do something with it. Thus the flat world requires individuals who are self-directed. As one corporate executive at Apple told us, in today's environment, "if a person needs to be managed they are no longer employable." The flattening of the organizations means there isn't room for the management layers of the past. Self-management is a requirement in the flat world. See Reflection Box 1.2.

We recommend reading Friedman's books. You might also consider providing copies to members of your leadership team and school board.

1.2 REFLECTIONS ON A FLAT WORLD

- How might these flat world trends affect your vision for education in your school or district?
- Have you envisioned each of your students in a flat world and flat organizations?
- What attributes would you want them to possess?
- Is your school or district creating environments where your students are encouraged to be self-directed or self-managed? Or are the structure and practices of your school or district actually so "top-down" that these skills are not encouraged?
- Is your own school organization "flatter" than it was 10 years ago?
- Is your school or district as intentional about flat world and flat organizational outcomes as you'd like it to be?

Perspective #3: The Service Economy

Another trend to consider is the 21st century shift to the service economy. Not too long ago, a primary purpose of education was to prepare students for jobs in fields such as agriculture and manufacturing. Those career opportunities continue to wane; now students must prepare for service-oriented careers. Today, 80 percent of the country's jobs are in the service economy, and that number is headed to exceed 85 percent ("21st Century Skills, Education & Competitiveness" 4).

We often ask educators, when they are gathered in large groups, "What percentage of you consider yourselves to be in the service economy?" Often only half of the educators raise their hands. We argue that *all* educators are in the service economy. For some reason, people tend to equate service economy jobs with low-end, fast-food jobs. But service economy jobs run the full gamut of our economy. Educators, doctors, lawyers, accountants, and bankers are all in the service economy. Pretty much everyone in health care and education is in the service economy. Anyone who engages with customers, clients, or patients is in the service economy. PhDs in electrical engineering who sell high-end computers are in the service economy.

One hundred years ago, we were largely an agrarian economy. Fifty years ago, we were largely a manufacturing economy. Today we are largely becoming a service economy. Our education model has not shifted to accommodate this profound change.

Consider the questions in Reflection Box 1.3.

Perspective #4: Citizenship

Each of the trends we have just described has focused primarily on jobs and the economy. These trends have also dramatically affected a primary pillar of our society—citizenship.

The question "What skills do young people need to be successful in the new global economy?" is incredibly important. But civic leaders and thought leaders in the civic engagement community rightly point out that the skills required of the modern workforce are essential for 21st century citizens. The complexities of 21st century public policies, campaigns, and initiatives are astounding. The role of the media in shaping public opinion has profoundly changed since the 1950s. The demands of citizenship are much greater today than they were 50 years ago. These challenges require more complex thinking, more empathy, more civility, and more

1.3 REFLECTIONS ON THE SERVICE ECONOMY

- What skills does someone in the service economy need? Listening skills? Empathy skills? Problem solving skills? Communication skills? Collaboration skills? Ability to customize solutions? Any others come to mind?
- If you know that four out of five of your students are going to be in the service economy, how might that affect your vision for the kind of education you want them to have? Does this suggest that you need to update your education model?
- Should our schools be more purposeful and intentional about the listening, empathy, problem solving, and communications skills of the service economy?
- Does this concept of the transition from agrarian to manufacturing to service sector jobs help frame the transformation that you would like to lead your school or district through?

1.4 REFLECTIONS ON CITIZENSHIP

- Have the leaders in your school or district considered how to prepare young people for 21st century citizenship?
- Have you had a discussion with the civic leaders of your community on how the demands of citizenship might have changed over the past 50 years?
- Have the leaders in your school or district acknowledged and transformed to accommodate the *global* nature of societal challenges?

sophisticated forms of interactivity than our education systems typically address. They also require a high degree of media literacy. Finally, many of the policy challenges that could be addressed as national challenges a generation or two ago have become global in scope.

Consider the questions in Reflection Box 1.4.

Perspective #5: Pace of Change

In the 1950s, "change" was not an identifying feature of our culture. In just two generations, it has become the hallmark of our culture. Earlier generations of educators did not need to consider a top goal to be "preparing students for a lifetime of change." For conscientious educators today, it is a must. Refer to Reflection Box 1.5.

Our grandparents prepared themselves for a single career and one or two jobs over a lifetime. Today's students are facing a very different reality. According to the U.S. Department of Labor, the average number of jobs between ages 18 and 42 now stands at 10.4.

1.5 **REFLECTIONS ON CHANGE**

- How much does your current model of education prepare students to adapt to change?
- How much does your school culture model change and continuous improvement?
- How comfortable are you as a leader in demonstrating flexibility and adaptability in the face of change? How about your leadership team?

In *That Used to Be Us,* Friedman and Mandelbaum put this observation in a very current context. They observe:

> When Tom wrote *The World Is Flat,* Facebook wasn't even in it; it had just started up and was still a minor phenomenon. Indeed, in 2005, Facebook didn't exist for most people. Twitter was still a sound, the "cloud" was something in the sky, "3G" was a parking space, and "Skype" was a typo. That is how much has changed in just the last six years. (59)

Perspective #6: Design and Innovation

Another perspective to consider as you address educational transformation is the growing importance of creativity, innovation, and design in our economy. For decades, we have been worried that jobs were being lost to China and India because of the lower cost of labor. But cost is not the only factor.

We recently asked a group of educators to share examples of products they purchased that were far more expensive than the least expensive option—in other words, an item that they could have gotten for much less, but they opted for a more expensive version. One teacher sheepishly raised her hand and said she recently paid $40 for a wastepaper basket. We asked her what she could have paid—and she said 99 cents. We then asked her why she was willing to pay 40 times more. She explained that the more expensive one had a design that matched the countertops in her bathroom. We all recognize this moment because we've all made a similar choice at some point. Most of us at some point choose something beyond the "low cost" option for aesthetic or other design-related reasons.

In his book *A Whole New Mind,* author Daniel Pink has repeatedly talked about this phenomenon. As the economy continues to evolve, design and creativity have become incredibly prized skills and, in fact, major drivers of our economy. This point is powerfully reinforced by Tony Wagner in his book about innovation in education, *Creating Innovators: The Making of Young People Who Will Change the World.* In the book, Tony explains the "culture of learning" necessary to foster innovation. He argues that the most successful schools will be called upon to create innovators who will be the drivers of the new economy. He observes that traditional education environments have five key traits that are at odds with innovative environments. They tend to be characterized by:

- Individual achievement;
- Individual academic subjects;
- Extrinsic instruction (e.g., grades);
- Risk aversion;
- Passive consumption of knowledge.

In contrast, he observes, highly innovative environments that embody a "culture of learning" exhibit:

- Collaboration;
- Crossing of boundaries (e.g., breaking down of silos);

8

- Intrinsic motivation (e.g., passion);
- Responsible risk taking;
- Creation of knowledge.

Look at this last list of five characteristics of a learning environment. Can an individual teacher create this environment in one individual classroom? Yes, but not without really being bold, courageous, and cutting against the grain. Tony observes that this is often the case. But these instances of innovation are sporadic and isolated. He refers to the innovators as "outliers." Refer to Reflection Box 1.6.

Perspective #7: Information

Another area that might influence your vision of 21st century education is the changing nature of information. Most of us older than 40 went to school at a time when the nature of information was largely static. The universe of information at our disposal seemed largely fixed. A textbook could be relevant in a field for one or even two decades. But the rate of information change has increased dramatically. One way to describe this is the "shelf life" of information—the length of time information stays "fresh." For example:

- When Ken learned the nine planets, the shelf life of that information was 50 years. (The information didn't change for most of Ken's lifetime.)
- When Valerie learned the nine planets, the shelf life of that information was 30 years.
- When Ken's daughter learned the nine planets, the shelf life of that information was 15 years.
- When Valerie's daughter learned the nine planets, the shelf life of that information was seven days; she learned the nine planets, and the very next week, Pluto was taken off the list!

It's not just an issue of the shelf life of information, either. The sheer volume of available information is incredibly different than it was just 10 years ago.

John Bransford, a leading researcher and academic in the field of cognition, has observed that in the United States today, we tell our kids the same thing 100 times and on the 101st time we ask them if they can remember what we told them the first hundred times, when in the 21st century the real coin of the realm is if they can look at material they have never seen before and know what to do with it.

Today students still learn within an educational system that is focused

---

1.6 REFLECTIONS ON DESIGN AND INNOVATION

- Do you accentuate creativity in the culture of your school?
- Would you like to make sure competencies like innovation and design capabilities are taught in your school or district?
- Is "design" a topic that is even addressed?
- Is the growing importance of creativity and innovation in our society a useful way of describing the transformation you want to lead in your school or district?

1.7 REFLECTIONS ON INFORMATION CHANGE

- What are the implications in your school and district of the short shelf life and rapid explosion of information?
- How might this issue effect how leaders in your school and district approach teaching and learning?
- Is your school or district still largely focused on content mastery?
- Is your school or district also focusing on skills like verifying, discerning, leveraging, synthesizing, and integrating information?
- Is the transformation from content mastery to "content and skill" mastery a helpful way for you to capture the transformation you want to lead in your school or district?

on memorization and content mastery. However, as we discussed earlier, we now live in a world of ever-increasing information where mastering content is just one of the many ways in which students need to work with content.

Consider the questions in the Reflection Box 1.7 on page 9.

Perspective #8: Technology

When it comes to everyone's list of "major societal changes," technology is always on top. Technological advancements are the easiest changes most of us see. They are tangible. We each have our own personal stories about how technology has changed our lives or how our children, grandchildren, nieces, nephews, or young friends are more technologically proficient than adults. The impact is unmistakable. Refer to Reflection Box 1.8.

Consider these data points as summarized in the P21 report "21st Century Skills, Education & Competitiveness":

- In 1967, the production of material goods (such as automobiles, chemical, and industrial equity) and delivery of material services (such as transportation, construction, and retailing) accounted for nearly 54 percent of the country's economic output.
- By 1997, the production of information products (such as computers, books, television, and software) and the provision of information services (such as telecommunications, financial and broadcast services, and education) accounted for 63 percent of the country's output.
- Information services alone grew from 36 percent to 56 percent of the economy during the 30-year period from 1967–1997.
- Today the United States is more than 15 years into the information age. In 1991, U.S. spending on information technology ($112 billion) first surpassed spending on production technology ($107 billion). In 1999, the largest sector of the labor force, 45 percent, was still in material services, but the proportion of the workforce in information services was not far behind, at 41 percent—and this sector has been growing at a much faster rate.

1.8 REFLECTIONS ON TECHNOLOGY

- Do you think of technology primarily as an "engagement" strategy? Is it simply a way to get students interested in topics they otherwise would not be interested in? Is it a way to make sure students have the necessary digital skills to succeed? Or do you see today's technological advances as a foundational driver of your 21st century education vision?
- Do you have a well-considered plan for the use of technology in your school or district? Is it tied to all the other 21st century outcomes you have identified as a way to enable them?
- Is technology something you think about on a spectrum that includes pencil, chalk, and blackboards? Or do you see today's technology as a wholesale shift in teaching and learning? Do you think of technology as a powerful driver you can harness to transform the nature of your organization?

When we began our work in 21st century education more than a decade ago, both of us believed wholeheartedly in education technology as a revolutionary shift in the educational process. At the time (in the late '90s), the Internet explosion appeared to be the single most important foundation for change we could imagine. Ken was working with the computer industry to encourage educators to adopt more technologically driven strategies and to reduce the digital divide. Valerie was actually using technology to build training and education curriculum for businesses and schools. We were pretty sure that technology was the next silver bullet for learning.

But along the way, we adjusted our views. Too often we saw technology being used for technology's sake. The excitement over the latest "new toy" sometimes clouded the focus on student outcomes. Paper and pencil still can be the best tools in the classroom, depending on the learning goal(s). We came to see that the promise of technology—that it would create a new foundation to address broadly shared challenges in schools and districts—often was not fulfilled. And we began to see technology skills as one competency (an incredibly important one, for sure) among many equals that students needed.

We still believe wholeheartedly in the power of technology to support transformational teaching and learning. We also know that some of the most brilliant, effective, innovative educators are ones who embrace technology and use it to its utmost potential—and we continue to highlight their successes, both in this book and in our work. But technology is not, nor should it ever be, the sole focus or the end goal. And we caution that it might not form the strongest foundation for your leadership vision.

We hope these reflections have encouraged you to consider a range of questions you might not have had the luxury of thinking through in your day-to-day work. Our goal is to help you identify the ways you want to explain the need for a new educational model in your school or district. We hope we have also helped you identify the kind of transformation that you want to lead. Now we want to shift to a discussion of what skills your students need to address all these shifts in 21st century society.

Where to Start: The 4Cs

If you're like most education leaders we've worked with, at this point you are impatient to move past the perspectives and reflections and roll up your sleeves to get some things done. You might be thinking, "Now that I've settled on my take on change, what do I need to do immediately to change my school or district?" A reminder: There is a tendency in education to focus too quickly on education strategies as the key issues of change. Many educators move immediately to strategies such as the length of the school day, the design of a building, or the implementation of a new curriculum. But in our experience, this skips over one very important step of your vision. Prior to settling on those strategies it is important to identify what *student outcomes* will form the core of your personal vision.

You can't really know what education in your school or district should look like if you don't identify what capabilities your students must have to succeed in life, citizenship, and work.

Having spent the past eight years focused on exactly this issue, we suggest a basic starting point for your consideration—the 4Cs:

- Critical thinking
- Communication
- Collaboration
- Creativity

We believe the 4Cs can serve as the foundational skills of your 21st century vision. We have seen many leaders use them as the starting point for their vision, so we would like to explore each of them with you.

Critical Thinking

From our perspective, critical thinking should be the first among equals when it comes to the topic of 21st century student readiness. Critical thinking is not a new skill, of course. What we mean is that critical thinking is, now more than ever, a skill that everyone must possess. There are at least three reasons for this.

First, everyone in the new economy must know how to continuously improve. Monitoring and improving one's individual performance, as well as the performance of one's team, are absolute requirements in flat organizations. You can't continuously improve without the ability to critically think. Refer to Reflection Box 1.9.

Second, being able to think critically is a matter of survival in the new economy. We were approached one day by a skeptical businessman who asked if we really thought *everyone* needed to be a critical thinker. He pointed to a woman behind the cash register nearby and wondered aloud whether the checker truly needed to think critically as part of her job. We responded by pointing out that routine jobs like hers are often being automated. What if that checker needed to redefine her role in the organization? How would she reposition herself to bring value to the organization and/or the industry? How would she position herself to find a new job if hers was eliminated? All of these would require effective critical thinking.

Third, everyone needs critical thinking skills to be successful in college. David Conley, the country's leading expert on college and career readiness, has observed that habits of mind such as analysis, interpretation, precision and accuracy, problem solving, and reasoning can be as or more important than content knowledge in determining success in college courses.

Perhaps not surprisingly, we hear often from teachers and business leaders that today's kids don't think. We hear that today's students want to know what is required to get an "A" but aren't interested in developing true understanding of the topic at hand. A hospital administrator in Indiana told us that the students he was hiring out of high school to work as entry-level intake clerks and orderlies didn't think for themselves and were, therefore, not useful as hospital employees.

We all share a responsibility to develop critical thinking skills among students so they can pursue successful careers, but it is also a serious issue for citizenship. In the current political environment, we must cultivate a generation of citizens who can use their critical thinking skills in electoral and policy processes. Today's citizens need critical thinking skills to operate in an environment cluttered with competing information that requires them to compare evidence and make decisions in complex policy areas from health policy to financial regulation policy to environmental policy.

When it comes to incorporating critical thinking into a school system, we have been particularly impressed by the example set by Superintendent Mary Kamerzell and her team at Catalina Foothills School District in Tucson, Arizona. Systems thinking and critical thinking are cornerstones of their model. They have worked closely with the Waters Foundation to integrate systems thinking throughout

1.9 REFLECTIONS ON CRITICAL THINKING

- Does more rigor in critical thinking make sense to you as part of your personal vision?
- Have you specifically considered the value of "systems thinking" strategies?
- Has your school or district adopted a rubric for critical thinking?
- Do you agree that bringing critical thinking to *every* student is an important strategy that might not currently be part of your school's or district's education model?

their curriculum and assessment systems. It is amazing to see elementary school students use the tools of systems thinking to figure out how a change in one part of a system will affect another part of the system.

We have also been impressed by the work by Superintendent Jeff Weaver and his team of educators in Upper Arlington City Schools outside of Columbus, Ohio. They spent a year refining their 21st century model with a district advisory group and then decided to prioritize the skill of critical thinking. They emphasized rigor by setting the expectation that every student would be an effective critical thinker. More details about this work can be found in Step 4, where we explain how the district uses 21st century skills coaches to advance the professional development of critical thinking with their teachers. Also, you can find more details about critical thinking resources in Appendix 3.

Communication

The other skill that is repeatedly deemed by employers to be inadequate in their employees is communication. This might seem odd because most K–12 education systems place considerable emphasis on written and oral communication skills, especially in the subject of English language arts. Nonetheless, we hear repeatedly that there is a major deficiency of all students, including graduates of four-year higher education institutions, in:

- Written communication skills
- Oral communication skills
- The use of technology to communicate effectively

In the report "Are They Really Ready to Work?" employers note that although oral and written communication are among the top four skills they seek in new hires, *all* graduates are lacking in these areas. High school graduates fare the worst, with 53 percent of employers citing this group's deficiency in oral communications and 81 percent citing their deficiency in written communications. Almost half of employers said employees with two-year degrees were still lacking skills in these two areas, while more than a quarter of employers felt four-year graduates continued to lack these skills. Refer to Reflection Box 1.10.

In the mid nineties, Napa Valley Unified School District responded to similar concerns by opening New Technology High School. (We explain more about this story in Chapter 2.) Its key characteristics included an emphasis on the skills identified in the SCANS report, particularly communication skills.

The new high school established a grade on student report cards for oral communication, along with intervention strategies to assist students in improving their skills. Communication skills are now part of every course grade throughout the New Tech Network.

1.10 REFLECTIONS ON COMMUNICATION SKILLS

- Do you feel that communication skills need a higher priority in your school or district?
- Do you need to specifically prioritize oral communications as a skill? Should students be required to regularly make oral presentations to audiences of adults and outside experts?
- Do you need a broader range of writing requirements, such as the ability to write business letters, memos, and other workplace applications, added to the standard academic writing requirements?
- Should technology competency be a part of the communications requirement of your school or district?
- Is revamping the communications requirement for all students a reasonable element of a 21st century education model for your school or district?

Finally, the ascension of the service economy makes oral communication skills absolutely essential. Almost no one in society will be able to hold their own economically if they can't effectively communicate. In Appendix 4 you will find a compendium of resources about the teaching and learning of communication skills.

Collaboration

How much work do you personally accomplish working in isolation? If you are like most of us, you are finding the answer to be "less and less." These days, it is rare for any work to be completed by a single person working alone. Yet we continue to place massive emphasis on individual performance in our pedagogy and in our assessments. Employers regularly comment that the individuals who are least successful in the workplace often fail as a result of an inability to work effectively with others. Even writers—who seem relatively isolated in their work—need publishers, editors, and publicists (to name a few) to effectively accomplish their goals.

But to take matters a step further, more and more work today is done in global teams. One auto manufacturing executive we know in Tennessee oversees a "regional team" that includes North and South America. The employees on his team not only speak a wide variety of languages, they also work in vastly different time zones and bring with them a wealth of diverse cultural experiences.

The author James Surowiecki has done a wonderful job of explaining how, in the 21st century, collaboration really leads to knowledge creation. He explains how the "wisdom of crowds" helps to develop new knowledge that is most often more accurate and useful than knowledge created by an individual: "Under the right circumstances, groups are remarkably intelligent, and are often smarter than the smartest people in them" (xiii). Surowiecki's work underscores the importance of collaboration; he makes a compelling case that large groups of diverse individuals can develop more accurate and robust forecasts and make better decisions than a single highly skilled decision maker.

1.11 REFLECTIONS ON COLLABORATION

- To what degree do you require your students to demonstrate mastery of working in teams to solve problems?
- Do you require each of your students to participate in "knowledge creation" projects? Is this something you believe should be included in a K–12 education?
- Do you consider a student's ability to work with people from diverse cultures and perspectives to be an essential skill?
- How important are collaborative skills to your vision of 21st century education?

One of the longest running and best examples of 21st century collaboration in schools is the Global Learning and Observations to Benefit the Environment (GLOBE) program. GLOBE is a worldwide hands-on, primary and secondary school-based science and education program that enables students, teachers, and scientists to collaborate on inquiry-based investigations of the environment. Each year, students in more than 100 countries collaborate on inquiry-based investigations of their local environment, sharing their results over the Internet. More than 1.5 million students have participated in GLOBE since it was set up in 1995, contributing more than 22 million measurements to the GLOBE database for use in their inquiry-based science projects. Projects like GLOBE are important to consider as you reflect on your approach to collaboration in the digital world (GLOBE, 2011). Refer to Reflection Box 1.11.

We have included additional resources on collaboration in Appendix 5.

Creativity and Innovation

We have long associated creativity and innovation with the arts. It seems ironic that as we realize the growing importance of creativity and innovation skills for our students, funding for arts in education is declining rapidly. But it is essential that we think about creativity and innovation even more broadly.

Thomas Friedman, the author of *The World Is Flat,* observed: "Your ability to act on your imagination is going to be so decisive in driving your future and the standard of living in your country. So the school, the state, the country that empowers, nurtures, enables imagination among its students and citizens, that's who's going to be the winner" (AASA). From our perspective, creativity and innovation are essential ingredients to economic success. You are either going to need to be creative and innovative yourself or be able to effectively collaborate with someone who is. Refer to Reflection Box 1.12.

This suggests that creativity and innovation should have a broader role than just being accentuated in the arts. Creativity and innovation should be embedded in every subject. This is a challenging proposition. Typical approaches to education do not allow much room for developing a culture of creativity and innovation in classrooms. Many schools and districts we have worked with have created book clubs or discussion groups within their professional learning communities around creativity and innovation. They have used the works of Sir Ken Robinson, Richard Florida, and Daniel Pink to spur discussion around these topics.

Daniel Pink's book *A Whole New Mind* has been particularly popular in K–12 settings for creating a discussion on the value of focusing on creativity and design. He has advocated that we work to develop an "artistic sensibility" in all students. His book can be very valuable in helping jump-start a discussion around these topics. You also might wish to explore the initiatives of Dale Dougherty, founder of the Maker movement. He has recently launched Makerspace, an initiative that aims to engage high school students in collaborative, distributed design and manufacturing experiments. Additionally, the New York Hall of Science has been a leader in trying to bring more creativity and innovation into science and math education. Some have referred to this as adding the arts to science, technology, engineering, and math education (STEM) and have termed the concept STEAM. Consider incorporating some of these ideas into your initiatives.

A number of helpful resources on the teaching and learning of creativity can be found in Appendix 6.

In this section, we hope we have helped you consider the importance

---

1.12 REFLECTIONS ON CREATIVITY AND INNOVATION

- Have you been able to maintain your investments in arts education?
- Do you need to rethink the position of arts and creativity in your school or district to place more emphasis on them?
- Do you aspire to include more creativity and innovation in classrooms across your school or district?
- Do you know of classrooms in core subjects that are hubs of creativity and innovation?
- How would we scale these approaches to make them present in more and eventually in all classrooms?
- Should you include courses on design and engineering in your curriculum?
- Is creativity and innovation a part of your vision for your school or district?

1.13 REFLECTIONS ON THE 4CS

- Do you think each of the 4Cs is critical to creating a 21st century citizen and worker?
- Which of these outcomes should each graduate be required to demonstrate?

of the 4Cs. You should be in a better position to determine what role critical thinking, communication, collaboration, and creativity should play in constructing your vision for a 21st century school or district. We believe the 4Cs should be core student outcomes in every school and district, but you will need to determine whether they fit into your vision and your community. Consider the reflections on the 4Cs in Reflection Box 1.13 on the previous page.

What to Add: Beyond the 4Cs

There is nothing magical about the 4Cs. Some schools and districts have chosen 5Cs. Some have adopted "compassion" and some have adopted "civility" as the fifth "C." We want to flag another possible "C"—"citizenship." In some communities, the 4Cs will be viewed as a dilution to core content even though they are intended to be integrated into core content. Give some thought to whether your school or district is being explicit about its commitment to content. You might want to consider adding "content" as your fifth "C" to make this commitment absolutely clear.

However, there is even more to consider beyond the four or five "Cs." There are many skills you could add to your list of student outcomes. While most schools and districts we have worked with and witnessed have started with the 4Cs as their core 21st century student outcomes, many have expanded their vision beyond just these competencies. In this section, we pose for your consideration three other skills that you might want to consider adding to your own personal list:

- Self-direction
- Global competence
- Financial literacy

Self-Direction

Some would argue that we are facing a national crisis in self-direction. They might be right.

As we mentioned earlier, an executive we know flatly stated that anyone who needs to be managed is no longer employable there. But everywhere we go, we hear that many of today's young people lack self-direction. It is not necessarily that students don't work hard, it's that they either want to be told what to do next or they simply can't—or won't—try to figure things out on their own. In the 21st century, that's a huge liability.

Daniel Pink, in his latest book *Drive,* has accentuated this issue under the label he calls autonomy. He explains that individuals have an innate drive to be autonomous. We would observe that the new economy is demanding it from them as well. The problem is that most schools are making this issue worse (to say nothing of the impact of "helicopter parents"). Most schools are top-down environments where the most successful students learn to follow directions *exactly,* to never "draw outside the lines" or take any risks for fear of failure or a substandard grade. There is little co-creation and collaboration and almost no self-direction encouraged in their coursework.

In a district we worked with in the Midwest, educators recognized the urgency of the issue and decided to tackle it by emphasizing self-direction in their curricula. Self-direction planning sheets were incorporated in many assignments. In addition to restating the assignment, each student is now asked to describe a personal goal for the assignment. After completing an assignment, each student is asked a series of questions about his or her performance:

- Did you set a good goal for yourself?
- Would you set a different goal the next time?
- Did you work efficiently?
- How should you work more efficiently the next time?
- Is there anything else you could do to improve your performance?

We watched this approach work extremely well in the context of a writing assignment; however it could have worked in almost any subject. What impressed us the most was how seemingly simple it was to frame the exercise at the beginning and at the end in a way that asked the student to self-direct, self-assess, and improve.

Other school districts have focused on project-based learning, in part to accentuate more self-direction skills. Because students are working actively in the context of a real-world project, they have more opportunities to make decisions and lead their own learning paths.

Once you determine whether to emphasize self-direction, there are a large number of ways to work to emphasize it. Refer to Reflection Box 1.14.

1.14 REFLECTIONS ON SELF-DIRECTION

- Does your school or district focus on self-direction today?
- Could you be more purposeful and intentional about self-direction as an outcome?
- Do you have a rubric for self-direction?
- Does this topic of self-direction resonate with you?
- Should it be incorporated into your personal vision?

Global Competence

Global competence is a concept that embraces language fluency, understanding of global perspectives, and the ability to work with people from diverse cultures. Ask any executive from a mid-size or large business, and they will tell you that the ability to work in complex global teams with individuals from many cultures who speak many languages is one of the key competencies in the business world today.

We have observed that, in some parts of the United States, the topic of "global competence" is controversial; it can be viewed by some as seeming unpatriotic. It is wise to be sensitive and careful about these kinds of sentiments, especially if they are commonly held in your region. At the same time, in the next two decades, one's ability to work in a global context will become increasingly important, if not essential, to career success for most students. As we have mentioned previously, the increasingly global nature of citizenship is also important to keep in mind.

Several schools, districts, and organizations around the country have focused their efforts on the issue of global competence. The Asia Society is a recognized leader on this subject. They have developed a network of schools that serve as examples for the teaching of global competence. They have also developed a guide to global competence (http://asiasociety.org). Becoming familiar with the work of Fernando Reimers, *the Ford Foundation Professor of International Education at the Harvard Graduate School of Education*, is also an excellent way to ground your leadership in this area (http://www.edweek.org/ew/articles/2008/10/08/07reimers.h28.html).

Additionally, several schools and districts we have worked with have adopted International Baccalaureate (IB) programs in their schools. The IB program has scaled globally and has gained impressive traction. Its leaders have been very open to work on integrating "21st century outcomes" into the IB approach. In fact, the Upper Arlington School District in Ohio is serving as a pilot project for merging 21st century outcomes into its IB schools.

We've also been excited to watch some districts partner with the international student travel company EF Education to emphasize global education. EF has designed world travel programs for teachers and students to help foster greater appreciation for global competence issues, including, but not limited to, language fluency. It is also working with education leaders in Ohio to establish a network of leaders working together to define what global competence should look like in their schools and districts.

Finally, check out the work of New Global Citizens. They are a very exciting 501(c)3 based in Phoenix, Arizona, that has created a resource guide on how individual classrooms can connect with and support projects around the world in need of help. New Global Citizen not only provides the resource guide but also identifies specific projects for individual classes to work with. You can find out more about them at: www.newglobalcitizens.org. These examples should give you some ideas of ways in which global competence could be more intentionally and purposefully pursued in your school or district. Refer to Reflection Box 1.15.

1.15 REFLECTIONS ON GLOBAL COMPETENCE

- What programs do you have today in your school or district that touch on global competence?
- Do you need to expand the reach of these programs?
- Do you need a rubric for global competence?
- Is "global competence" for every child a central component of your personal vision for your school or district?

Financial Literacy

The worldwide recession that began in 2009 has highlighted the topic of financial literacy. As we look back on that financial crisis, we see a real missed opportunity in its wake. Millions of consumers didn't have the basic knowledge and skills to be wise consumers of basic financial instruments. Many individuals did not, and still do not, understand the basics of loans and borrowing. Many individuals did not understand the basics of mortgages and financing for housing. Many individuals had no knowledge of how much debt they could afford. There is clearly an urgent need for financial literacy programs, but they only exist on a very small scale. We are asking whether financial literacy should be treated as optional or as a new basic requirement of 21st century education.

In at least one school, financial literacy is a needed part of the curricula. At the MET school in Providence, Rhode Island, students spend half the week working in jobs in the community and in school-run businesses. We met a student who was the director for sales and marketing for the school-run local beverage bottling and distribution company. We asked him to share his attitudes about the school. He really liked it but felt he was not being taught enough math. Stunned, we told him he was the first student we had ever met who told us he wasn't getting enough math. He responded quickly by saying: "You don't understand. I'm the director of sales and marketing and they are not teaching me the math I need to do my job."

Students are more than willing than you might think to learn rigorous subjects like math—when they are presented in applied contexts, that is. The MET school student understood why he was learning formulas, and he wanted more. Unfortunately, many mathematics educators do not consider financial literacy to be a part of math.

We respectfully disagree. Whenever we've asked math teachers what percentage of the subject could be taught in the context of financial and business literacy, the responses ranged between 70 and 90 percent. We simply don't understand why educators are refusing to incorporate financial literacy into mathematics curricula.

We also believe it would be helpful to include entrepreneurship studies in K–12 education. The Network for Teaching Entrepreneurship (NFTE) is an organization that works with students from low-income communities to focus on entrepreneurial activities. The program includes a textbook on entrepreneurship as well as requiring students to work on a business plan. They can submit their plan to local, state, and national competitions. This focus on entrepreneurship is one that ought to be adopted more broadly.

Another exciting approach has been taken by Superintendent Donna DeSiato and her team in the East Syracuse-Minoa School District in East Syracuse, New York. They focus on financial literacy through the student-run credit union that was established on the high school site. Some days the high school credit union completes more transactions than the actual credit union, which sits right across the street. Not only are high school students working at the credit union, they are also teaching elementary and middle school students the basics of financial literacy.

In still other districts, Junior Achievement (JA) is a helpful resource for financial literacy teaching and learning. Through partnerships between JA and schools, business executives help students with courses and projects related to business and financial literacy. Additionally, the consortium for Entrepreneurship Education has compiled many resources that might be helpful to you in the area of entrepreneurship education. These are all exciting examples of what is possible in the realm of financial literacy. Refer to Reflection Box 1.16.

While we have highlighted global competence, financial literacy, and self-direction, there might be other skills that you'd like to add to your personal model. We recommend that you look at the Partnership for 21st Century Skills' full framework, which we've included in Appendix 1 and which you can find at www.P21.org. You will see a number of other skills that we have not highlighted in this step:

- Information, media, and technology
- Flexibility and adaptability
- Productivity and accountability
- Leadership and responsibility
- Civic literacy
- Health literacy
- Environmental literacy

1.16 REFLECTIONS ON FINANCIAL LITERACY

- Is financial literacy an area your school or district currently emphasizes?
- Should financial literacy be a part of your personal vision for education in your school or district?

You might wish to consider all of these, and others, as you develop your own personal vision. Although we have highlighted the 4Cs and three additional options, others might be more suitable for your school, district, and community. The important thing is that you as an education leader identify those skills that you consider central to your vision for your school or district. For the purposes of this book, however, we'll continue to refer to the vision you have adopted as the 4Cs, recognizing that the competencies that define your vision for 21st century education will be unique.

FINAL THOUGHTS

You've now spent quite a bit of time thinking about your own personal vision. Over the years that you have been an education leader, you have considered this topic previously and brought a great deal of experience to this exercise. Now you've read this step, thought about the perspectives and reflections it has raised, and used that thinking to help you decide which student outcomes you want to incorporate into your education model.

The vision you settle on won't be fixed in stone. But we suggest starting your 21st century education journey from a place of personal excitement and conviction. You can't do the work of Steps 2–7 if you haven't settled on your own starting point. Once you have it, you can co-create and collaborate with others and continue to critically think, problem solve, and adjust as you work with your leadership team and all the other stakeholder groups inside and outside your school and district. But it is essential to begin this work by establishing your own vision, your own personal starting point.

Before you finalize your own vision, we thought it would be helpful for you to see some examples of ones that other education leaders have created (see the three examples in Figure 1.2). These graphics represent the end result of extensive community-wide consensus building (something we cover in Step 2), but we thought it would be helpful to give you a preview. The first is Compass to 2015, the vision for Virginia Beach City Public School District in Virginia Beach, Virginia (see Figure 1.2a). The second is the Catalina Foothills model, the graphic for which was designed by high school students in the district (see Figure 1.2b). Finally, we want to highlight the model for Upper Arlington, Ohio (see Figure 1.2c).

The three models in Figure 1.2 demonstrate that this work looks different in every school and district. There are no cookie-cutter approaches here. The leaders in each district have developed customized models to suit the unique needs in their communities. These models also demonstrate how helpful it can be to produce a graphical representation of your 21st century vision for education. We encourage you to work toward that end.

FIGURE 1.2A   Model for Virginia Beach City Public Schools District

Virginia Beach City Public Schools
Compass to 2015
Our Outcomes for Student Success

Our primary focus is on teaching and assessing those skills our students need to thrive as 21st century learners, workers, and citizens. All VBCPS students will be:

- Academically proficient;
- Effective communicators and collaborators;
- Globally aware, independent, responsible learners and citizens; and
- Critical and creative thinkers, innovators, and problem solvers.

FIGURE 1.2B   Model for Catalina Foothills

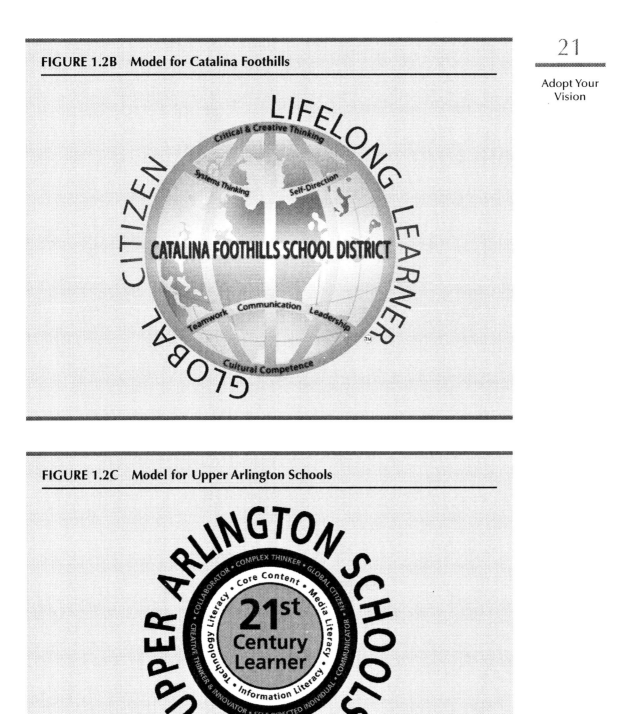

FIGURE 1.2C   Model for Upper Arlington Schools

In order to help you, we have one final reflection exercise to help you to synthesize some of the key thoughts in this step.

If you fill out both of these charts, you should be able to:

1. Determine which of the societal and educational changes are driving your commitment to a 21st century model of education for your school or district;

2. Determine which of the student outcomes you will present as part of your personal vision that will "kick off" your dialogue with your stakeholders.

REFLECTION ON THE 21ST CENTURY PERSPECTIVES

Perspective	Interesting but not compelling	Important	Central to my vision
The Workforce			
The Flat World			
The Service Economy			
Citizenship			
The Pace of Change			
Design & Innovation			
Information			
Technology			

REFLECTION ON THE STUDENT OUTCOMES

Student Outcome	Interesting but not compelling	Important	Central to my vision
Critical Thinking			
Communication			
Collaboration			
Creativity			
Self-Direction			
Global Competence			
Financial Literacy			
Other			
Other			
Other			

A Broader Vision for Teaching and Leadership

The work you are completing in Step 1 provides a unique direction for student outcomes; it also, however, provides a strategic direction for teaching and leadership in your school or district. This is because the 4Cs are not just good outcomes for students. They are also the attributes of great teachers and great leaders. As you refine your vision for 21st century learning, keep this in mind:

- The 4Cs are not just student outcomes;
- The 4Cs are not just the dimensions of good pedagogy;
- The 4Cs are the attributes of 21st century leadership.

FIGURE 1.3 The Role of the 4Cs in 21st Century Education

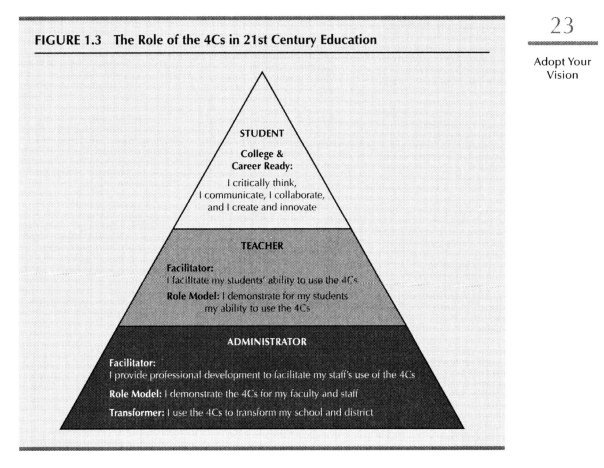

The importance of the 4Cs is apparent when it comes to all three of these areas: student outcomes, teaching, and leading, as depicted in Figure 1.3, The Role of the 4Cs in 21st Century Education.

Note that student outcomes (at the top of the pyramid) remain the primary focus for the 4Cs. Students in the 21st century must possess these skills. But in order to accomplish this vision for students, teachers must embrace the 4Cs in their teaching practices and education leaders must embrace the 4Cs in their leadership practices.

Recently a superintendent told us, "I love this model. It has a beautiful symmetry about it. Our students need the 4Cs as outcomes. Our teachers need the 4Cs to teach. But this also makes clear that our leadership team needs to possess the 4Cs. The entire organization can use the 4Cs as their respective organizing concept." This was music to our ears. It should be music to your ears, too. You now have a model that not only provides a frame of reference for where you want to take student outcomes, but you now might also have a sense about where you would like to take your teachers and your leadership team as well.

We know you have done a lot of critical thinking in Step 1. Thank you for all of this hard work. We hope it helps you produce a useful starting point for your journey as a 21st century education leader.

Now let's move to Step 2 and determine how you will build consensus around a co-created vision of 21st century education for your school or district.

REFERENCES

Figure 1.1 Autor, David H., Frank Levy, and Richard J. Murnane. "The Skill Content of Recent Technological Change: An Empirical Exploration." *Quarterly Journal of Economics* 118 (2003): 1279–1334.

AASA. *The School Administrator* 65.2 (Feb. 2008) http://www.aasa.org/SchoolAdministratorArticle.aspx?id=5996.

"AMA Critical Skills Survey 2010." American Management Association. http://www.p21.org/storage/documents/Critical%20Skills%20Survey%20Executive%20Summary.pdf.

"Are They Really Ready to Work?" *Partnership for 21st Century Skills,* 2006. Washington: DC: P21. Web. Jan 2011.

Autor, David H., Frank Levy, and Richard J. Murnane. "The Skill Content of Recent Technological Change: An Empirical Exploration." *Quarterly Journal of Economics* 118 (2003): 1279–334.

Bransford, John. Personal interview. Jan. 2010.

Conley, David T. "Toward a More Comprehensive Conception of College Readiness." Education Policy Improvement Center. 8 Feb. 2008. Web. 12 June 2011. http://www.collegiatedirections.org/2007_Gates_CollegeReadinessPaper.pdf.

Friedman, Thomas. *The World Is Flat: A Brief History of the Twenty-First Century.* New York: Picador/Farrar Straus and Giroux, 2005.

Friedman, Thomas, and Michael Mandelbaum. *That Used to Be Us: How America Fell Behind in the World It Invented and How We Can Come Back.* New York: Farrar, Straus and Giroux, 2011.

GLOBE. Web. July 2011. http://globe.gove/about

"Learning for the 21st Century." *Partnership for 21st Century Skills.* Washington, DC: P21, 2002.

Makerspace: Creating a Space for Young Makers and Educators. O'Reilly Media's Make division, in partnership with Otherlab, 26 Feb. 2012. Web. Jan. 2012. http://makerspace.com/.

Merrill, Jim. Personal Interview. January 2011.

New York Hall of Science. *Proceedings from the "Innovation, Education, and the Maker Movement" Workshop.* 26–27 Sept. 2010, Queens, NY. Web. Jan. 2012. http://www.nysci.org/media/file/MakerFaireReportFinal122310.pdf.

Pink, Daniel. *Drive: The Surprising Truth About What Motivates Us.* New York: Riverhead, 2009.

Pink, Daniel. *A Whole New Mind.* New York: Riverhead, 2006.

"Skills and Tasks for Jobs: A SCANS Report for America 2000." *Secretary's Commission on Achieving Necessary Skills.* Washington, DC: Department of Labor, 1999.

Surowiecki, James. *The Wisdom of Crowds,* New York: Anchor, 2005.

"21st Century Skills, Education & Competitiveness." *Partnership for 21st Century Skills,* 2008.

U.S. Department of Labor. "Number of Jobs Held, Labor Market Activity, and Earnings Growth Among Younger Baby Boomers: Recent Results From a Longitudinal Survey Summary." Bureau of Labor Statistics, 2004. Web. Feb. 1, 2011. http://www.bls.gov/nls/nlsy79r20.pdf, published 2004.

Wagner, Tony. *Creating Innovators: The Making of Young People Who Will Change the World.* New York: Scribner/Simon & Schuster, 2012.

STEP

Create a Community Consensus

THE 4CS FOCUS

The 4Cs focus for Step 2 is:

- Critical thinking: You will need to think critically about how to design your outreach and consensus building strategy.
- Communication: You will need to effectively tell the story of why your school or district needs a new model of education and what your vision is.
- Collaboration: You will need to facilitate authentic collaboration among all stakeholders to build the broadest base possible for your vision.
- Creativity: You will need to be creative and innovative in every aspect of your outreach strategy.

Introduction

Having a vision is terrific—building upon it with others makes it a reality. Now that you've considered your personal vision in Step 1, it is time to utilize your communication and collaboration skills as you work to build consensus around it.

Leading your school or community from a personal conviction to a *shared vision* among all the key stakeholders in your school or district and community is the next step—and it is an important building block. If this were 50 or 60 years ago, it might have been enough to simply set the policy and expect others to follow your lead. But creating any kind of change in today's school systems requires broad and deep layers of consensus. We believe this engagement dialogue of Step 2 is absolutely critical. This "buy-in" phase for your vision is a lot of work, but it will enable you to co-create a vision for 21st century education that can create a supportive environment for the transformations you want to make in your school or district.

First, we recommend you be intentional and purposeful about your *leadership*. In each district where we have seen 21st century education implementation, strong leadership has always been the key ingredient for success. Committed groups of teachers and/ or administrators can make progress, no question about it. But when the head of the school or district strongly embraces the work, it reaches many more students, is more sustainable and, we believe, is critical to overall success. So take your position as an education leader seriously. This work can't happen without you.

Our first suggestion is to showcase your commitment. Think about all of the ways you can highlight your support for 21st century education and the 4Cs. You would be surprised by the number of schools and districts we visit where teachers and staff say to us: "Well, we know the curriculum director cares about this, but we are not really sure how important this is to the principal or superintendent." As a leader, showing visible, consistent dedication to this work is a must.

There are many ways to demonstrate your support for 21st century education. You can produce blogs and newsletters or describe it (even if briefly) in your public appearances. You can ensure it is a regular agenda item in leadership team meetings. You can share articles through your digital networks. You get the idea. Your team will be trying to read the depth of your commitment. If they suspect it is shallow, then there is no need to reprioritize their own work. Don't leave them up in the air—*showcase* your commitment.

Second, we recommend *modeling* the outcomes. If students are to think critically, communicate, collaborate, and be creative, you and your leadership team need to model these skills for teachers, staff, and students.

We have interviewed dozens of education leaders who are leading 21st century education initiatives in their schools or districts. Whenever we ask them to identify the skills that have been most helpful *to them* in moving their 21st century education initiatives forward, they describe some version of the 4Cs.

Mary Kamerzell, the superintendent of Catalina Foothills School District in Tucson, Arizona, names systems thinking as her top choice. Her students learn systems thinking, and her teachers teach systems thinking. But, in addition, she has used systems thinking in every aspect of her leadership from the very beginning. Because the foundation of her work as a leader relies on this skill, it has made it much easier for her team to live and breathe it as well—they have developed a common definition of systems thinking that has been integrated into all curricula, assessments, and professional development in the district. Her leadership team uses a common set of systems thinking literature and research to guide and improve its work.

Superintendent Jim Merrill of Virginia Beach City Public Schools puts it this way: "Communication is the most important skill. Right behind it would be collaboration, but you can't do a darn thing if you can't express what you are trying to accomplish." Superintendent Pam Moran of Albemarle School District in Virginia also notes the importance

2.1 REFLECTION ON LEADERSHIP

- Are you prepared to offer dynamic leadership for your 21st century education initiative?
- Do the 4Cs provide a helpful framework for you as you consider the attributes of the 21st century leader?
- Are you prepared to serve as a "role model" of the 4Cs for your school or district?
- Are you prepared to challenge your leadership team to adopt and model the 4Cs as the attributes of their leadership?

of communication and collaboration skills. In her opinion, if she can't articulate it and can't have two-way conversations with people about it, it doesn't matter how good she is at innovation or problem-solving work. It doesn't matter how flexible and adaptable she is. To her, as the superintendent, it all comes down to communication and collaboration skills because that's how good things get built with other people. Superintendent Donna DeSiato of the East Syracuse Minoa Central School District takes the perspective that each of the 4Cs is important. In her opinion, it is not helpful to focus on one over another; they are all interconnected and equally necessary.

As you can see, these leaders are using the 4Cs as central leadership skills. These are not just key outcomes for students. They are also key attributes of 21st century leadership; modeling them for your entire community is essential. Refer to Box 2.1.

Communicate the Importance of the 4Cs

As you work to build a consensus around 21st century education, you will utilize your communication skills a great deal. Finding a way to tell a compelling story about the need for 21st century education is critical.

One effective tactic is to engage your audiences in the conversation. We often use what we call the "three questions" exercise. This exercise is a great lead-in with stakeholders when you are starting a dialogue about change, student outcomes, and your school or district. The speaker asks the group each of the questions below in sequence, asking participants to respond to each one aloud:

1. What are the two or three biggest changes in our society in the past 25 to 30 years? [allow for feedback to be shared]
2. What two or three skills do your students need in order to address these changes in society? [allow for feedback to be shared]
3. Looking at the skills you listed in answering the previous question, how intentional is your school or district in helping your students develop these skills? [allow for feedback to be shared]

We often ask participants to share their responses to questions 1 and 2 with the entire audience, then to discuss their responses to the third question in small groups. This exercise helps people think critically about their roles as educators and stakeholders and the needs of today's students. There is always a moment when the group concludes that much more could be done within the school to produce 21st century student outcomes. That's always one of our favorite moments in the discussion.

Another effective communication strategy we have employed is storytelling. As we've traveled the country speaking about 21st century education, no matter how many different ways we have talked about it, people always remember the stories we tell. So our first piece of advice is to become a consummate 21st century education storyteller.

Below is one example of how this kind of device works when we employ it. As you read the example, think about what story you could use to communicate a key element of your initiative, the way we have done below to demonstrate the importance of partnerships.

Story Example

This story involves the beginning of the New Tech High School model in Napa, California, as we mentioned in Step 1. When we were invited to visit to learn about their model, we asked the school to describe how they started this work.

As part of a local economic development initiative, business leaders were researching how to bring businesses to Napa Valley. One of the biggest issues they discovered was the lack of a skilled labor force needed to attract high technology companies. Employers were looking not just for technologically literate employees, but employees who were self-starters, problem solvers, creators and collaborators. Napa schools, on the other hand, were turning out a few college ready students and lots of low skill workers. The business leaders approached the school district and basically said, "fix this."

In 1996, after repurposing an old elementary school, Napa Valley Unified School District opened New Technology High School. Its defining characteristics were one-to-one computing, a digital collaborative platform, cross curricular team teaching, block scheduling, an emphasis on 21st century skills like critical thinking, and, of course, project-based learning.

About two years later, we returned to see how the new high school was assessing the 4Cs. A student walked up to us and announced himself as our guide. He walked us around the building for a while, and we asked him to show us how his knowledge and skills were assessed. He took us into the student lounge, and we logged into his class on American history and literature. On the top page a column read:

- Work ethic 30%
- Literature and history content 50%
- Communication skills 10%
- Technology skills 10% (A report card such as this one is featured in Step 5 (on page 83).)

He explained that the school board required 30% of each grade to be devoted to work ethic. The teachers set the rest of the percentages. We realized right then and there that the 30% work ethic reflected the school board's partnership with the business community. The young man told us that every time he logged into the course, this page appeared first—always reminding him what knowledge and skills were being measured.

As he generously shared his online report card progress, we noticed that while all the grades were 80–85%, he was failing communication skills with a grade of 55. We asked him to talk a bit about that. He told us the following: "Well, two years ago, in the old high school, if I asked someone what to do about a low grade, they'd say, 'study harder.' At this school, because my grades were online, by the time I got home, my mom had already seen my grades. My mom had already called my teacher and said, 'My son flunked communication skills, what are we going to do about it?' The teacher recommended two things. First, she had the drama coach meet with me and some other students who had the same challenge to help us with our presentation skills. The teacher also had me serve as a high school tour guide!"

So we said, "You flunked communication skills three months ago? You are terrific!" And he didn't miss a beat—he asked, "Will you come down the hall and tell my teacher?" Which we very happily did.

We like this story for three reasons:

- It's a great example of a business–education partnership working together to focus on important student outcomes.

- It shows how in less than one year the school could develop an effective plan to build the outcomes it cared about into a new high school.
- It shows how innovation and creativity can help develop useful interventions to make a difference.

This school is not an isolated example, by the way. The New Tech High School in Napa has now grown into a network of more than 90 schools around the country. Visiting places like this is a powerful way to build your storytelling toolkit. It helps make your vision much more concrete when you can share stories with others in your school, district, and community. Also, consider other ways to enhance your storytelling abilities, such as:

- Visit with business leaders and ask them their view of what skills are most important for your students to develop. These discussions can provide excellent material for your storytelling.
- Tell stories from your own experiences about the importance of the 4Cs in your own life and career.
- Talk to the students in your school or district and ask them how they feel about 21st century skills like the 4Cs.
- Talk to your own children, grandchildren, and nieces/nephews about their views of the need for a new education model. These can be turned into powerful stories.
- Engage in conversations with members of your school board, parents, and community members. The stories you hear from them will enrich your own storytelling.
- Engage in conversations with your teachers. Find those teachers who are doing the best job of currently teaching the 4Cs in your district and weave their experiences into your own stories.

Now that you have some storytelling ideas, here is a suggestion for organizing them:

- Take two 5" × 8" index cards.
- At the top of one, write "The reasons for change." On this card, list three or four concrete stories you can tell about the need to change the education model.
- On the second card, write "21st century outcomes." On this card, list three or four stories you have about teachers, schools, or districts you know that are actually putting 21st century education in action.

As you talk to the various groups, add interesting stories to your two lists. And when you're out talking to folks about your vision, don't forget to regularly fit these stories into your presentation. Also, try a little test. After your presentations, ask a few folks what part of your presentation was most effective. Invariably, they'll tell you it was one of your stories. This will reinforce for you the need to keep collecting and telling stories.

A third communication strategy that we have employed is the use of videos to complement our presentations. Many of you are already using videos as part of your presentations; some of our favorites are included in Figure 2.1.

We have recently completed working with the Pearson Foundation and EdLeader21 on several videos. One is "The Role of Leaders in 21st Century Education." It includes some insightful interviews with superintendents who

---

FIGURE 2.1 **Videos on 21st Century Education**

- EdLeader21 videos that focus on the role of leadership in 21st century education: **http://www.youtube.com/edleader21**
- P21 and Fablevision's "Above and Beyond;"
- "Did You Know?" series A vision of Students Today (**www.youtube.com/watch?v=dGCJ46vyR9o**)

are currently leading 21st century education initiatives in their districts. Others (available on the EdLeader21 YouTube channel) focus on the 4Cs, curriculum and assessment.

One of our other favorites is the "Did You Know?" series developed originally by Karl Fisch and updated by Howie DiBlasi (he updates the video every year or so). You might remember the videos from the well-known tagline "shift happens!" The Partnership for 21st Century Skills (P21) also has an excellent collection of relevant videos you might use. P21's contest on 21st century readiness resulted in two winning videos, both of which are quite effective. One is an animation, and the other is a set of testimonials from young people. P21 also recently released an animation titled "Above and Beyond" that is a powerful conversation starter about the 4Cs (see Figure 2.1).

Finally, we've recently noticed more and more schools and districts have been facilitating large group discussions about the state of education. This is another effective communication strategy. The structure and focus of these gatherings vary broadly. Some involve conversations with stakeholders inside the school or district; some have taken the form of community conversations about education. Often, these meetings have been organized around a movie or a book. The movies *Two Million Minutes, Waiting for Superman,* and *Changing Education Paradigms* have all been used this way. Five books on 21st century education that have commonly been used by reading groups around the country are included in Figure 2.2.

FIGURE 2.2 Selected Books On 21st Century Education

The list below is by no means exhaustive, but each one is an excellent contribution to the literature on 21st century education.

- *21st Century Skills: Learning for Life in Our Times* by Bernie Trilling and Charles Fadel. This is a comprehensive book about the Partnership for 21st Century Skills Framework for Learning.
- *The Global Achievement Gap* by Tony Wagner. This a particularly helpful book in the context of education leader and business leader dialogue on 21st century education. We are aware of several school boards and community groups that have used this book to stimulate a business–education community dialogue.
- *21st Century Skills: Rethinking How Students Learn* edited by Jim Bellanca and Ron Brandt is a fairly recent publication. It is more of a compendium of articles on 21st century education, and Ken Kay contributed the foreword. The book includes pieces from Howard Gardner, Linda Darling-Hammond, Jay McTighe, Bob Pearlman, and Rebecca and Richard DuFour.
- *A World-Class Education: Learning from International Models of Excellence and Innovation* by Vivien Stewart presents what some of the best examples from other school systems around the world are doing to prepare students for an innovation-based world.
- *College and Career Ready* by David Conley. Conley takes his four dimensions of college and career readiness (contextual skills and awareness, academic behaviors, key content knowledge and key cognitive strategies) and articulates how these can and should be used as a blueprint for high schools to prepare students for 21st century success.

As you consider communication strategies, consider the strongest, most compelling messages you can develop as well as the kind of "pushback" you are likely to receive.

First, let's start with your most positive message. You can build consensus among stakeholders by staying focused on 21st century student outcomes. You will be able to build a rich consensus on what the 21st century outcomes of your school or district should be. In 2002, when we began working on 21st century education, one simple question was the key: "What skills do young people need to be successful in the 21st century?" As we asked the question over and over, it became clear that there was overwhelming consensus about the answer. The skills that people named in response to this question were identical 90 percent of the time. We would go into a group of 200 business leaders, parents, administrators, or school board members, and we would hear the same answers, without fail. Big picture issues can be quite contentious in education circles, but in this case, there is rarely disagreement about what students needed to be able to do to be successful in work, college, citizenship, or life.

We recently facilitated a stakeholders' meeting in Springfield, Missouri, in southwest Missouri. Attendees included business leaders, school board members, teachers, administrators, parents, and students. In a relatively short amount of time, they agreed that *all* of their students need to be able to critically think, problem solve, communicate, and collaborate. Even in such a diverse group, these conclusions were not at all controversial.

But here we offer a word of caution: Be careful to fully understand what this kind of consensus really means. If you ask your stakeholders whether all students need these skills, you will find general agreement. But if you ask the same people to identify the best ways to teach and assess these skills, or the best ways to reorganize schools to prioritize these skills, you will not find much consensus—in fact, very rapidly you'll start to see a wide range of conflicting opinions. We cannot stress the importance of this enough. If you are an effective and engaging communicator and collaborator, you will be able to forge a clear consensus around the student outcomes. It will be much harder to build consensus around the strategies for implementation. So we advise you, in your initial stages of consensus building, to focus first on the student <u>outcomes</u> people can agree upon. By focusing on the direct impacts for students, everyone should be able to agree on the vision and to find it energizing and inspirational. For example, it is refreshing to discuss with students and their parents these kinds of questions:

- Should every student who graduates from this school or district be a critical thinker and problem solver?
- Should every student who graduates from this school or district be an effective communicator?
- Should every student who graduates from this school or district be an effective collaborator?
- Should every student be creative and innovative?
- Should every student who graduates from this school or district demonstrate a minimal level of global competence?
- Should every student who graduates from this school or district be fluent in a second language?
- Should every student who graduates from this school or district be financially literate?
- Should every student who graduates from this school or district be self-directed?

We have seen these questions energize audiences in a broad range of communities. And it provides a welcome departure from current educational debates that focus far too often on tactical arguments about things like standards or educational data quality. Debates about implementation are important—but they have their place. When you are building consensus about the vision, try to avoid getting trapped in the issues of the day. Build, instead, an energetic dialogue about the future of your school system, and use this dialogue to energize your students, parents, and citizens in a commitment to revitalize education.

Second, we have counseled leaders we have worked with to emphasize critical thinking as the first skill among equals. This is an important piece of advice because it potentially addresses the whole tone of 21st century learning initiatives. We need young people who are effective problem solvers to apply the knowledge they have to contexts with which they might not be familiar. These are key 21st century capabilities. Our current educational system rarely challenges students in such rigorous ways. You are committing to address this shortcoming by raising the current bar in education. Your initiative is, therefore, more demanding than current education models. "Applied learning" and "critical thinking" in the context of core academic subjects represent a highly rigorous and demanding education model.

We like describing this approach as "21st century rigor." Using such language can help you emphasize your commitment to advancing the capacities of your teachers and students. To those—and there will be some—who will claim that 21st century education is simply about "soft skills," you can and should counter that critical thinking is much more rigorous than the rote memorization that often passes for rigor in today's dominant model of education.

Questions from the AP biology exam shared below can help your audiences understand this notion of 21st century rigor. After a decade of encouragement by many, including the National Academy of Sciences, to go beyond its traditional focus on content mastery, the College Board has revised many of their AP exams to place more emphasis on critical thinking, problem solving, and applied learning. A released question from the old AP exam and a sample question from the redesigned AP exam are contrasted below.

The creeping horizontal and subterranean stems of ferns are referred to as:

1. Prothalli

2. Fronds

3. Stipes

4. Roots

5. Rhizomes

Notice this question is basically a factual recall question.

Now, in contrast, look at a question from the redesigned AP exam for biology:

$$H^+ + HCO_3 \quad H_2O + CO_2$$

The equation above shows a reversible reaction that occurs in blood. An Olympic marathoner training at high altitude in Colorado feels dizzy and begins hyperventilating while taking a run. Her blood pH is elevated, resulting in alkalosis. How will normal blood pH be restored?

1. An increase in O_2 concentration in the plasma will lead to a decrease in H^+ concentration

2. An increase in CO_2 concentration in the plasma will lead to an increase in H^+ concentration

3. A decrease in sweating will lead to an increase in HCO_3 concentration

4. A decrease in respiration will lead to an increase in plasma O_2 concentration

Notice that the revised question gives students a formula. In the past, students were asked simply to recall the formula. Now they are asked to apply it in a real-life situation.

We show audiences these two exam questions and then we ask them about the difference in the education styles. What would a school system that emphasizes "question 1-type" education look like? What would a school system that emphasizes "question 2-type" education look like? We also ask them which question is more challenging. These exam questions are a great way to give audiences a mental image of 21st century rigor. We think it will help you tell your story that the 4Cs are about more rigor, not less.

Along the same lines, it is important to emphasize your support for accountability as you reach out to stakeholders. 21st century education *is completely consistent with attempts to increase accountability in education.* It is a good thing to hold students, teachers, and administrators accountable for performance. However, there are two problems with the accountability strategies being used today. Most of them are administered in a punitive context. How many of us think our students are best served in an environment of blame and punishment? Can we really expect teachers to perform well in hostile environments? Shouldn't the goal of the accountability be a mutually supportive environment of shared accountability? Accountability in its dominant form today does not support continuously improving cultures of high performance.

This problem exists because the most commonly available accountability systems rely on 50-year-old metrics, not the ones that truly matter for students today. The metrics we are using in current accountability systems are overly focused on content knowledge only.

When educators raise valid complaints about No Child Left Behind (NCLB), we always ask them how they would feel if they were being held accountable for the 4Cs. We ask what would happen if accountability metrics actually measured students' critical thinking, communication, collaboration, and creativity skills, in addition to their content knowledge. Educators almost always respond in the affirmative that accountability would make sense if it focused on such meaningful outcomes.

Thinking about accountability from this perspective means measuring more of the things that really matter. It leads you to ask whether every student is ready for 21st century life, citizenship, and work. This kind of accountability system doesn't allow for the use of outdated measurements. It calls for measuring the real performance-based competencies that students need for success in college, career, and work—things like critical thinking, collaboration, communication, and creativity.

The Common Core State Standards (CCSS) represent a step in a positive direction for accountability, in our opinion. The CCSS in English and mathematics will result in more critical thinking, problem solving, and applied learning strategies being embedded into state assessments (and the state-based accountability systems). We welcome this emphasis. It is consistent with the goals of 21st century education. The CCSS has also accomplished an important goal for 21st century educators—the new standards are more focused on depth of understanding and less breadth of content, which permits deeper exploration of academic content. This is a welcome development in the standards movement.

It is important *not* to view the CCSS as *the* path to your 21st century education goals, however. Even if the new standards represent an improvement in addressing critical thinking, problem solving, and communication skills, they do not address many of the student outcomes that you might have embraced in your school or district model. In many states, their implementation will not adequately address collaboration, creativity, global competence, financial literacy, technology literacy, and self-direction, for example. This means that you as a leader and your school or district need to view CCSS as the floor but not the ceiling in terms of how you support students in becoming 21st century citizens and workers. To see an analysis of CCSS as they relate to 21st century outcomes, see the Partnership for 21st Century Skills Common Core Toolkit. It is a helpful resource in understanding the CCSS in terms of higher-order thinking skills (www.P21.org).

In summary, accountability can be a powerful, positive part of your messaging. It is wise to support and expect accountability for the things that really matter: 21st century student outcomes.

In addition to promoting your positive messages, you should be prepared to respond to arguments that might be made against your 21st century education initiative. In our experience, opposition to 21st century education falls into three main categories. The first is that you are undermining core academic content. The argument goes that if you emphasize critical thinking, communications, collaboration, and creativity, you will undermine the teacher's ability to teach what is really important. This argument is often stated in hierarchical terms: you can't begin to think critically in a content domain unless you've mastered the basic (or even advanced) content of that domain. These advocates contend that content mastery is a step that must be accomplished *before* critical thinking takes place.

This argument relies on the false dichotomy that we actually have to choose between teaching content and skills. The correct answer is that the best teaching and learning actually blend rigorous content mastery with higher-order thinking skills. The two can and should be mutually supportive of one another.

Another category of criticism is that 21st century education is too focused on the needs of business. One dimension of this argument is that education is designed to do more than prepare young people for the workforce, that citizenship is important, too. Another variant of this argument is that the advocates of 21st century education are largely tech vendors trying to sell more tech products. The interesting thing about the 4Cs is that it is impossible to argue that they only prepare students for the workforce. Imagine an individual who is a critical thinker, a problem solver, a collaborator, a communicator, and creative. Isn't this person also likely to be an effective citizen? Isn't a student with these attributes likely to be effective in her/his personal life? Imagine someone with those attributes working for a non-profit or being elected to public office. The 4Cs are skills that apply far beyond the needs of the 21st century workforce. They are needed in every element of modern, civilized society.

Finally, the most daunting challenge to 21st century education leaders is the fundamental resistance to change. This general approach takes a myriad of specific forms:

"We're already doing it."
"We don't have the money."
"We're overloaded."
"This is nothing new."
"We're already well into the 21st century."
"The old system worked just fine for me."
"This is an educational fad that will just go away."

This cluster of responses requires special attention because resistance to change is the biggest hurdle you will encounter. It requires patience, humor, and persistence on your part. In education, many important stakeholders (teachers, administrators, parents) take a "check the box" attitude about new initiatives. If teachers feel they occasionally teach critical thinking or communication, then they can "check the box" and don't need to address your initiative seriously. You can challenge them with a different approach:

- Are they as intentional and purposeful about their teaching as they could be?
- Are they on a path of continuously improving their pedagogy?
- Is the school or district consistent in its approach to the 4Cs?
- Could we work collectively to improve the delivery of the 4Cs to *every* student in *every* classroom?

These questions often turn the natural inertia within education systems in a more active direction. It is important for you to telegraph your optimism and energy for your approach. We hope that our focus on communication strategies has provided you with the tools and arguments you need to feel well prepared for launching your outreach efforts. Before we focus on your collaboration activities, let's have you do an inventory of your communication tools.

2.2 CHECKLIST ON COMMUNICATION TOOLS

- Do you have two or three stories to tell about your perspectives on changes in the 21st century?
- Do you have two or three stories to tell about your perspective on the importance of the 4Cs?
- Have you selected a video or two to use in your presentations?
- Have you selected a movie or book to use as the basis of a stakeholder outreach meeting?
- Have you created a visual presentation outlining your vision?

As you create your presentation, the following checklist of ideas might be helpful:

Key Ideas	Central to my vision	Included in my presentation
Changes in the 21st century:		
The Workforce		
The Flat World		
The Service Economy		
Citizenship		
The Pace Of Change		
Design And Innovation		
Technology		
Information		
Other:		
Other:		
Key Messages:		
21st Century Outcomes		
21st Century Rigor		
21st Century Accountability		
Other:		
Other:		

Please keep in mind our challenge to you. You are not only making the case for your vision of 21st century education—you are also showcasing your communication skills. Use this effort as a way for "modeling" effective communication skills for your school and district. Now let's turn to what exactly you are going to do with these great tools and arguments.

Collaborate Around the 4Cs

You not only need to bring your communication skills "A" game to this effort, you also need to bring your collaboration "A" game. As all stakeholders begin to feel they are an authentic part of the process, the more likely they will embrace it. And the more you model collaboration skills, the more collaborative an environment your school or district will become.

We recommend reaching out to four key groups: students, educators, the business community, and community groups. If you reach out to each of these constituencies, you will have created a very impressive base of support for your 21st century education initiative. You will have received much valuable input to help you revise and improve your initiative and you will have enlisted many people who can help you implement the proposal. You want to use this outreach period to create a sense of energy and common purpose so that you and each of these important groups feel you are working together to co-create a 21st century education model in your school or district. This phase of your work is very time consuming. It requires a tremendous amount of shoe leather, grit, and patience, but in the long run, it will pay off with deep support and enthusiasm among your team members.

We hope it won't come as a surprise, but we believe the starting point for your collaborative efforts should be with your students themselves. You will have the most fun engaging with your students on this topic. Everywhere we go, students are among the most dynamic participants in the conversation about the future of education. They see how many of their fellow students are disengaged in school. They are quick to acknowledge how much their current learning environments lack when compared to the excitement they feel for their out-of-school pursuits and interests. Yet they are astute at identifying the school programs that are truly relevant and challenging. In our work with schools and districts, it is the student leadership that has been the most heartening to see. Students should be one of the most important elements of your outreach strategy.

To help set the frame for thinking about student involvement, we recommend reading the "My Voice 6–12 Student National Report 2010." It contains excellent data from the MyVoice survey on student aspirations, which was completed by more than 19,000 6th to 12th graders nationally. Focusing on student self-confidence, desire to achieve, and perceptions of school, the survey asked students to answer questions in categories such as belonging, sense of accomplishment, curiosity and creativity, leadership and responsibility, and confidence to take action.

While there are some positive trends noted in the survey, here are a few of the more concerning highlights for 21st century education leaders:

- Less than half of students think their teachers care about their problems and feelings, feel they are a valued member of the school community, or are proud of their school.
- Less than half of students enjoy being at school.

- Only slightly above one-third think their teachers make school an exciting place to learn. Roughly half think school is boring. At the same time, seven in 10 believe learning can be fun.
- Barely four in 10 feel their classes help them understand what is happening in their everyday lives.
- Approximately one-quarter of students are afraid to challenge themselves because they are afraid they might fail.
- Two-thirds of students reported confidence in their own leadership skills, but less than half feel they have a voice in decision making at school or believe that teachers are willing to learn from students.

If even some of these attitudes are reflected in your school or district, the student's role in your 21st century initiative will be critical for your success. Students are not merely the recipients of your 21st century vision, however. They should help craft and implement it. If they are involved in authentic ways, they can be some of your most powerful implementation partners. See Appendix 10 for the Student Outreach Toolkit.

As you think about involving students in helping to refine your vision, it is important to understand where they are today. What are their attitudes about learning? How do they perceive their teachers, their classes, and their school environments? What are their expectations about what they need and want to learn? Do they see the school as a place that supports their aspirations for learning?

Engaging students around such questions is a logical step in the process of refining your vision. Also, consider these questions:

- Have you talked directly with students about 21st century education?
- How have the perceptions and attitudes of your students influenced your vision for 21st century education?
- Do students believe they play an active role in decision making in the school/district?
- Do all students perceive themselves as fellow implementers of the 21st century education initiative?

In general, we recommend reaching out to students consistently about your 21st century education initiative. Have them help define what "seat(s)" they want at the table, how they can help, and what challenges they see. As you consider how to reach out to your student population, reflect on these questions:

- In what ways are education leaders and students currently discussing and/or working together to implement 21st century education initiatives?
- What regular forums are in place to allow students to reflect on and participate in the transformation work you are pursuing?
- What barriers exist between students and education leaders that make such collaboration a challenge?
- Is your outreach strategy focused on all students or a specific subset of students? (If it is a subset, such as the student council, is there a strategy for reaching out to the full student population?)

These dialogues with students should give you a good sense on how to design their participation in the consensus-building phase as well as the ongoing 21st century work of your school or district.

In addition to thinking about students, you should also consider a group that is often enthusiastic about 21st century education—teachers. In many districts and schools we have visited, teachers have rallied around this work. Think about reaching out to your early adopters. These are the teachers on the cutting edge who enjoy improving their practice and are often adept at integrating new technologies into their work. Elementary school teachers in particular will tell you that the 4Cs are already incorporated into their practices. By recognizing the teachers who are already doing this work, you will begin with a group of vociferous advocates who support your 21st century vision.

A number of teachers within specific disciplines have been actively supporting 21st century education as well. The national associations that represent teachers—English (NCTE), Social Studies (NCSS), Science (NSTA), Geography (NCGE), along with arts education groups and mathematics educators, to name a few—have already developed "21st century skills" maps within their content domains. (The maps can be found at www.p21.org; also see Appendix 2.) These maps provide examples of what the 4Cs look like when they are integrated into 4th grade science, 8th grade English or 12th grade mathematics. Consider sharing these maps with the heads of departments in your school or district and use them as "awareness" tools with teachers. Educators in specific disciplines might well become champions of your effort because they understand the value of building the 4Cs more intentionally into their academic subject area.

Teachers of gifted and talented students will also be some of your strongest advocates for 21st century education. They will be important resources for you as you take their traditional focus on complex thinking skills and rigorous application of knowledge and make it more available for every student. Similarly, administrators and teachers in Career and Technical Education (CTE) programs believe their work is nicely aligned with 21st century education outcomes. CTE teachers have been teaching personal and career skills extremely effectively for decades. However, those programs are often viewed as resources for non-college-bound students. Yet, the skills that CTE programs emphasize are needed by every student. "Up to the Challenge: The Role of Career and Technical Education and 21st Century Skills in College and Career Readiness," published by P21, ACTE, and NASDCTEC, is a wonderful basis for considering the strengths of CTE and the way it can be used as a platform for 21st century education work. You can use resources like these as background materials and then ask your constituents to consider this scenario: Think about a school in which every child is taught in a manner consistent with the way gifted students are taught. And imagine, in the same school, that every student participates in CTE classes. How would that affect each student? What would it take to make this kind of transformation?

Librarians are another group of educators who are likely to embrace your vision. Nationally, librarians have been among the most vocal proponents of 21st century education. They are natural advocates for information, media, and technology literacy. The American Association of School Librarians (AASL) has created "Standards for the 21st Century Learner" that are world class and well aligned with 21st century education outcomes. In some districts, librarians act as 21st century skill coaches.

Also, be sure to work with your teachers' unions, if they are a part of your system. In many districts and states, the National Education Association (NEA) affiliates have been the leading advocates for 21st century education. John Wilson, the former National Executive Director of the NEA, commented that "NEA members want to teach in a manner envisioned by the framework for 21st century learning. That is a vision many of us in teaching are excited about. Teachers and administrators should be able to come together around this shared vision for learning."

Your school board can and should be an ally in this work as well. Good school board members intuitively think about the future of the district and ask themselves "where should our district be in five years?" and "Are we thinking about what our kids will need in five to 10 years?" Most school boards play central roles, obviously, in charting the strategic direction for the district.

In districts like Upper Arlington, Ohio, and Fairfax County, Virginia, the momentum for 21st century education originated with school board members. Your 21st century vision can be presented as part of a board retreat or strategic planning discussion.

Catalina Foothills School District had been working on strategic planning for a decade when, in their third strategic plan, they began to focus on what they started calling 21st century learning outcomes. Hamilton School District, outside Milwaukee, Wisconsin, had a very similar set of experiences. Its superintendent and school board members began a strategic planning approach more than 15 years ago. It wasn't until their fourth strategic plan that they began their focus on 21st century student outcomes. Leaders in each of these districts had traditions of strategic planning that were successful in making substantial improvements and changes. They built upon such traditions to then move their 21st century education initiatives forward.

It might help you and your board to look at discussion questions such as: "What student outcomes are really critical to our students' future success?" and "Is our school or district intentional and purposeful enough about those outcomes?" You might want to lead your school board through the "three questions" exercise highlighted earlier (see p. 37). Most school boards will not only actively engage in such a conversation but are also often willing to host such a conversation with the broader community as well.

The parent community is a complex one to engage in on this subject. Some parents will intuitively understand the changing needs of the workforce—they are active participants in it. They can bring a particularly helpful perspective to the conversation. Other parents, however, might be inclined to support the system as they knew it—they will need to be brought along in the process. Either way, it is important to emphasize the involvement of parents in the conversation.

If you reach out to all of these groups diligently, a vibrant conversation will begin to take place in your school or district. Thus far we have focused on teachers, librarians, teachers' unions, school boards, parents, and students. Are there other internal stakeholder groups you might add to your list? You might want to consider convening a group of internal stakeholders and begin to cultivate general support for your vision.

Next it will be important to look outside your school or district and engage "external" audiences. In almost every district we have visited, the business community has been an ally the school or district leader can count on. Business leaders understand how much things have changed and understand that their employees need more than mere content mastery. They have the expertise on what skills are most important for current and future jobs in your community, and they are often willing to consider a wide range of possible collaborations.

In Tucson, over 20 local businesses employ math and science teachers for the summer to work on real company projects. The program was created by UA College of Education and is now a regular, and expanding, opportunity for early career STEM teachers. Teachers are paid market rates for six to eight weeks and develop a deeper understanding of the challenges their students will be facing when they enter the workforce. One teacher who spent her summer at Raytheon, one of the largest employers in the program, observed after the eight-week stint that it changed her perspective on the way she should teach math. She understood more instinctively how important it was to challenge her students with real world math problems.

Internships are nothing new, of course. But some internship-based school models that have emerged in the past few years are worth noting. One of these is the Cristo Rey Network of 24 schools across the country, including Chicago, Portland and Tucson. The San Miguel High School in Tucson is sponsored by the Brothers of the Christian Schools; there, students attend class four days per week and spend one day a week employed by a local business in an internship setting. Students are paid for their work, which helps to pay for school tuition. These internships are designed to reinforce student academic knowledge, critical thinking skills and workforce preparedness.

Another excellent model is Big Picture Learning schools. At the MET School in Providence, Rhode Island and at all Big Picture Learning schools, every student is required to design and implement an out-of-school learning experience/project in a business or community organization. Students spend about two days each week learning and working in these "Learning through Interests/Internships" experiences, with the support of on-site mentors and their school advisors. The in-school and the out-of-school learning are aligned and integrated, and learning in both settings is awarded academic and graduation credit. But even if your school is not set up that way, encouraging businesses to offer workplace internships is an important way businesses can help participate in a 21st century education environment.

Another effective tactic is to partner with key business leaders in your community. As we mentioned earlier, the CORE Federal Credit Union in East Syracuse, New York, has partnered with the East Syracuse Minoa School District to operate a student-run credit union in the high school. A drug company in the same district partnered to create a science course for juniors and seniors on how to develop a life-saving drug and get it approved by the FDA. Finally, a number of companies are able to financially contribute to innovative school district efforts. Some schools and districts have created foundations that businesses can contribute to and the money can be focused on targeted efforts like "mini-grants" to teachers who propose innovative ideas to advance 21st century education in their classroom or in the district.

It isn't enough to reach out to the business community, however. The broader community needs to be cultivated as well. Community and state organizations focused on workforce development and economic development can be helpful allies. Local workforce development boards, for example, understand the need to promote critical thinking, communication, collaboration, and creativity as essential requirements of the 21st century workforce. Once you begin reaching out to these kinds of organizations, it becomes possible to imagine your work fitting within a regional economic development initiative. Regional initiatives have started in Cleveland, Cincinnati, and northwest Indiana; many of these are already using the 4Cs as a theme for organizing their communities around 21st century economic success.

Leaders in youth development and informal education are another group to consider for outreach. There are innovative youth development programs all over the country that already recognize the importance of the 4Cs. (See, for example, http://www.readyby21.org/.) Such groups are using innovative strategies to prepare at-risk youth for the challenges of the workforce. One such example is the Year Up program in Boston. Companies in Boston fund scholarships for individuals to participate in the Year Up preparation program and make a commitment to hire the individual when the program is completed. It makes great sense for traditional K–12 districts to align themselves with programs like these. The 4Cs vision provides an excellent platform for a cooperative partnership such as this.

Informal education providers are also important partners. After-school programs, youth programs, summer school programs, museums, and public libraries all fall into this category. In some cases, these programs have integrated 21st century skills into their strategies more quickly and more intentionally than their K–12 counterparts. Students who participate in after-school programs—Boy Scouts, Girl Scouts, Little League Soccer, YMCA, YWCA, 4-H, and so on—are all honing their critical thinking, communication, collaboration, and creativity skills.

The North Salem Central School District in New York is in the midst of a 21st century education initiative focused on creative problem solving. Participants have been pleasantly surprised to find that the youth development programs in their area have been very enthusiastic and feel very well aligned with the district's new initiative.

Most recently many public libraries and museums have thought about their role in supporting 21st century skills in their communities. An initiative of the Institute for Museum and Library Services (IMLS), *21st Century Skills, Museums, and Libraries*, can provide a very effective kick-start for a conversation around how K–12 public libraries and museums could work together more closely to foster the development of the 4Cs in your community.

You might also think about approaching adult education programs. In some communities, you as a K–12 leader might have jurisdiction over those programs. In many communities, they are separate. In any event, many adult education experts have found the 21st century framework to be helpful to their development. A notable one is Comprehensive Adult Student Assessment Systems (CASAS). CASAS works with state and local programs to assist youth and adults to improve basic skills, earn a nationally recognized high school diploma (National External Diploma Program), and develop essential skills to ensure success in the 21st century workplace.

Finally, we encourage you to reach out to the higher education community. The most obvious connection is with colleges of education. Engage them around your vision for the future of education in your district. After all, you'll be recruiting their graduates who, ideally, should be able to teach and assess the 4Cs. Also, forward-thinking colleges of education can be a resource for you in providing professional development for your teachers around critical aspects of 21st century education. The Partnership for 21st Century Skills and AACTE published "21st Century Knowledge and Skills in Educator Preparation," which can be a helpful resource as you reach out to these partners. And The National Council for Accreditation of Teacher Education (NCATE), the accreditation entity for colleges of education, has also prepared a new vision that embraces 21st century education strategies for colleges of education. In California, K–12 and higher education leaders worked together to develop the California Early Assessment Program, which has done a remarkable job of improving college readiness among high school graduates (http://www.calstate.edu/eap/index.shtml).

Beyond colleges of education, college presidents and chancellors are also key potential partners you might want to engage in a broader dialogue on your vision:

- What kind of students is higher education really looking for?
- How are they thinking about changes in their admission's strategies over the next five to 10 years?
- How are they thinking about how they deliver 21st century skills to their own students?
- What changes in pedagogy and assessment are they envisioning within higher education?
- What kind of partnerships can they envision with K–12 schools and districts?

Now let's consider how you would bring together some representatives from the business community, after-school programs, summer programs, youth development programs, adult education programs, public libraries, museums, and higher education. You might share your vision for K–12 education with them and facilitate a discussion around questions such as:

- How can we in K–12 education better align our work with the workforce and economic development needs of our community?
- How can all of you help us better understand the economic and workforce capabilities that our students will need to possess?

- How could we work together to develop a common vocabulary that K–12 educators and the broader community could use in working together to produce students more prepared for the economic needs of the community?
- How can we better align the work of formal with informal education in our community?
- Can we develop strategies more intentionally purposeful with one another to produce a better set of 21st century education strategies for our young people?

If you've followed this outreach strategy, you have made a very robust set of contacts within your community. You've taken your vision and brought it to:

- Your own education community in your school or district.
- Those in the community involved in business, economic development, formal education, informal education, and youth development.

You should come away with a very good sense of who your allies are. And you've laid a groundwork for the community being receptive to your vision.

Once you have gone through these informal collaborations, you will need to consider how to use another set of collaboration skills. You will need to design a *process* for your school or district to more formally consider your new education model. There is no single process we should or would recommend. Your process should be customized around your personal strengths and the needs expressed by your community. Some leaders will work better in smaller groups, and some leaders can envision functioning effectively in very large group settings. We can, however, share examples we have observed that are effective.

In Catalina Foothills School District, Superintendent Mary Kamerzell created a representative advisory board of 40 individuals who worked for almost a year to create a vision for the 21st century outcomes of their school district. The advisory group represented both internal (teachers, administrators, and parents) and external (business community, community groups) representatives. The work of the group involved accessing a wide array of information and resources and also coming to closure on the skills that district leaders would build into the next five-year plan.

A similar advisory group was deployed by Superintendent Jeff Weaver in Upper Arlington School District (Ohio). The group had 35 members that included teachers, administrators, board members, community members, and parents. While community members and school board members did participate, the bulk of the representatives were from the key internal audiences within the district including the district's entire leadership team.

In Superintendent Merrill's initiative in Virginia Beach City Public Schools, Virginia, there was a heavy emphasis on creating a broad community consensus. The process eventually resulted in a meeting of more than 1,000 citizens who met at the Virginia Beach Convention Center. This left the school leadership feeling that they had truly been given a mandate to take the schools in the direction of the student outcomes that the community meeting had ratified.

These are just a few examples of potential process strategies that you could employ. Knowing which one to use depends in part on what strategic goals you are trying to accomplish.

- How much input do you feel you need from the internal school community? What about outside stakeholders?
- How much are you trying to get the community to "buy in" to your vision?
- How fragmented is the community? How much is there a need to "pull the community together"?
- How much has the community delegated the decision to educators and are they prepared to live with the consensus of your own internal education community?

The answers to these questions will determine the type and depth of the advisory process you choose. Whichever path you choose, the goal is to achieve broad community consensus. It is also important to realize that the school board must consider the work of your advisory process and formally adopt the final model.

We have included outreach toolkits for community groups, business leaders, school boards and students in Appendices 7-10; we encourage you to take advantage of these resources as you plan your outreach activities.

2.3 REFLECTION ON COLLABORATION

You have hopefully evolved from thinking about your own vision to focusing on how you will work to co-create a common vision with all of the key stakeholders needed to carry this vision forward. Consider completing this summary exercise to help take stock of all the potential ways to build support for your initiative:

- Which are the three or four groups *inside* your school or district that are likely to be most supportive of your 21st century initiative?

Internal Supporting Group	Strategy to Approach Them	Best Arguments
1.		
2.		
3.		
4.		

- Which are the three or four groups in the broader community *outside* of your school or district that are likely to be most supportive of your 21st century initiative?

External Supporting Group	Strategy to Approach Them	Best Arguments
1.		
2.		
3.		
4.		

- Which are the three or four groups (*internal or external*) that are most likely to offer resistance to your vision and initiative?

Opposing Group	How to Approach	Best Arguments
1.		
2.		
3.		
4.		

These three grids will give you a roadmap on how to build the strongest allies to help you create the shared support for the initiative as well as to anticipate those that are likely to be toughest to bring along. Your job is to build the support you need, but also try to anticipate those places where resistance might come and try to neutralize or lessen the intensity of the resistance. Most importantly, though, we hope you leave Step 2 with a sense that you now have not only identified but have secured a broad base of support in and out of your education community. You now should have a broad base of allies to work with in implementing your 21st century vision.

FINAL THOUGHTS

So here's how far you have come in building the foundation for your new vision:

- You've adopted a personal vision.
- You've created communication tools and messages to communicate effectively about your vision as well as to "model" your communication skills.
- You've adopted a collaboration strategy to do general outreach both inside and outside the school community, to create a process for formal consensus building around your vision, and to model your collaboration skills.

We hope Steps 1 and 2 have been helpful. It is important—and challenging—to create broad and deep consensus around a transformational initiative in your school or district. We commend you for taking on this challenge. More inspirational work is coming next. This is because the improvements that truly affect your students directly happen with Steps 3–7. With Steps 1 and 2, you have laid the groundwork for the next stages of the work where education, learning, and assessment for your students will really change. That's where the payoff will be for your students—and you.

REFERENCES

DeSiato, Donna. Personal interview. June 22, 2010.

Merrill, Jim. Personal interview. June 15, 2010.

Moran, Pam. Personal interview. June 10, 2010.

"My Voice National Student Report 2010." Quaglia Institute for Student Aspirations. http://qisa.org/publications/docs/NyVoiceNationalStudentReport(6-12)2010.pdf.

NCATE. http://www.ncate.org.

"Standards for the 21st Century Learner." American Association of School Librarians. http://www.ala.org/aasl/guidelinesandstandards/learningstandards/standards.

"Up to the Challenge: The Role of Career and Technical Education and 21st Century Skills in College and Career Readiness." P21, ACTE, and NASDCTEC. http://www.p21.org/storage/documents/CTE_Oct2010.pdf.

Wilson, John. Personal interview. June 6, 2010.

"21st Century Knowledge and Skills in Educator Preparation." Partnership for 21st Century Skills and AACTE. http://www.p21.org/storage/documents/aacte_p21_whitepaper2010.pdf.

STEP 3

Align Your System

THE 4CS FOCUS

When it comes to the "big intersections" between the 4Cs and the topic of alignment, think about these ideas:

- Critical thinking: Analysis and systems thinking will be necessary as you align curriculum, assessment, and instruction systems with the 4Cs.
- Collaboration: The work of alignment requires active collaboration among educators at all levels of the system.
- Communication: The goal of alignment—to make the 4Cs a part of teaching and learning for every student—should be communicated clearly at every stage of the process.
- Creativity: Alignment work requires leaders who can be flexible and innovative!

Alignment: Bringing the Work to Scale

We hope that, in Steps 1 and 2, you have established your personal vision for 21st century learning and that we have convinced you of the importance of building consensus around this vision with all stakeholders throughout your institution and community. Now comes some of the most difficult work—taking real steps toward aligning your system to ensure *all* students are benefiting from this vision. When your vision is being implemented in a systemic, coordinated way across the school or district, that's when you will start to see powerful results: the 4Cs integrated into daily teaching and learning for *every* student.

These next few steps will, we hope, provide necessary guidance as you integrate the 4Cs into curricula, assessments, and instruction in a more aligned, efficient way.

But let's clarify what we mean by alignment. If you've ever had your spine out of alignment, you know how performing the simplest tasks becomes much harder—tying your shoes or getting out of bed. If you put off going to the chiropractor and try to increase your activity level, the problem doesn't go away. It just gets worse. When we are working with educators on this issue, we try to demonstrate an out-of-alignment system. We look up and to the right, turn our shoulders to the left, and try to walk straight. When different parts are heading in different directions, nothing works in harmony. Coordinated movement is very difficult. We explain that if your vision for student success is focused on the 4Cs, but your professional development is primarily delivered through stand-and-deliver formats and your assessment systems are composed of low-level multiple choice tests, your system is not aligned. Your initiative will not progress effectively or efficiently, and it will be very difficult to expand its impact beyond a few pockets of students.

On the other hand, when the 4Cs are integrated with curricula, assessments, instruction, and professional development, your vision can be carried out at scale. All parts of the system align to reinforce the goal of ensuring 21st century success for every student.

So consider us your personal chiropractors, at least for the next few steps.

What Does an Aligned System Look Like?

The goal of Step 3 is an aligned system that looks something like this:

- The district has developed a clearly defined set of student outcomes that includes the 4Cs.
- The 4Cs are integrated throughout curricula.
- Assessments measure student performance across the 4Cs, as represented in the curricula.
- Principals, teachers, and other leaders have the professional development and support they need to teach and assess the 4Cs.
- Education leaders are sharing their 4Cs-related work through regular communications and collaborations with parents, community members, and other stakeholders.
- Education leaders are monitoring and improving 4Cs implementation over time.

No matter which set of skills you have chosen to begin your initiative—the 4Cs or some other set of knowledge and skills—embedding your vision into daily teaching and learning requires alignment across all major elements of the system: assessments, curricula, instruction, professional development, and more. Without a systemic approach to 4Cs alignment, you are unlikely to move beyond what our colleague Ray Pecheone of Stanford calls the "jewel box" phenomenon in education: wonderful "oo-ah!" examples from individual classes and schools. As Ray puts it, we like to carry these "jewel boxes" around and show them off as proof points. The problem is that in most of these cool examples, only a very small percentage of the student population is reached. As education leaders and advocates, we get so excited about these individual examples that we sometimes neglect to engage in the hard discussions about implementing these ideas on a larger scale to benefit all students. In other words, if we're going to get serious about 21st century systems of teaching and learning, we cannot be satisfied with isolated success stories—no matter how exciting they are. The best work requires a systems-thinking approach if we are to accomplish 21st century readiness *for every student.*

As you no doubt realize, aligning school and district resources around a vision for 21st century student outcomes is incredibly difficult work. This stage of your work is a perfect example of what Robert Marzano calls "second order change" (65–68). His notion of first order change is something you might think of as "low hanging fruit," or changes that can be made using existing systems and resources. If you're reading this book, chances are you've been working on first order change in your school or district for some time and are interested in going further. "Second order change" requires a fundamental rethinking of the enterprise, going beyond existing knowledge, skills, and resources. As a school leader embarking on such a transformative effort, your district or school will wrestle with a number of key questions around aligning your education system with the 4Cs, such as:

- How can we teach and assess these skills in all grades and all subjects?
- What resources do we currently have to support this kind of teaching and learning?
- What additional resources do we need?
- How can we make this work scale beyond a simple pilot project?

Thinking about Step 3 as a "second order" type of change helps set your team's expectations for how comprehensive the work must be to reach all students.

It is worth repeating here that reaching all students equitably, in the end, should be a top priority. Step 3 helps you go beyond pilot projects and individual (but isolated) teachers doing extraordinary things to an aligned system that ensures every student benefits equally from your 21st century education initiative.

What Is 4Cs Alignment?

Now that we've described the concept of alignment in general terms, it's important to note how common it is (in high-performing districts, especially) to have an aligned system that has nothing at all to do with the 4Cs. The basic idea of alignment in education systems is not new; most often, it is associated with aligning curricula and assessments with state standards. This kind of comprehensive alignment among standards, content, and assessments is a fine goal, especially when it is paired with a systems thinking approach. (For more information, we recommend Peter Senge's work, which is often cited by education leaders who are implementing a systems thinking approach.) But in most of the work we have seen performed in the name of alignment, there is a surprising lack of attention to *21st century student outcomes*. It isn't all that uncommon, of course, to have an aligned system of standards, content, instruction, and assessment in which students achieve rote mastery of content extremely well! That is not 4Cs alignment. The goal of Step 3 is to ensure that all parts of your system support your vision—*specifically in terms of the 21st century student outcomes you have defined*.

As we've outlined in Figure 3.1 on page 48, Step 3 asks you to consider each element of your system and reflect on *how comprehensively the 4Cs are integrated*.

FIGURE 3.1   21st Century Alignment: Systemic 4Cs Integration

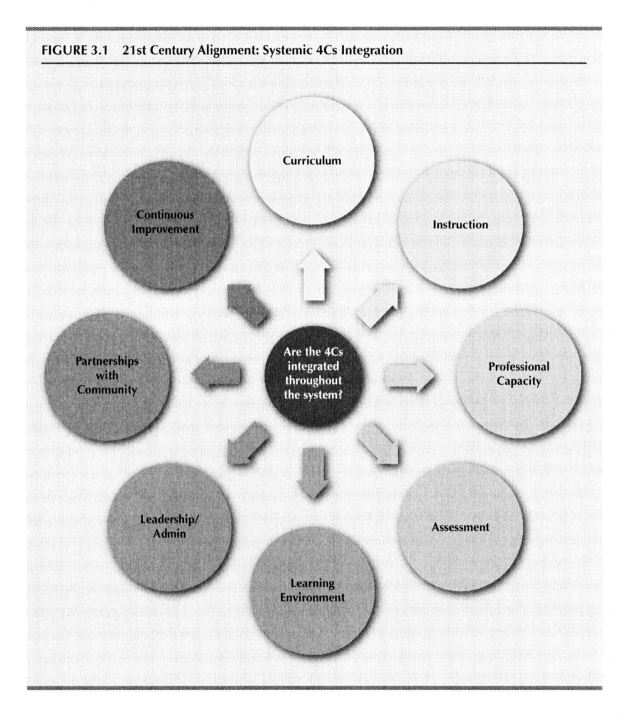

Example Box 3.1   What Does Alignment Look Like? A Snapshot from Virginia Beach City Public Schools

The following example provides a profile of how one district is pursuing the issue of alignment. The work being done in Virginia Beach City Public schools (mentioned previously in Step 2) demonstrates the diversity and complexity of alignment work.

In Virginia Beach City Public Schools, Superintendent Jim Merrill and his leadership team are actively pursuing system-wide alignment around their 21st century learning goals. The district has about 69,000 students, more than 15,320 full-time, part-time and substitute employees, and 81 schools. Superintendent Merrill and his cabinet created and are leading **Compass to 2015,** the district's strategic plan for 21st century education. Their approach offers a helpful model for anyone interested in 4Cs alignment. The VBCPS team's alignment work is always being adjusted in real time, but generally speaking it can be summarized in four major areas of activity:

- Community alignment
- Strategic plan alignment
- Implementation team alignment
- School alignment

In addition to these areas of work, some key values have emerged that have contributed to the successes to date. District leaders have committed to:

- Prioritizing a culture of openness, transparency, collaboration, and continuous improvement
- Supporting principals and their unique needs at individual sites—for example, always remembering that every school's path is different
- Starting with the strengths that exist in each school, rather than focusing on gaps as a first step
- Using the cabinet-level leadership meetings to continually ask, and re-ask, whether each implementation step is aligned to the goals of Compass to 2015
- Communicating relentlessly—stopping along the way to acknowledge members of the organization individually and collectively for their support and progress toward the overarching goal

We have described these areas of activity in brief, along with some thoughts on the lessons learned, below.

COMMUNITY ALIGNMENT

The district's first step was to establish a clear definition of 21st century student outcomes and create alignment in the community around these expectations. (You can see a graphical representation of their vision in Step 1.) The vision for student outcomes, which is now broadly supported throughout the community, is:

The district's primary focus is on teaching and assessing the skills students need to thrive as 21st century learners, workers, and citizens. All VBCPS students will be:

- Academically proficient;
- Effective communicators and collaborators;
- Globally aware, independent, responsible learners and citizens; and
- and creative thinkers, innovators, and problem solvers.

A Lesson Learned:

- Superintendent Merrill believes strongly in the importance of building broad and deep consensus with the entire community around the student outcomes (see Step 2 where consensus building is covered in great detail.) As we mentioned in Step 2, the initial vision-setting process took over a year and involved hosting many

(continued)

community-wide meetings, with the culminating event attracting more than 1,000 participants. As a result of this early work and continued communication and collaboration with stakeholders, especially parents, the district's work around 21st century student outcomes is both well-understood and strongly supported—educators and stakeholders across the community understand and "buy in" to the vision. Superintendent Merrill makes a point of saying, however, that consensus building is great but that it must be followed by real action. As he puts it, "The community is very astute and can separate 'talk' from 'action' in a minute. Your credibility with the community is a direct result of meaningful action—change they can understand and support or come to support" (*EdLeader21 Blog*).

Strategic Plan Alignment

Compass to 2015 identifies five strategic objectives that are directly aligned with the district's vision for student outcomes. Refer to their web site http://www.vbschools.com/compass/index.asp. The plan for each strategic objective is developed specifically to enable the student outcomes as defined in Compass to 2015.

The strategic objectives are:

1. *Engage Every Student:* All teachers will engage every student in meaningful, authentic, and rigorous work through the use of innovative instructional practices and supportive technologies that will motivate students to be self-directed and inquisitive learners.
2. *Balanced Assessment:* VBCPS will develop and implement a balanced assessment system that accurately reflects student demonstration and mastery of VBCPS outcomes for student success.
3. *Improved Achievement:* Each school will improve achievement for all students while closing achievement

gaps for identified student groups, with particular focus on African American males.
4. *Create Opportunities:* VBCPS will create opportunities for parents, community, and business leaders to fulfill their essential roles as actively engaged partners in supporting student achievement and outcomes for student success.
5. *Capacity Building:* VBCPS will be accountable for developing essential leader, teacher, and staff competencies and optimizing all resources to achieve the school division's strategic goal and outcomes for student success.

A Lesson Learned:

In the first year of implementation, Professional Learning Communities were chosen as a key activity to support Strategic Objective 5, capacity building. They didn't succeed at first. Principals were provided with some basic information and were expected to "run with it"—but it didn't happen in part because of issues with alignment. The following year, district leaders evolved the plan from its position of "thou shalt have PLCs" to one that provides schools with resources to systematically develop a collaborative learning culture in their buildings. School principals and their teams were given rubrics and processes that helped them address key questions as a regular part of doing business, such as: *What do we want students to learn? How will we know that they learned it? What will we do for students who . . . . didn't learn the material? . . . . have already mastered the material? What parent and community resources will we utilize to support student learning?* Also, the district now provides copies of Richard and Rebecca DuFour's book *Learning by Doing*, which establishes a shared definition for PLCs. District leaders also host a Principal's Collaborative meeting every month to keep everyone's work on Compass to 2015 connected. It was in some of these meetings that the principals first developed a system-wide approach to learning walks (http://www.vbschools.com/compass/learningWalks.asp) and defined the "look fors" (http://tinyurl.com/794387k) for that first, all-important 21st century skill—critical thinking. With centralized staffing and support, this collaborative now operates as a true PLC, and issues of alignment are kept "front and center" in everyone's work. (For more details about professional learning communities, please see Step 4; for more information about learning walks and supporting teachers, please see Step 6.)

Implementation Team Alignment

To implement Compass to 2015, a Strategic Planning Implementation Steering Committee was established with an eye toward alignment and accountability. (Superintendent Merrill, in a nod to the naval base where his district is located, calls this group his "SEAL Team.") Each of the five strategic objectives is co-chaired by a cabinet-level leader and a school principal so that the work is done collaboratively with site leaders. Superintendent Merrill actively participates in the group, which meets monthly to ensure a coordinated approach.

A Lesson Learned:

The Strategic Objective 2 action team—led by the associate superintendent for educational leadership and assessment and a high school principal—took on what it regarded as an important task: the development of a tool to help evaluate student progress in each of the identified 21st century skills. The team came up with a continuum (a kind of high-level rubric that is used to guide curricula and assessment activities) that identified levels of attainment of these skills, so teachers could identify what critical thinking looks like as a student progresses from a basic skills level to advanced. However, as that group proceeded with its work, it made a big shift, and what began as an assessment

tool became an instructional planning tool. The big "*aha*" in all this came when the action team "test drove" the document with about 40 teachers. The overwhelming commentary was that this document should be used as a front-end strategy for planning instruction. And that is what it became. It was also determined that benchmarks were needed to assist teachers in developing rubrics to assess these skills; these are currently being developed in collaboration with teachers across the district. The alignment that is emerging between instructional planning and assessment at the school level is a direct result of the alignment that exists within the implementation team. Working together, these team members make sure the work is always focused on the student outcomes in Compass to 2015.

School Alignment

Each school in the district must align its Plan for Continuous Improvement (PCI) to the strategic plan and outcomes for student success. While this continues to be an important method for aligning all schools to Compass to 2015, the issue of accountability and scale led to the concept of "Vanguard" schools. These schools are early adopters for key initiatives related to Compass to 2015. The program is proving to be a powerful tool for scaling the work of alignment in schools.

The Vanguard program identified three categories of focus as immediately crucial to the success of the strategic plan: integration of instructional technology, balanced assessment, and responsiveness to student need. Eight Vanguard schools per category (a total of 24 schools) were selected based on their self-assessment as being ready to implement the initiative. That self-assessment included eight criteria:

- School culture of continuous improvement
- Responsiveness to student needs
- Alignment to the student outcomes in Compass to 2015

(continued)

- Implementation of a collaborative learning community (PLC)
- Instructional leadership
- Parent and community connections
- Integration of instructional technology
- Utilization of resources (human, fiscal, and material) to support Compass to 2015

These schools work with specialized support teams to provide professional development that is innovative, job-embedded, and research-based to their teachers. In the coming year(s), the schools in the initial Vanguard group will be partnered with schools that are joining Vanguard during the 2011–2012 school year. After an inaugural year, leaders in each Vanguard school will serve as mentors and coaches to their peers in partner schools. As a result, principals will have the benefit of learning from one another to achieve district-wide alignment with 21st century student outcomes.

Some Lessons Learned:

The cabinet-level leadership recognized early on that all schools are not at the same comfort level with the five strategic objectives of Compass to 2015. Recognizing this, the Vanguard program began with a select group of 24 schools that had rated themselves as "ready" to implement certain components of the strategic plan. These initial Vanguard schools served as important field test sites for key initiatives; the leaders

in these schools are now serving as coaches and mentors for the next group of schools in the Vanguard program. The vision is that the program will become mostly peer-led over time as it scales to include all 81 schools in the district.

In every instance of the Vanguard program, the school's principal is asked: "Where's your entry point? Where do you want to start?" District support teams try to understand the unique context at each school to find out what programs are already working well in order to build on them. In one school assigned to the Balanced Assessment component, collaborative learning had been a strategic focus for several years—but site leaders noted that collaboration skills were not being assessed. So the first step focused on connecting the great work being done around collaborative learning to an assessment model. In another case, an elementary school (also focused on Balanced Assessment) had already established a strong set of practices around Habits of Mind. The Vanguard team's first step in this case was to make the connection between Habits of Mind and Balanced Assessment. Teachers saw the connection right away—it was a logical extension of the work they were already doing. In both of these examples, the work was perceived as a natural fit—it was not seen by teachers as a brand-new initiative. As a result, it was much easier to establish high levels of engagement and alignment.

The significance of the Virginia Beach City Public Schools example is twofold: (1) it demonstrates how broad your view must be as a leader to connect all the dots and really implement this kind of initiative across an entire system; and (2) it should also reassure you that there is no single "right" way to pursue this work—a spirit of experimentation, iteration, and openness to learn from mistakes is probably the most helpful mindset to have when you focus on Step 3.

We think you'll find this step of alignment an exciting and rewarding part of the work because an excellent tool is readily available. Many districts have used the MILE Guide with great success. In this section, you'll see how this tool can be used to generate dynamic action to produce a more systemic, aligned 4Cs initiative. The MILE Guide, developed by the Partnership for 21st Century Skills, is an excellent resource to guide your work around alignment. It is included at the front of this book.

In Kansas, for example, educators in some school districts have used the MILE Guide to organize their thinking and chart their strategic planning. In Kansas, Blake West, in his role as president of the Kansas National Education Association, has used the MILE Guide to help lead strategic planning with district teams. The tool helps educators prioritize areas for further work, share exemplary practices among educators, and benchmark progress across the system. He believes the MILE Guide helps provide teachers and education leaders with meaningful, practical guidance in planning the kinds of system-wide learning experiences that will help students apply 21st century skills to solving real world problems.

In addition to being reprinted in the beginning of this book, the tool exists in two forms:

- A PDF version for download (that you may print at no cost on large-format paper here: http://p21.org/documents/mile_guide_tool_091101.pdf) or a print version that can be purchased from P21. This MILE Guide tool provides a highly detailed way to self-assess your school's or district's progress in 21st century skills integration.
- A streamlined version of the self-assessment portion of the MILE Guide can be accessed online, free, at http://p21.org/mileguide. This quick 17-question survey is a much faster way to begin the self-assessment process; it is a condensed version of the print version of the self-assessment.

Each of these versions of the self-assessment is designed to help you determine where your district sits on the spectrum of 21st century skills integration and then use that information to plan a *systemic, aligned* path for future work. It also can help you and your team set specific benchmarks and goals as part of the alignment process. The MILE Guide self-assessment tool—whether you're using the print or interactive questionnaire—allows you to identify the areas of your system that are "out of alignment" quickly and guides your next steps.

In addition to being an excellent tool for alignment work, the MILE Guide is extremely useful as you pursue outside funding such as grants—the tool's framework provides a compelling structure that helps you identify and prioritize objectives for funding via grants and other sources.

What the MILE Guide Does Best

The MILE Guide self-assessment tool is best used as a guide for aligning your entire system around your 21st century vision. Getting your leadership team and faculty aligned around the same vision for teaching and learning is a monumental task. This work is made much, much easier when there is agreement up front about the "current state" of things. So the MILE Guide is designed to provide a structure for focused dialogue about where each element of your system is today on the spectrum of 21st century learning, without being prescriptive or punitive.

How to Use the MILE Guide

We have seen the MILE Guide used in many different settings with various audiences. There is no one "right" way to use it; we've included a few scenarios below.

1. Consider having all team members complete the online MILE Guide (http://p21.org/mileguide) before attending a brainstorm/strategy meeting. It takes about 10 minutes to fill out the 17-question survey online, after which results can be printed. Ask each participant to bring the printout to the strategy session. Organize them into small groups to discuss their individual results. It's pretty common to find that educators in the same building rate the school or district very differently—some will say they're "transitional," and others will be surprised at that, claiming there's no way they are beyond "early." The differences in responses, more than the similarities, are where the richest dialogues can occur. Once there is a general understanding in the room around the online MILE Guide results, the paper-based tool can be used to drill down into areas that might not be aligned currently, such as assessment, continuous improvement, or partnering.

2. Consider using the paper-based MILE Guide as one element of a two-part session on 21st century education. At the end of the first segment, assign as homework the MILE Guide. Ask each participant to circle the most accurate descriptor (early/transitional/21st century) for each column in the tool. Request that they come to the next day's segment prepared to discuss the results. When they arrive for the second part of the session, organize them into groups of eight and ask them to share their observations with each other. Ask each table to assign a spokesperson to report out to the larger group; use the large group synthesis to highlight any interesting tensions, differences, and/or similarities that come up. You'll likely hear a wide range of perceptions among the participants—some will describe the system as "early"; others will be just as adamant that the school or district is "21st century." The ensuing discussion should be focused on developing a shared understanding of current practices. Understanding *why* different educators have such divergent views is incredibly illuminating. And, of course, if you're in the rare circumstance of having complete unanimity about the current state, you can move quickly on to a discussion about how to move to the next stage of the work!

3. Regardless of whether you start with the online or the paper-based tool, consider how you can use each column of the tool to craft working groups and specific action plans that can be tracked and reviewed for progress over time. The MILE Guide exercise should be seen as a clarifying, unifying step in the journey; it is a preliminary stage activity that should be followed with specific, prioritized action steps.

4. Use the Implementation Recommendations in the back of the MILE Guide publication (http://p21.org/documents/MILE_Guide_091101.pdf) to brainstorm specific actions and review best practices from districts that have already begun this work. Consider, for example, what activities your team will tackle when it comes to the columns of the tool: Student Knowledge & Skills; Education Support Systems; Leading and Teaching; Policymakers; Partnering; and Continuous Improvement/Strategic Planning.

5. Use the self-assessment results to generate a shared vision for future progress (see Steps 1 and 2 for more about the vision-setting process). Most districts we've worked with have developed their own logos and other visuals (as you saw in Step 1) to depict their vision for 21st century student outcomes and how they are addressing them. The task of creating a visual depiction of the 21st century vision and supporting strategies is another way to extend the MILE Guide activity and produce tangible, helpful results that can be shared with all stakeholders.

What Does the MILE Guide Self-Assessment Tool Cover?

Looking at the MILE Guide matrix out of context might seem a little overwhelming, so we've included a brief description of the main elements here in case it is helpful. The MILE Guide basically covers the following areas of a typical 21st century skills initiative:

- **Student Knowledge and Skills.** The first column in the MILE Guide represents a full range of 21st century student outcomes: the skills, knowledge, and expertise students should master to succeed in work and life in the 21st century (based on the P21 Framework).
- **Education Support Systems.** The second major column of the MILE Guide represents the support systems necessary to ensure student mastery of 21st century knowledge and skills. Twenty-first century standards, assessments, professional development, curricula, instruction, and learning environments must be aligned to produce a support system that produces 21st century outcomes for today's students.
- **Leading and Teaching.** This section of the self-assessment tool focuses on the role that education leaders play in ensuring 21st century skills mastery among students. If you are just now beginning your planning work, this column can be a helpful place to start in and of itself.
- **Policymakers.** This section articulates the critical stages of work policymakers can pursue in advancing the dialogue about 21st century learning.
- **Partnering.** At the ground level, district leaders need clear descriptions about the early stage, transitional, and 21st century level indicators of partnerships with parents, higher education, community, businesses, and other entities. This column in the MILE Guide self-assessment tool gives districts a straightforward way to engage these stakeholders around partnering opportunities as part of the 21st century skills initiative.
- **Continuous Improvement/Strategic Planning.** Accountability to a 21st century skills initiative is critical. In this final column, the MILE Guide self-assessment tool lays out a description of the end goal for 21st century learning and measures for continuous improvement and strategic planning to guide the way.

In summary, the MILE Guide helps you get the "big picture" of where you stand with alignment of your system around 21st century skills like the 4Cs. Once you have established a baseline of where your system is currently, you can use the MILE Guide periodically to gauge progress along your journey.

FINAL THOUGHTS

We hope this step has helped you exercise your critical thinking and systems thinking abilities as you consider the issue of alignment. We believe the MILE Guide is a powerful tool to help you create the momentum you need to enact systemic changes in your school or district. Implementing a 21st century education initiative that can be sustained, and that can be brought to scale, requires 4Cs alignment across every key dimension of the system: student outcomes, system leadership, stakeholders, policies, learning environments, partners, and continuous improvement.

Going back to our chiropractor analogy: If your entire spine happened to be out of alignment, you wouldn't expect to correct the issue in a single treatment. Aligning your school or district should be viewed the same way. The work being done in districts like Virginia Beach City Public Schools, Catalina Foothills School District, and many others is often difficult and painstaking, as you can imagine. It is also some of the most dynamic and interesting work being done in education today.

3.1 REFLECTION

We strongly suggest that you use the print version of the MILE Guide, along with the online MILE Guide, to get a big picture view of your system's alignment to the 4Cs. In the meantime, the grid below might help organize your thoughts around alignment as a way to quickly get started with this step.

As you fill in the right-hand column with your best sense of your progress, note whether your system appears to be aligned. If each step is at a different stage (early/transitional/21st century) in the process, chances are your system is out of alignment. Do you have a sense of what steps you should take to make alignment more likely? Is there one area that needs immediate attention, or will you need to work more systemically?

Step	STAGE OF IMPLEMENTATION Describe each step as follows: "E" for "early" (beginning) "T" for "transitional" (intermediate) "21" for "21st Century" (advanced)
Step 1: Adopt Your Vision	
Step 2: Create a Community Consensus	
Step 3: Align Your System	
Step 4: Build Professional Capacity	
Step 5: Focus Your Curriculum and Assessment	
Step 6: Support Your Teachers	
Step 7: Improve and Innovate	

We intend the next section of the book—Steps 4, 5 and 6—to be framed as an aligned implementation exercise. For readability purposes, we have separated the topics of professional development, curricula, assessment and teacher support into separate steps; it is important, however, to keep the overall goal of alignment in mind. While these next steps will tackle highly specific areas of your teaching and learning system, we will continue to ask you to think critically and systemically about how each area is connected to, and is dependent upon, the others to work. Refer to Reflection Box 3.1.

REFERENCES

DuFour, Richard, Rebecca DuFour, Robert Eaker, and Thomas Many. *Learning by Doing: A Handbook for Professional Learning Communities at Work.* Bloomington, IN: Solution Tree Press, 2006.

Marzano, Robert J., Timothy Waters, and Brian A. McNulty. *School Leadership That Works.* Aurora, CO: McREL, 2005.

Merrill, Jim. *EdLeader21 Blog on Community Consensus,* Mar. 2011. Web. Aug. 2011.

West, Blake. Personal interview. Jan. 15, 2010.

STEP 4

Build Professional Capacity

THE 4CS FOCUS

The 4Cs focus of Step 4 is:

- Critical thinking: Professional development should help every educator enhance his or her own critical thinking skills.
- Communication: Professional development should allow educators to focus on their own communication skills.
- Collaboration: Professional learning communities are some of the most powerful ways for educators to collaborate around 4Cs teaching and learning.
- Creativity: The culture of professional development should support creative and innovative approaches to 4Cs teaching and learning.

Introduction

It seems like such a simple observation, but we cannot expect students to learn the 4Cs (critical thinking, communication, collaboration, and creativity) unless these competencies are modeled by educators. And, by extension, we cannot expect educators to alter their practices if we don't give them the training and support they need to be effective. Colleges of education, as a rule, do not focus on the 4Cs as student outcomes; as a result, it is unlikely that the teachers you are hiring and the teachers already on your team have received the training necessary to implement your 21st century vision. Practically speaking, it falls to individual districts and schools to create the communities of practice that lead to effective professional learning.

Your ability to successfully train and support educators in teaching and assessing the 4Cs is a critical factor in your success. Making sure your PD strategy is effective is challenging because:

- Good professional development is hard to do.
- Professional development today has such a bad reputation—most of it richly deserved.
- Professional development has largely focused on the teaching of core academic subjects to the exclusion of how to teach the 4Cs.

It will take a powerful and sustained effort to transform any traditional professional development program into a set of PD strategies that align with your vision. In our education reform work, we regularly use the expression: "We're flying the plane while we redesign it." We've heard this phrase more and more often from district and school leaders, and there is no aspect of education to which it is more applicable than professional development.

When it comes to PD, we not only have to change the culture surrounding professional development, we have to rethink the content focus of it as well. In this way, the 4Cs have two very important roles in professional development: The 4Cs should serve as the principles of PD redesign and the 4Cs should also represent the primary content focus for PD.

The 4Cs as the Design Principles for Professional Development

So here is the problem of trying to fly the PD plane and redesign it at the same time: The PD plane is in such a state of disrepair no one wants to get on. Most educators have a pretty dim view of what constitutes professional development today, and with good reason. We have all had the experience of attending a seminar where none of the 4Cs is present: No critical thinking is required, no collaboration is expected, and no creativity is encouraged. Stand-and-deliver lectures are surprisingly common. It's ironic—if not outright depressing—to encounter educators who have attended training sessions about inquiry-based learning where they sit through a series of lecture slides. When this is the kind of "professional development" being provided, how can we possibly engage educators in lifelong professional learning?

This state of affairs isn't hopeless, however. As you will recall, in Step 1, we asked you to be open-minded about the concept of accountability. Yes, accountability can be draconian. But, remember, we asked teachers how they would feel if accountability were focused on critical thinking, communication, collaboration, and creativity. They said they'd have a very different point of view.

Here similarly in the area of professional development we need to ask faculty to have an open mind: What if professional development had the attributes of the 4Cs? How would you feel about professional development if:

- It challenged you to think critically?
- Helped you communicate more effectively?
- Involved true collaboration with colleagues around authentic work?
- Inspired you to be more creative and innovative in your practices?

If these were the characteristics of all PD, we think most teachers would embrace it.

Assuming you adopted these design principles, how would PD in your school or district change? Would stand-and-deliver lectures be the norm? We doubt it.

Instead, we imagine a PD setting where teachers are asked to redesign a unit of instruction, are working in a group to constructively improve each other's work, trying out the new strategies in their classrooms, and then are returning to the group to learn from each other's successes and failures. Does this sound like an environment that encourages critical thinking, communication, collaboration, and creativity? We think so.

Fortunately, over the past decade, two major PD organizations in education have been helping educators move in this direction. Learning Forward (formerly The National Staff Development Council) has done excellent work overall helping the field rethink professional learning. Their standards emphasize the importance of learning communities that promote a culture of continuous learning and shared responsibility. The standards also highlight the important role of leaders in developing support systems for educators to enhance professional knowledge and skills ("Learning Forward Standards for Professional Learning"). This definition represents an excellent move toward a more 21st century-oriented vision of professional development.

The Association of Supervision and Curriculum Development (ASCD) has also long promoted the need for enhanced professional learning and 21st century education. They have published several volumes related to 21st century curriculum, including the work of Robert Marzano, Grant Wiggins, and Heidi Hayes Jacob. Additionally, several of ASCD's state chapters have been promoting 21st century education. The New York, Texas, Virginia, and Wisconsin chapters have been particularly active on behalf of 21st century education, and New York ASCD devoted an entire issue of its publication to 21st century education.

While the attempts by Learning Forward and ASCD are most helpful, we also recommend a simple message to your PD staff about utilizing the 4Cs: Gather your PD staff together and have them work with you to develop a PD transformation plan that utilizes critical thinking, communication, collaboration, and creativity as organizing principles.

Challenge your professional development staff to address questions such as:

- How can professional learning (both for teachers and administrators) challenge our educators to critically think and reflect deeply on their practice?
- How can professional learning opportunities integrate 21st century communication strategies and tools?
- How can the professional learning model encourage creative and innovative teacher practices?

These ideas can serve as a solid and helpful set of "design elements" for your professional development strategies.

In this process, the "C" we really want you to emphasize in thinking about PD redesign is *collaboration*. Simply focusing on collaboration can help you transform current PD practices. Most professional development today still treats the teacher working in isolation. Professional learning opportunities should, instead, integrate your team so it is natural to learn and work "collectively." Professional learning should help educators collaborate with each other in their day-to-day practices.

We have been very impressed by the capacity of the professional learning community (PLC) movement to really accentuate the need for collaboration and collective practice. PLCs are effective at breaking the isolation of the individual teacher and, instead, instituting a more collaborative, transparent community of practice. PLCs are also very helpful in creating a culture of collective responsibility where every educator shares a sense of responsibility for every student, throughout the system.

Richard and Rebecca DuFour are the preeminent national leaders when it comes to PLCs. Their model includes three big ideas that merit your attention:

- The fundamental purpose of the school is to ensure that all students learn at high levels. The school exists not merely to see to it that all students are taught, but to ensure that all students learn.

- To fulfill their purpose of helping all students learn at high levels, educators must work together collaboratively in a collective effort rather than in isolation.
- Educators must create a results orientation in which they constantly seek evidence of student learning and use that evidence to respond to the needs of individual students and to inform and improve their individual and collective practice.

In the DuFours' construct, which we fully support, the isolated teacher is replaced by a team of teachers working together. The members of the team hold themselves collectively responsible for the progress of all students. The school day is structured to include time for collaboration. In the old model, teachers might be given some materials along with a lecture and be left to their own devices. In this new model, teachers learn and work collaboratively; they use a common set of indicators to gauge collective progress. They work together to address the individual needs of students. Education leaders are instrumental in establishing this kind of model. In *Leaders of Learning,* Richard DuFour and Robert Marzano (2011) stress the importance of collaborative teams and shared leadership to ensure PLCs are effective. In our view, the DuFours' PLC model is an essential component of any district's 21st century professional learning strategy. That's why we employ many of these same principles within our own PLC (EdLeader21). We describe our PLC approach as follows:

- We are dedicated to creating true communities of practice through co-creation, collaboration, and member-to-member learning.
- We believe the best learning happens when it is authentic—meaning it is job-embedded, relevant, differentiated, and timely.
- We emphasize a culture of continuous learning and shared responsibility for the PLC's progress.
- We focus on continuous improvement within the PLC by using evidence that can be tracked over time to strengthen progress and success.

Superintendent Pam Moran in Albemarle, Virginia, also embraces collaborative professional development. Her district has abandoned stand-alone, one-time professional development workshops and made staff development collaborative, seamless, relevant, and job-embedded. In her district, professional learning encourages teachers to see themselves as part of a collective intelligence model, rather than as individuals working in isolation.

Albemarle leaders initially focused on face-to-face professional learning communities. These are now supported by a vibrant online community in a private social networking environment. It is common for Moran and other educators to come across an idea, share it with their online community, and watch it go "viral." In one recent example, Moran came across a blogger's post on Twitter about establishing "paperless" teaching on Earth Day. She copied and pasted the post on the PLC website, at which point the rest of the faculty took the idea and ran with it. Soon afterward the district held a "teach paperless" week that was a big success, all from the initial "copy-and-paste" that took Moran about two minutes. More recently, she connected with education leaders in Michigan through Twitter and developed a virtual collaborative project around the 10th anniversary of 9/11. Teachers and students across two states and several districts worked together to record and share 9/11 remembrance stories and find ways to comprehend the event.

Moran also relies on Richard and Rebecca DuFour's work on PLCs to nurture what she calls a "web of leadership" rather than a hierarchical approach to PD. What that means, in practice, is horizontal or vertical teams where principals, teachers, and technology coordinators pursue professional learning together. Principals are often just participants; they are not necessarily the focus nor do they lead the sessions. She describes her principals and teachers working as teams to identify essential understandings for students, for example, or better approaches to standards-based grading. Moran has tried to flatten the entire hierarchy so that people realize they are all on this journey together and that they must build understanding collectively and struggle through it side by side.

Another interesting example of how to emphasize collaborative professional development is from the New Tech Network (mentioned previously in Step 2). The schools all use a project-based learning model that requires significant professional support and capacity building. The success of every school, therefore, centers on robust professional learning opportunities that are highly collaborative.

A significant part of the NTN PD strategy is the requirement that every new teacher participate in professional learning communities (PLC). Each new teacher participates in a PLC within his or her school and participates in a PLC that involves teachers in schools across the network. The teachers are able to use New Tech Network's online platform to engage in a virtual PLC. This online work is complemented by in-person meetings where the collaborative culture is reinforced through regular sharing of best practices. Teachers are able to share over 800 projects, find resources for just in time learning and participate in meetings and groups for specific feedback among peers. The New Tech Network believes that the principles of collaboration and communication are central to the success of their professional development programs and that their PD programs are central to the success of their schools.

The examples provided by Albemarle and New Tech are powerful because of the way they emphasize collaborative learning among educators. We believe they are the wave of the future in that they will set the tone for how "cutting edge" districts will work together on collaborative professional capacity building. And they are sterling examples of how collaboration and, in fact, all the 4Cs can serve as the organizing principles for transformed professional development.

The 4Cs as the Content Focus of Professional Development

From our perspective, it is not enough to change the culture and strategies of PD. The focus of PD needs to be refined as well. Here is just one quick example: We visited a district that was utilizing PLCs. One of the participating teachers remarked that she loved focusing on student outcomes like critical thinking and collaboration but was frustrated that there wasn't time set aside to train teachers about these skills. We were surprised by this because the district's PLCs appeared to be functioning quite well. She went on to explain that while the PLCs were very active, the PLC work was organized around core academic subject-related professional development. It was a great moment to ask her to reflect on the PLC strategy. We encouraged her and her colleagues to shift the focus of their PLCs to support the teaching of core academic subjects *along with* the 4Cs.

The vision for 21st century outcomes must be a primary focus for the content of PLCs. Some PLC advocates and peer coaches remain neutral about what content is "delivered" through the PLC. There is nothing wrong with that. But for you, as a leader of a 21st century district or school, it is important to make clear *what the essential purpose* of any revamped PD strategies should be. The PD program and its practitioners must understand that they should be focused intensely on the 4Cs and the other outcomes that your educational community has embraced as its vision for 21st century education.

The DuFours also make this point in their work. They emphasize that it is not enough to simply define the existence of PLCs; providing the time for PLCs to meet won't guarantee the success of professional development or your vision. The PLCs must truly be focused on the 21st century challenges that the school or district has embraced. The PLCs themselves must create clarity around the definitions of the 4Cs and other 21st century outcomes. They must have a common understanding of how progress will be measured for the agreed-upon outcomes. They must have a common understanding of what student success looks like and how to accomplish it together (DuFour, 2012).

In sum, the PLCs must be the place where 21st century outcomes are integrated into PD so that teachers can integrate these competencies into daily practices. Some resources that might help you embed the 4Cs into the work of your PLCs are worth considering. As part of our work within EdLeader21 (our PLC for leaders), we have developed resource guides for each of the 4Cs, which are included in the Appendix 3-6. These documents include a definition for each outcome and a wide range of resources focused on that student outcome. These are excellent resources for your PLCs to use in their professional development activities.

Yet another resource tool that will help with integrating the 4Cs into PD is the first guide to the 4Cs specifically designed for teachers. It is titled "Preparing Our Students for the 21st Century: An Educator's Guide to the 4Cs" and is being published by the National Education Association (to request a copy, please email 21stcenturyskills@nea.org). It can help you design effective professional development sessions with your teachers around the 4Cs. It includes material on why the 4Cs are important and what steps teachers can take to embed the 4Cs in their practice. It includes many specific examples from each of the academic disciplines.

If you need more specific examples in your PD efforts of "what it looks like" in core academic subjects, please see the "21st Century Skills Maps" that we mentioned in Step 2. They were developed by national associations for teachers of math, science, social studies, English, geography, the arts, and world languages and, as a result, will have credibility with educators in those subjects. The maps may be found at www.p21.org under the "Tools and Resources" tab. They are also described in Appendix 2.

Because of our conviction that critical thinking is the most important of the 4Cs, we'd like to share a brief example from our network. In Upper Arlington, Ohio, Superintendent Weaver and his team focused the first two years of their 21st century education PD on critical thinking. Imagine for a moment that every teacher in your district working in professional learning communities focused on critical thinking, all at the same time. Imagine teachers in every department, school, and grade simultaneously and collaboratively sharing their critical thinking strategies with each other—this would result in a commitment to improving the rigor of the district's thinking and learning on a grand scale. It would be quite inspiring. And that's basically what Upper Arlington did.

In order to "kick off" their two-year focus on critical thinking, they developed the idea of a traditional day-long PD event focused specifically on critical thinking. But their 21st century skills coaches took a very powerful step. They spent months recruiting 38 teachers in the district who had compelling examples of teaching critical thinking in their classroom. These teachers were asked to serve as the faculty at the event. Their leadership at the event communicated very clearly that the critical thinking work in the district was founded on the deep expertise that already existed within the district. The entire faculty was interacting with its own experts on how to pursue more effective critical thinking pedagogy. The resulting levels of engagement were high, as you can imagine.

The 21st century skills coaches in Upper Arlington now report that the day-long event created incredible demand for ongoing implementation around critical thinking practices. The coaches now support the critical thinking work of the PLCs in their schools while also supporting individual teachers who are integrating critical thinking practices in their classrooms.

Additionally, Upper Arlington has used groups of teachers each summer to focus their professional development around critical thinking. They had a group one summer convened specifically to develop their rubric for complex thinking. The work included identifying six components of complex thinking as well as a progression from Stage 1 to Stage 4 describing the development of each of the six components. This rubric has been an incredibly helpful contribution to the district's focus on critical thinking.

Another outstanding example of a focus on critical thinking is the work of the Center for Authentic Intellectual Work (www.centerforaiw.com). They have been serving as the primary consultants to the Authentic Intellectual Work (AIW) in Iowa Project. Their work is based largely on the research of Fred Newmann, Bruce King and colleagues at the University of Wisconsin-Madison (Newmann et al., 1996; Newmann, King, & Carmichael, 2007; King, Schroeder, Chawszczewski, 2006). Education leaders in Iowa recognized about five years ago, as part of its focus on their 21st century core curriculum, that the state needed special focus on the capacity of Iowa teachers to effectively teach higher order thinking skills. They asked schools who were interested in forming professional learning communities around critical thinking and authentic student achievement to apply to participate. Over the five years of the program it has now spread to over 100 schools.

Bruce King, one of the designers of the approach, underscores the importance of having a common instructional framework for teachers at a school to use. These common definitions (in the form of rubrics) are critical, according to King, to assure that all teachers are on the same page with respect to critical thinking (as well as in-depth conceptual understanding and connections to the real world, the other AIW dimensions). What is exciting in Iowa is that now dozens of schools across the state are setting into motion a critical thinking professional learning community designed to specifically focus on the improvement of pedagogy around higher order thinking skills. Imagine how well this will prepare teachers and students to address the new Common Core standards and new AP exams focused on critical thinking, problem solving, and applied learning. It is a great tribute to the state of Iowa that it is focused on helping their schools and teachers develop their collective capacity for critical thinking practices.

These examples underscore the importance of placing the 4Cs as a primary content focus for your professional development efforts. Although in this section we have used critical thinking as an example, you can imagine a similar focused approach helping teachers to work collectively to improve their pedagogy of communication, collaboration, or creativity skills.

So now we have covered using the 4Cs as organizing principles of your PD as well as establishing the 4Cs as the focus of your PD. We have one last topic we want to raise with you: What are the PD resources you will deploy to make it happen?

The Resources for Professional Development

The prospect of moving past traditional stand-and-deliver PD to one that is more vibrant, interactive, and collaborative is an exciting one. But how do you accomplish this at a time of shrinking budgets? Do you really have the resources to accomplish such lofty goals? In the current economic climate, it might feel as if you do not have the resources you need. However, there are a number of tactics you have at your disposal that might be helpful.

1. Inventory your current PD allocations and consider whether they can be deployed more effectively.

Professional development is one of those places where it makes a lot of sense to inventory your current strategies and expenditures and determine whether you're really getting a good return on your investment. You can also determine whether you can just alter the current approaches or need a full-scale overhaul.

In Virginia Beach, Virginia, district leaders determined that their existing professional development division needed an overhaul. They restructured the existing department and used those resources to support the professional development needs around the 21st century education initiative. This was a major step. They didn't provide new spending on PD; rather, they redeployed their PD resources so that they truly supported their 21st century learning outcomes.

2. Review the roles and responsibilities of all current personnel that are, or could be, focused on PD.

Consider reviewing all the positions in the district that currently have professional development responsibilities and determining how that might translate into staffing of your 21st century education initiative. In Catalina Foothills School District, leaders transitioned the existing librarian positions into curriculum integration specialist positions that now support teachers in 21st century learning practices. Other districts we are familiar with have changed existing job descriptions in order to staff 21st century education implementation work. In Upper Arlington, Ohio, technology coaches became 21st century skills coaches.

We don't advocate any one of these strategies above the other. Each community's situation is unique, and the solutions will vary. However, we have been observing districts around the country as they conduct audits to determine how existing personnel might be deployed differently. The following positions are ones that have often been reconfigured, in our experience:

- Technology coaches
- 21st century skills coaches
- Librarians
- Curriculum integration specialists
- Professional development specialists

If your school or district employs many different specialists such as these, it is worth considering whether they can work in a more unified way. Shouldn't all these support personnel be working closely together and supporting the district's overall 21st century vision? Many schools and districts have merged the responsibilities of these specialists, in part for cost savings, but also to improve professional development support for their 21st century education work. We strongly suggest you undertake such a review.

3. Determine the degree to which you can rely on outside partners (such as educational service agencies or "county" offices) for their PD capabilities.

Some schools and districts rely on the work of their regional educational service agency (ESA). Where they exist and are effective, ESAs can provide robust professional and technical support for a wide range of 21st century implementation activities. The regional agency in central New York, the OCM BOCES, offers specialized 21st century professional development activities for participating districts. They produce annual events, seminars, workshops and virtual communities focused specifically on 21st century education.

4. Consider the potential for outside groups, including state and national professional learning communities like EdLeader21, to support your PD initiatives.

Many 21st century districts, of course, rely on professional development resources from outside consultants. There are a myriad of opportunities for teachers, but not as many for leaders. For that reason, last year we initiated EdLeader21, a professional learning community for leaders committed to building the 4Cs into their school or district strategies. You can learn more about EdLeader21 on our website, www.edleader21.com and in the introduction to this book.

5. Consider peer coaches as an alternative to new personnel.

Finally, there is one particularly cost-effective strategy that we recommend: peer coaching. It is premised on the notion that, rather than hiring new professional development personnel, you can instead identify teachers that have the most potential to serve as peer coaches and train them for that purpose.

Les Foltos is a pioneer in the peer coaching field. As director of technology for the Seattle Public Schools in the 1990s, Foltos had great difficulty getting teachers to learn new technology integration skills using traditional professional development methods. What he found, which is now a fairly commonly used practice throughout the United States and the international education community, is that teachers instinctively look first to trusted colleagues for professional guidance. Preferably, the colleague is someone who is just down the hall and who is not a mentor or master teacher.

As Foltos describes it, these are peers who might have stronger collaboration skills and maybe know a bit more about best practices in technology integration, but they are not experts. They are facilitators. They are collaborators. Frequently, they are co-learners. At the heart of Foltos' model is ensuring that all peer coaches have strong communication and collaboration skills. Foltos emphasizes that it is the communication and collaboration skills in the coaching that really make an impact, where you see teachers developing a deeper understanding of the strategies and practices that will better meet the needs of their students.

It is important to point out that peer coaches are full-time teachers. Ideally, the school strongly supports collaboration among teachers and provides sufficient time each week for the coaches to collaborate with teachers, in addition to common planning time, grade level meetings, and PD days built into the school schedule. There is no additional compensation. When Foltos has asked the coaches why they coach, they say they do it because of the satisfaction they get from working with other teachers and helping them to develop and gain skills and confidence. As you'll no doubt notice, these are the same reasons all good teachers decide to go into teaching in the first place.

Peer coaching might or might not be helpful in your particular situation, but whatever specific activities you pursue, it is important to complete a comprehensive review of your professional development resources and determine how best to configure them to support your 21st century education initiative.

FINAL THOUGHTS

We have stressed four things in this chapter:

- Focus on professional development as an essential component of your 21st century education initiative.
- Use the 4Cs as the "design principles" for your evolving professional development work.
- Focus your PD on how teachers teach and assess the 4Cs.
- Deploy or redeploy resources to support your professional development.

It's absolutely critical that your PD has an impact on all of your educators' abilities to produce 4Cs outcomes among *all* students consistently in each and every classroom.

As a helpful exercise, use this chart to help you focus on how the 4Cs can help you "build out" your professional development strategy. Our hope is that the 4Cs will become central to your 21st century approach to professional development.

THE 4CS AND PROFESSIONAL DEVELOPMENT STRATEGY

The 4Cs and PD Strategy	Reflection	Next Step
Critical Thinking	How will your educators' capacity to critically think and reflect deeply on their instructional practices be reflected in your redesigned professional development?	
Communication	How will your redesigned professional development model 21st century communication strategies?	
Collaboration	How will your redesigned professional development be based on collective activity and decision making?	
Creativity	How will your redesigned professional development foster creativity and innovation in teaching and learning strategies?	

THE 4CS AND PROFESSIONAL DEVELOPMENT WORKSHEET

The 4Cs	PD Focus	Next Steps
Critical Thinking	What materials and strategies on critical thinking have you included in your PD program? (*See Appendix 3: Resources on Critical Thinking.*)	
Communication	What materials and strategies on communication have you included in your PD program? (*See Appendix 4: Resources on Communication.*)	
Collaboration	What materials and strategies on collaboration have you included in your PD program? (*See Appendix 5: Resources on Collaboration.*)	
Creativity	What materials and strategies on creativity have you included in your PD program? (*See Appendix 6: Resources on Creativity.*)	
Self-Direction	What materials and strategies on self-direction have you included in your PD program?	
Global Competence	What materials and strategies on global competence have you included in your PD program?	
Financial Literacy	What materials and strategies on financial literacy have you included in your PD program?	
Other Student Outcomes	What materials and strategies on _____ have you included in your PD program?	

4.1 OVERALL REFLECTIONS ON PROFESSIONAL DEVELOPMENT

- How would you rate the quality of professional development today in your school or district? Is it largely the traditional approach to PD? Are teachers still working largely in isolation on their PD?
- Have you established a culture of collaboration for your PD? Have you established professional learning communities? Have you established a culture of collective responsibility for the results of *all* students?
- Have you undertaken a review of all your PD resources and personnel and considered consolidating and streamlining them? Are you utilizing peer coaches?
- Do you have a strategy to focus each of your PD strategies (PLCs, PD personnel, peer coaches) on the 4Cs and the other 21st century outcomes that you have embraced?

REFERENCES

DuFour, Richard. Personal interview. Mar. 10, 2012.

DuFour, Richard, Rebecca DuFour, Robert Eaker, and Thomas Many. *Learning by Doing: A Handbook for Professional Learning Communities at Work.* Bloomington, IN: Solution Tree Press, 2006.

DuFour, Richard and Robert J. Marzano, *Leaders of Learning: How District, School, and Classroom Leaders Improve Student Achievement* (pps. 23–24, 56–58). Bloomington, IN: Solution Tree Press, 2011.

M. B. King, J. L. Schroeder & D. Chawszczewski. "Authentic Assessment and Student Performance in Inclusive Secondary Schools," in F. W. Parkay, E. J. Anctil, & G. J. Hass (Eds.) *Curriculum planning: A contemporary approach,* 8th edition. Boston: Allyn & Bacon, 2006.

"Learning Forward Standards for Professional Learning." *Learning Forward.* Jan. 5, 2012. http://www.learningforward.org/standards/standards.cfm.

Moran, Pam. Personal interview. June 10, 2011.

F. M. Newmann, M. B. King, & D. L. Carmichael. *Authentic Instruction and Assessment: Common Standards for Rigor and Relevance in Teaching Academic Subjects.* Des Moines, IA: Iowa Department of Education, 2007.

New York State ASCD. "Impact on Instructional Improvement." 36.1 (Mar. 2011). http://www.newyorkstateascd.org.

STEP

Focus Your Curriculum and Assessment

THE 4CS FOCUS

When it comes to the "big intersections" between the 4Cs, curricula, and assessment, think about these ideas:

- Critical thinking: When it comes to the most important student competency to include in curricula and assessment, critical thinking is the "first among equals." If you are not teaching and measuring critical thinking skills, it borders on educational malpractice in the 21st century. You'll also rely on your own critical thinking skills to pursue Step 5.
- Collaboration: Curricula and assessments should be designed collaboratively and focus on student collaboration as specific outcomes. Curricula and assessments should help students work together to produce high-quality products and self-assess collaborative performances.
- Communication: Communication skills should be highlighted in curricula and assessments. Also, the 4Cs should be *clearly communicated* to educators and students via the curricula and *explicitly reported* to relevant stakeholders through assessments and assessment data.
- Creativity: Curricula and assessment systems should support diverse opportunities for students to perform and master creative thinking skills, which are difficult to teach and measure using traditional methods. Additionally, education leaders who are designing curricula and assessment systems that measure the 4Cs will need to use their creativity and innovation skills constantly because there are no pre-packaged "off the shelf" ways to perform this work—it takes new ideas and a lot of flexibility.

On your journey through this book, we've asked you to consider the 4Cs in light of your vision, community, system, and professional development. Step 5: Focus Your Curriculum and Assessment is one of the most interesting, we think, because it is often the place where education leaders instinctively begin working. You might find, like some of the leaders we have worked with, that the best way to get your people grounded in your initiative is to dive right in to a 4Cs curricula or assessment project. There is nothing wrong with this approach, as long as you recognize it as a small starting point that will lead you very quickly on your way to the broader alignment work as described throughout this book and most notably in Step 3.

Step 5 covers 4Cs curricula and assessment in separate sections. You'll notice that these topics are, of course, quite interconnected—for example, are curricula-embedded assessments an element of curricula or assessment? (They are both.) We'd like to stress that 4Cs curricula and assessments should be viewed as interlocking components in a highly aligned system, even though for practicality's sake we have separated them here.

What Is 4Cs Curricula?

Curricula can be described as the content, knowledge, skills, and aptitudes that are written, taught, and learned within a school system. 4Cs curricula are simply curricula that cover core academic subjects with an intentional focus on skills such as critical thinking, communication, collaboration, and creativity. These kinds of curricula:

- Are quite rigorous, going beyond rote factual recall.
- Focus on student understanding, often using Understanding by Design (UbD) principles.
- Are embedded with a balanced combination of core academic content, performance-based tasks, and assessments *for* learning.
- Are never considered "complete" in a traditional sense because it serves as the platform for educators and students to teach and learn in iterative, continuously improving cycles.
- Enhance professional capacity through the design process; educators at every level of the system are engaged in refining curricula and improving daily practice.

In describing what we mean by 4Cs curricula, it is important to point out the different levels of curricula that exist within schools and districts: the intended, written curricula (such as high-level curriculum and unit guides), the taught curricula (such as units/lessons/instruction), and the learned curricula (such as student performances)—see Figure 5.1.

Effective integration of the 4Cs into curricula means attending to *all three areas* in Figure 5.1. Often, district and school leaders focus their transformation efforts on the intended, written curricula (#1 in Figure 5.1). But in an age when teachers have ready access to a multitude of curricular resources including commercially published, district-published, self-created, web-based, student-created, and more, a regimented "top-down" approach to 4Cs curricula doesn't have much chance of becoming an integral part of the taught, let alone learned, curricula (#2 and #3 in Figure 5.1). As many leading curriculum experts have pointed out for years, even if central office leaders write a guaranteed, viable curriculum that integrates the 4Cs, how can you make sure every educator uses it as it is intended? Frankly, you cannot, and you should not, because this is not the right mindset.

A better approach is to design 4Cs curricula with a mindset of continuous improvement and co-creation. Principals, teachers, and specialists can and should be directly involved in collaboratively creating substantial, authentic, performance-based curricular experiences so that all students have deeper and more consistent opportunities to learn. This approach is nicely demonstrated by the work being done by Mary Kamerzell's team in Catalina Foothills School District, where curricula are backwards-designed among the faculty in a highly collaborative, ongoing process. The work of 4Cs curricula design actually *is* the content of their professional development.

FIGURE 5.1   Levels of Curricula

The 4Cs should be integrated into each of these levels:

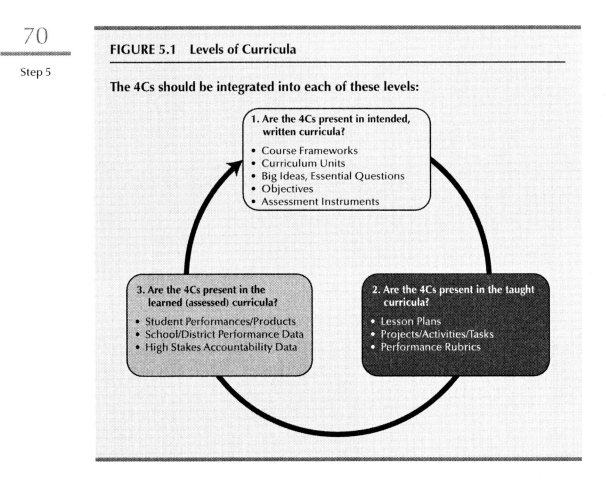

1. Are the 4Cs present in intended, written curricula?
 - Course Frameworks
 - Curriculum Units
 - Big Ideas, Essential Questions
 - Objectives
 - Assessment Instruments

2. Are the 4Cs present in the taught curricula?
 - Lesson Plans
 - Projects/Activities/Tasks
 - Performance Rubrics

3. Are the 4Cs present in the learned (assessed) curricula?
 - Student Performances/Products
 - School/District Performance Data
 - High Stakes Accountability Data

Special Comment on Common Core State Standards (CCSS)

While Step 5 is about curriculum and assessment, not standards, it is important to note the effects of the Common Core State Standards as they are being adopted by most states. The level of consensus achieved in the CCSS documents is an important point of progress in the standards movement (especially for those of us who are familiar with the "content wars" of the past); there is now a rigorous academic set of standards that can be viewed as the "floor" from which 21st century educators can build upon. This is good news. The CCSS in English language arts are particularly strong in their attention to critical thinking and communication. The CCSS in mathematics also point out the importance of skills such as reasoning and communication, though we wish the document provided clearer guidance on how to integrate these skills into mathematics content. For more on this topic, we recommend an excellent resource developed by the Partnership for 21st Century Skills, the P21 Common Core Toolkit, available at **www.p21.org.**

Understanding by Design (UbD) and 4Cs Curricula

A commonly used methodology we recommend for this kind of curricula design is Wiggins and McTighe's *Understanding by Design* (UbD). UbD is well-suited to 4Cs curricula design for two primary reasons:

- **UbD is not agnostic about the goal of teaching and learning—it focuses exclusively on student understanding.** The goal of UbD—student understanding—is to help students transfer knowledge and skills creatively, flexibly, and fluently in unique situations. (For an extensive treatment of the definition of "understanding," see Wiggins and McTighe pages 35–55, and Bransford, Brown, and Cocking, *How People Learn*.) This is an excellent framework for education leaders interested in building students' complex thinking skills such as the 4Cs—critical thinking, communication, collaboration, and creativity.
- **UbD requires a backward-design methodology.** Using backward design is a no-brainer for education leaders developing 4Cs curricula. Identifying the exact student outcomes you are hoping to achieve and working backward from there is a proven best practice for designing curricula that enhances understanding, not just content coverage. UbD's comprehensive, well-documented, and widely implemented methodologies are some of the most accessible and 4Cs-aligned resources available.

UbD's emphasis on identifying essential questions, enduring understandings, key performance tasks, and rubrics in curricula design will help you create a more effective, aligned 4Cs curricula and assessment system.

The challenge with UbD in our experience is getting a handle on its complexity and translating it into action. Given the sheer breadth and depth of UbD "how to" guides, it can be hard to isolate the most effective way(s) to pursue a backward-design approach to 4Cs curricula design. In the next section, we have attempted to highlight the action steps that have been cited most often by the district and school leaders who have implemented UbD in the context of their 21st century education initiatives.

4Cs Curricula Action Steps

As we just mentioned, UbD methodologies can seem overwhelming. Even leaders who have been utilizing backward-design methods such as UbD ask us to recommend the most helpful action steps for creating and refining 4Cs curricula, so we have tried to isolate a few of them here. The activities described below are derived from UbD methods and should illustrate the importance of using a backward-design process in your design.

These action areas below assume that, first and foremost, the school system has established a clear vision around 21st century learning outcomes and that there is a common view among all educators around student learning goals. Once there is consensus around a common 21st century learning vision, the steps below can help you integrate the 4Cs into curricula. Every district we have seen uses a wide variety of tools and methods. Therefore, the list below is not prescriptive; we encourage you to customize these approaches to fit the needs of your district and school.

Action Step: Use 4Cs Curricula Design as Professional Development

When it is done well, the process of backward-designing 4Cs curriculum becomes the primary platform for professional learning throughout the district. Educators should have regular opportunities to reflect on and refine the curricula.

At Catalina Foothills School District, many of the district's teachers participate every summer in curricula and assessment design work as well as in professional development offerings related to the work. Both of these areas are essential components in the district's strategic plan. Assistant Superintendent Mary Jo Conery told us, "we've always had teachers directly involved in developing our curriculum and assessments. There are either district-based teams or site-based teams collaborating on the work. During any given summer, we have up to 100 or more teachers involved in either curriculum or assessment design, or professional development, one of which was a redesign of inquiry based assessments in science at the middle and high school levels. Why? Because they want to use the information/data from their work with students to figure out what's working and what's not. Specifically related to the science inquiry assessments, they revised them to ensure they effectively measure the learning. They are engaged in the work because they understand the district's mission and believe it's the right approach for our students. They are invested in creating that which directly impacts their work in the classroom with students."

A similar approach is used in North Salem Central School District. In the first year of its 21st century education initiative, Superintendent Kenneth Freeston and his deputy superintendent, Mike Hibbard, had educators work together to develop a critical thinking and creativity–infused curriculum. In the second year, the team reviewed student performance data and identified areas for improvement. They worked in collaborative teams to refine the curriculum and intend to repeat the process each year. As Assistant Superintendent Hibbard describes it: "Our focus in the second year was: let's look back at the curriculum and figure out where we need to pay more attention. What was a challenge? What's the good, the bad, and the ugly?" The collaborative sessions among teachers occur during the school year, using release time and scheduled PD days. Educators find the sessions worthwhile because the work is authentic and timely. Curricula refinement has become the primary framework for professional development in the district.

As educators across the system work together to refine the curricula, their understanding of their own academic subjects deepens, along with a heightened awareness of cross-disciplinary approaches to teaching and learning. This approach also reinforces the importance of all educators co-owning and co-developing the 21st century education initiative.

Action Step: Create Common 4Cs Performance Tasks

District leaders can enable system-wide 4Cs student work by creating and implementing common 4Cs performance tasks (see Example Box 5.1). These tasks can then be written collaboratively among vertical and horizontal teacher teams and implemented across the system in specific courses and/or grades. In a typical implementation, every student will complete from one to four essential tasks (focused on the 4Cs) across one or more academic content area(s). Student performance outcomes can then be shared with teachers, parents, and administrators as appropriate. Student performance data, along with feedback from teachers, should then be used to improve the design and use of the 4Cs performance tasks in subsequent years.

In North Salem Central School District, New York, the UbD framework is used to guide curricula design. The North Salem vision for teaching and learning is for every student to become an effective problem solver; with this as the overarching goal, district leaders, site leaders, and classroom educators collaborated on the following curricula design activities:

- Mapping (and "unpacking") the standards
- Identifying essential questions for
  - Each discipline
  - Each course
  - Each unit
- Creating common course-level "problem solving tasks" (PSTs) that enable problem solving skills (every section of the same course has to integrate the same PST)

The items above have become the central elements of curricula all teachers are expected to use. Teachers have a great degree of autonomy in developing their own approaches to addressing the essential questions, unit objectives, and PSTs. North Salem's use of PSTs is notable—the PSTs are the primary vehicle for ensuring the 4Cs become integrated into regular teacher practices.

The PSTs are embraced by classroom educators because, like all elements of the curricula, teachers are intimately involved in co-creating them. In most cases, vertical teams of teachers meet in workshops to create a common PST. In the design workshop, teachers share one of their favorite performance tasks. Then the group assesses each task for the degree to which it aligns with the district's design characteristics and then votes to select one for further refinement. The group then collaborates to re-engineer it according to the district's criteria (for example, each PST must include items such as defining the problem, gathering information, analyzing information, presenting a work product, and meta-cognition). The resulting PST becomes a common learning experience for students in a particular grade or subject band. The most important aspect of this process, in our opinion, is that the PST is agreed upon by everyone before it is implemented, which results in a high degree of adoption and use.

One 21st century PST in North Salem is for middle school science, called "Creature Capture." It addresses the following unit question: *How do the external structures of an organism help it find, get, and consume food in its home habitat?* The task itself is described as follows:

> *The task: You will imagine and create a newly discovered creature and its planet earth home habitat and invent a way to catch it for humane, scientific study. Then you will create a three-minute video presenting your creature, your invention to catch it, and what you plan to learn about that creature. (The creature might have been discovered in a terrestrial habitat, a water habitat, or a combination of the two.)*

As a concluding step, students are asked to reflect on their work and identify areas for future improvement. (See Appendix 12 for a copy of this PST.)

Action Step: Focus on Project Based Learning

We have discussed the strengths of Project Based Learning (PBL) throughout this book and it deserves special mention here. PBL is an effective way to design and organize curricula around the 4Cs, especially when it is a primary focus for teaching and learning.

The Buck Institute for Education (BIE) is an invaluable resource for exploring PBL curricula (as well as the professional development needed to implement it). BIE Essentials of PBL (2012) defines rigorous, meaningful and effective Project Based Learning as follows:

- PBL is intended to teach significant content.
- PBL requires critical thinking, problem solving, collaboration, and various forms of communication.

- PBL requires inquiry as part of the process of learning and creating something new.
- PBL is organized around an open-ended driving question.
- PBL creates a need to know essential content and skills.
- PBL allows some degree of student voice and choice.
- PBL includes processes for revision and reflection.
- PBL involves a public audience.

For curricula specialists, we highly recommend two excellent resources published by BIE (www.bie.org):

- PBL Starter Kit: To-the-Point Advice, Tools and Tips for Your First Project in Middle or High School, John Larmer (Author), Buck Institute for Education; 1ST edition (2009)
- PBL in the Elementary Grades: Step-by-Step Guidance, Tools and Tips for Standards-Focused K-5 Projects (Project Based Learning Toolkit Series, Volume 2) by Sara Hallermann; John Larmer; John R. Mergendoller. (Buck Institute for Education; 1ST edition (2011).

Action Step: Collect and Share Student Work Examples

Sharing and reflecting on student work examples is critical for establishing common understanding among teachers of "what it really looks like" for students to master the 4Cs. We cover this topic in detail in Step 6, but the main idea is to ask educators to collaboratively review student work with these questions in mind:

- Does the student work illustrate mastery of at least one of the 4Cs? Why or why not?
- In cases where there is widespread agreement about the presence of the 4Cs in a piece of student work, what instructional practices appear to have helped support this outcome?
- What additional instructional strategies might have enhanced a particular piece of student work? Why?
- What similarities exist among 4Cs examples of student work, if any?
- What big differences exist among the student examples that are shared?

Action Step: Create 4Cs-Focused Curriculum Maps, Guides, and Units

We recommend creating 4Cs curriculum maps and guides to articulate where and when higher-order competencies should appear across subjects and grades. Once the maps are created, vertical and horizontal teams typically work to identify and address gaps. As we have mentioned previously, many district leaders use co-creative and participatory processes because they provide authentic professional development opportunities while also resulting in high-quality 4Cs curricula. We'd like to underscore this point. Curriculum mapping *should not result in a rigid teaching schedule* all educators must adhere to religiously. While valuable as an end product, curriculum maps are most valuable when they strengthen professional learning communities and when they provide flexible guidance, not prescriptive direction. When the goal is to create deep understanding of and shared professional commitment to 21st century teaching and learning, 4Cs curriculum mapping is a valuable and important action step. Refer to Example Box 5.2.

In Albemarle School District, Virginia, Superintendent Pam Moran and her team use concept-centered learning and backward design to guide curricula mapping. Moran compares the concept-centered approach to using a special camera filter; using a conceptual lens for curricula provides educators with a way to look at the curricula, much like using a filter in photography. It doesn't change the pieces of the picture, but it does affect how it looks.

All units, themes, and topics are organized around concepts, which are then connected to essential questions and student understandings. For example, a language arts unit on "Coming of Age" is focused on the concept of change, continuity, and culture. This concept might lead to the enduring understanding that change and continuity in language and literature reflect individual and societal evolution. Figure 5.2 represents one of the curriculum mapping tools Albemarle educators use to plan curricula. It illustrates how the enduring understandings, essential understandings, and essential questions might connect for a specific unit.

When Albemarle teachers begin unit design using concept-based thinking and backward-design strategies, they use a number of resources including the district's Framework for Quality Learning, the Division Curriculum Framework the Virginia Standards of Learning Curriculum Framework and other disciplines' Curriculum Frameworks to help identify interdisciplinary learning opportunities.

Here is how one language arts educator described the process of designing a concept-centered unit:

> "So, if I were to plan a unit starting with several of Poe's short stories, I need to consider, in relation to other units I will teach throughout the year, the lens through which students will study those short stories. If I select a thematic approach, I might have students read and discuss short stories with a central theme of fear of the unknown. I might structure their study around their personal fears of the unknown. I could then relate these stories to a larger work or other short works with the same theme. In this way, students would look at fear of the unknown as a universal experience.
>
> "Or I could choose a conceptual lens of author's craft. Although students would still discuss the central themes, we would spend more time analyzing Poe's use of sentence structure, vocabulary, figurative language, and such to determine how he brings a story to life. We could compare Poe's craft with that of other authors we have studied. Students could write emulating Poe's style and syntax, which would also bring in the lens of aesthetics."

No matter which conceptual lens is selected, the others are still relevant and should be explored as appropriate. Selecting a conceptual lens does not mean ignoring the others; it means elevating one to use it as a filter for studying a topic.

FIGURE 5.2 Albemarle Curriculum Mapping Example

Enduring Understandings

- Language is dynamic—multiple factors affect the evolution of language.
- Change and continuity in language and literature reflect individual and societal evolution.

↓

Essential Understandings

- An author's cultural context affects his or her perspective and, thus, his or her writing.
- An author's frame of reference influences his or her message.
- A reader's or listener's experiences affect understanding and enjoyment.
- Understanding historical and cultural context enhances and emphasizes meaning.

↓

Essential Questions

- How is an author's cultural context reflected in his or her writing?
- How does an author demonstrate bias?
- Why is an author's cultural context important?
- How do a reader's experiences change the text at hand?

Action Step: Use 4Cs Data and Analysis to Refine Curricula

The effectiveness of your 4Cs curriculum depends upon your ability to document how well students are learning what is intended. That's why curricula and assessment development often happen simultaneously. So while we haven't gone into detail about 4Cs assessment quite yet (coming later in this step), we should note the importance of creating a balanced and comprehensive approach to 4Cs assessment as a key part of the curricula design process.

We are, as we have said, adamant that rigid structures of compliance (and the over-emphasis on standardized test scores these often entail) can be detrimental to a true 21st century skills initiative. But quality data and reporting structures are incredibly important, along with a thoughtful system for professionals to reflect and analyze this data and use it to inform teaching and learning. In other words, teachers should be given meaningful opportunities to share, and reflect upon, their work in light of how their students are performing. Teachers should use such data to refine 4Cs curricula over time. One common method used by 21st century education leaders is to facilitate annual working sessions where educators use student performance data as a lens through which to review and refine the curricula.

Final Thoughts on Curricula

In summary, 4Cs curriculum advances your education initiative through "what" gets taught. Curricula refinement is a significant step in shifting from a rote memorization, content-only focus to a more balanced curricular approach that emphasizes both content and skills. This work goes a long way toward engaging teams of educators in your 21st century vision. The most important distinctions we have summarized are in Figure 5.3.

FIGURE 5.3   20th Century Curricula versus 21st Century Curricula

	20th Century Curricula	21st Century Curricula
Content Model	Content mastery with emphasis on discrete facts	Deep understanding of knowledge and skills with focus on essential questions
Adoption/ Authorship Model	Curricula selected by administrators with little input from teachers; written by commercial publishers with little customization by school or districts	Curricula selection, design, and development are highly customized using a wide range of source materials
Standards Model	Aligned to standards that focus on breadth of academic content coverage	Aligned to standards that emphasize essential understandings (with a focus on depth of knowledge and skills)
Revision Model	Revisions based on textbook adoption cycle; student performance data rarely used	Continual revisions led by collaborative teacher teams using current student performance data
Student Work Model	Student work demonstrates factual mastery	Student work emphasizes complex performances that demonstrate deep content understanding along with competencies such as the 4Cs

4Cs and Assessment

As you begin designing 4Cs curricula, questions around assessment will be your constant companion. Questions about how to measure the 4Cs are among the most common ones you will encounter on your 21st century journey. You will likely hear comments such as:

- These skills cannot be measured.
- Nobody agrees on how to define "critical thinking."
- Even if we could measure these skills, the current field of assessment is such a mess that there's nothing we can do.

Sound familiar? If so, our take on assessment will be encouraging. There are a number of exciting and dynamic ways to measure 21st century skills. The assessment landscape is not intractable and is, in many ways, headed in the right direction.

This is good news for 21st century education leaders. There are excellent reasons to feel confident as you begin the work of 4Cs assessment; there are many constructive models to use, and the big trend lines in assessment, while they have been negative for the past decade, are trending in a better direction. In this section, we'll share our thoughts on how to establish a positive tone around the issue of assessment and the 4Cs, and we'll point you toward some helpful action steps and models.

The Good News About Assessment

We know some days it doesn't feel like the rest of the education field is headed in the direction of 21st century education. But if one looks at recent developments in the Common Core State Standards, the AP exam, and the PISA exams, it is clear that the assessment world is slowly but surely beginning to emphasize assessment of higher-order thinking skills like the 4Cs.

Before we get into the current trends, however, let's go back a decade and consider how we got to the current point. When the accountability movement hit its height with the incarnation of NCLB, the emphasis was on having an assessment (any assessment) for accountability purposes. It was inevitable that the first wave of accountability would use measurement instruments that were widely in use—primarily multiple-choice tests. In this way, assessment for accountability was tied to the types of metrics that had been common for the past 30 or 40 years. These metrics appeared to do a decent job of identifying underperformance, and so they were embraced.

But it did not take long for educators to ask hard questions about the unintended consequences of such measurement tools—the narrowing of the curriculum and teaching to the test, for example. Eventually, educators, parents, and students themselves began to start asking the obvious: "Are we holding people accountable for the right things?" Policymakers soon began working on making state standards more rigorous—specifically, standards that would be internationally benchmarked and supportive of college and career readiness. This resulted in the Common Core State Standards that have now been adopted by more than 40 states. Regardless of how one feels about the Common Core, it is important to note that more states' ELA and mathematics standards will be aligned with critical thinking and communication skills than in the past. This is a positive development overall, in our opinion. Districts and schools that emphasize critical thinking and communication skills will now be supported by a majority of state standards. And those states that do not adopt the Common Core standards will hopefully place more emphasis on critical thinking, problem solving and communication skills. While the new state exams are not expected until 2014 or 2015, you should feel comfortable that the results of the Common Core process will lead to new state standards and exams much better aligned to the 4Cs that you are already emphasizing.

A similar set of developments is under way in the redesign of the AP exam, as we discussed in Step 2.The College Board is pursuing a multi-year process to de-emphasize rote memorization and increase the emphasis on critical thinking, problem solving, and applied learning in many AP exams.

The Programme for International Student Assessment (PISA) also helps validate the strategic direction in which you, your school, and your district are headed. The Organisation for Economic Co-operation and Development (OECD) has spent years trying to align the educational systems of Europe to the 21st century workforce needs of its countries. The PISA exam has consistently placed more emphasis on critical thinking, applied learning, and communication skills than its U.S. counterparts. This explains, in large part, the reason U.S. students have continued to place lower and lower relative to other countries on the PISA exam. The most recent results of U.S. students in the PISA exam should provide strong evidence to you in support of your 21st century education initiative. In 2012, the PISA exam will be adding financial literacy and dynamic problem solving (systems thinking). In 2014 or 2015, PISA will be adding collaborative problem solving questions to its exam. These developments should provide validation to you in two ways:

- It underscores the growing importance of these skills; and
- It suggests that the United States will face increasing pressure to teach and assess these skills as our international counterparts do because this is what high-performing education systems should be doing.

Even more encouraging news is that OECD is creating a school-based version of PISA, which we cover in detail later in this step. The PISA-Based Test for Schools will help participating schools support their benchmarking efforts, providing an important school-level perspective and links with the policy analysis and insights gleaned from the main PISA assessment.

Assessment Action Steps

Action Step: Pursue Benchmarking Assessments

Some leaders and school boards often ask, "Do we know how well our students compare to their peers on 21st century outcomes?" For these purposes, you might want to consider using a benchmarking assessment. This is a tool you can use simply to take a snapshot of where a sample of your students are, relative to a larger pool of students nationally or globally.

One tool that is focused on benchmarking U.S. high school students is the College and Work Readiness Assessment (www.cae.org/content/pro_collegework.htm). It measures

Example Box 5.3   CWRA Example

In the CWRA, a typical problem looks something like this:

The mayor of your town has had five years of a continuously increasing crime rate. She is considering two proposals: to build a new prison or to increase the police force by 250 people.

Attached to this question are three documents that are relevant:

- an academic study comparing the two strategies
- a press release from a city council member on the subject
- part of a transcript from a state legislative hearing on the subject

After reviewing the three documents, answer the following three questions:

1. What's the best case for building the prison?
2. What's the best case for increasing the size of the police force?
3. The mayor is presenting her budget to the city council at 3:00. Which proposal should she support and why?

Students who take this exam report high levels of engagement. They actually like taking this exam because it does not ask them to regurgitate facts from a textbook. It asks them to look at material they've never seen before and use it to solve a problem. The exam expects students to analyze and organize information and then communicate and problem solve— exactly the kinds of skills that are important in the 21st century.

---

critical thinking and communication skills at grades 9 and 12. Refer to Example Box 5.3. It asks students not to recall facts, but to look at material they have never seen before and attempt to analyze, communicate, and problem solve using the material. School leaders receive data that allow them to benchmark their ninth graders against other ninth graders across the country; in the 12th grade assessment, student data are benchmarked against other 12th graders and also compared with first-year college students as a way of gauging college readiness.

If your interest is in benchmarking your students against their international peers, districts and schools will soon be able to use the *PISA-Based Test for Schools*, which is expected to be available in late 2012. Please see Example Box 5.4.

Action Step: Create 4Cs Rubrics for Educators

Perhaps the most important tool at your disposal for assessment of 21st century outcomes is the simplest: rubrics. It always amuses us when people say "you can't measure 21st century skills." If you can create a rubric for the 4Cs, you can assess them. We think what people mean when they say, "You can't assess 21st century skills," is that you can't put all the skills in a large-scale summative assessment (and this point can be debated, of course). None of this means these skills cannot be measured.

For example, think about how all oral presentations are assessed in a K–12 setting. Typically, a rubric is used that includes items like posture, projection of voice, clarity

Example Box 5.4   PISA for Schools

There has been increasing demand in the U.S. for a student assessment that can be administered locally and that allows benchmarking with international results of the main Programme for International Student Assessment (PISA). In response to this, the Organisation for Economic Co-operation and Development (OECD) is currently developing a PISA-comparable test that can be administered by schools, networks and districts.

The results of this test, known as *PISA-Based Test for Schools*, will be comparable to the main PISA scales to allow for benchmarking with international PISA results for countries and economies when the test is administered under appropriate conditions.

Schools, school networks and districts will thus be able to administer the assessment and obtain results that will allow them to compare the performance of their schools internationally. *PISA-Based Test for Schools* is based on the same assessment frameworks as the main international PISA study. It includes items that measure students' abilities to successfully meet complex demands in varied contexts through knowledge and skills, motivation, and attitudes. The PISA frameworks focuses on literacy skills, defined as the capacity of young adults to access, manage, integrate, and evaluate information, to think imaginatively, to hypothesize and discover, and to communicate their thoughts and ideas effectively. PISA focuses on whether students can extrapolate from what they have learned and apply their competencies in novel situations in reading, mathematics, and science. *PISA-Based Test for Schools* results will be comparable to international PISA scales, in order to improve and support international benchmarking efforts by school and district leaders. As an increasing number of schools from different countries administer the assessment, participating schools and districts could form an international network where practices can be shared, issues discussed, and different tools made accessible.

of message, etc. There isn't a teacher in the country who should have trouble using such a rubric to evaluate a student's communication skills. Already, a number of school districts across the country are using rubrics for the 4Cs. Building on some of these excellent rubrics, districts, schools and organizations that have joined our organization, EdLeader21, are creating a master set of 4Cs rubrics that will be available to non-members in 2013 (you can learn more about this initiative in the Introduction). A wide range of rubrics for higher-order thinking skills can also be found by searching "rubrics" on Route 21, a website managed by P21 (http://route21.p21.org/).

Action Step: Create 4Cs Rubrics for Students

Rubrics are not just tools for teachers. Rubrics can and should be used by students themselves. We have visited numerous classes in which students have used rubrics to guide daily work. In one science class, students were using a rubric for "inquiry." One student had correctly identified a weakness in her questioning strategy—she was revising her inquiry statements to get at a deeper exchange of information about the topic. In her case, she was using the rubric to self-assess and improve her work in real time. In another example, fifth-grade students filled out a rubric at the end of a

Example Box 5.5 Detailed Example: Fairfax County Public Schools, Students as Global Learners Project

In Fairfax County Public Schools, Virginia, Superintendent Jack Dale and his team are in their fourth year of a district-wide global learners initiative that employs a common rubric used by educators. Every fifth grader in the district completes a technology-based student project that focuses on world cultures and world interdependence. Every fifth-grade social studies teacher uses the same rubric and online assessment system to record student outcomes.

To create the project, the project team (a diverse group of district and site administrators, teachers, and specialists) worked together to create essential questions and student project choices that enable students to meet the goal of demonstrating global awareness. Essential questions were first developed, and then projects were designed to address those essential questions. An array of choices was created to allow students to select a project matching their interests, multiple intelligences, and learning styles.

Then a common rubric was developed for use by all educators involved in the project. Teachers use this common rubric to assess the student projects. Results for all students are reported to the central office for analysis and reporting purposes. Because the projects are submitted electronically, schools are able to send a random sampling of student work to the central office each year; these are used as the basis for ongoing training and to ensure scoring reliability. Data related to the number of students successfully passing the benchmarks are reported to the school board.

Fairfax County's ECART tool, an electronic system that allows grading of these projects in an online environment, is used by teachers to grade and record student performance on the projects. All educators use the same online system for assigning student projects grades (on a rubric scale of 1–4). Central office leaders can easily access district-wide assessment data for use in reporting—but more importantly, for refining the project's design and the instructional strategies that best support it. ECART is currently being used to store exemplary student work in the global learners project for use in professional development sessions, where educators will work together to refine their approaches to instruction and grading of the global learner projects.

social studies class, which included some direct instruction followed by collaborative team work, to assess their skills during the day's lesson; the rubric asked students to rate themselves on a four-point scale across dimensions such as:

- I used facts to support my conclusions.
- I communicated clearly.
- I managed my time effectively.
- I contributed to my team's success.

In yet another class, students were practicing lines as part of a Shakespeare lesson. Students had written their own versions of a soliloquy. Each student filmed himself or herself delivering the soliloquy, reviewed the footage, rated himself or herself on "oral presentation" skills using a rubric, and re-did the exercise until the performance met his or her expectations. In classes such as this, it is common to watch students direct their own learning. What seems most impressive to us in these kinds of classes is how rich the dialogue is between the teacher and student; it is rare to witness a conversation that is solely about a grade on a particular piece of work. It is far more common to watch students asking teachers for advice about how to improve. That is the power of expecting students to evaluate and refine their own performances, and rubrics are an excellent tool for this kind of learning (or what is often called "assessment *for*, not *of*, learning). Please see the EdLeader21 YouTube channel to see our video about 4Cs rubrics.

Action Step: Highlight 4Cs in Grading and Reporting

Once your educators are collecting assessment data on the 4Cs, the next step is to consider how to reflect this information on the student report card. Anyone who has toyed with report cards knows that this is not an easy proposition. Teachers and parents all have their own ideas of what a report card should look like, and what is comfortable to them is often based on what is most familiar (i.e., the kinds of report cards they had in school). Nonetheless, if you want your system to focus on the 4Cs, communicating such outcomes to students and parents is critically important.

The team at Catalina Foothills School District has revised the district's K–12 report cards to align with its 21st century education initiative. An example of its middle school report card is included in Example Box 5.6. Note how the district's 21st century student outcomes are included in context within each subject area; all subjects have the same format (we have included a few as a representative sample on the next page).

Action Step: Implement Portfolio-Based Assessments

Portfolio-based assessments are incredibly helpful for educators interested in measuring the 4Cs. We've known for years that artists and architects have made and carried portfolios of their artistic or design work. Why shouldn't every student assemble a portfolio of the best examples of his or her core academic subject mastery along with 21st century outcomes? Imagine a student who had collected the best examples of his or her work demonstrating deep understanding of content, critical thinking, communication, collaboration, and creativity skills. This portfolio might demonstrate financial literacy (a student's budget, for example) or global competence (a paper written in another language or focused on another country's perspective on an international issue). Portfolios, when aligned with 21st century education outcomes, are compelling examples for students to share with prospective colleges and/or employers.

The Envision Schools in Northern California (www.envisionschools.org) have made major progress developing a system for portfolio assessment for the 4 C's. This approach is explained in detail in Example Box 5.7.

The Envision approach stands out for several reasons. Most of the student population (65%) qualify for free or reduced lunch. Envision students are often the first in their families to graduate high school and attend college; 90% attend college after graduation. All students work with an advisor throughout high school to collect and curate their most exemplary work. In the senior year, the student presents his or her portfolio in a public "defense," much like a dissertation defense with his or her advisors. A typical senior defense is held in the presence of teachers, advisors, student peers, and invited guests, such as parents and community members. The public presentation aspect of the

Example Box 5.6   Catalina Foothills 21st Century Report Card— Middle School

MIDDLE SCHOOL REPORT CARD
Catalina Foothills School District

Student: Johnny Smith   School Year: 2011–2012   Grade: 7

Esperero Canyon Middle School

REPORTING KEY

4   **Exceeds the Standard (Advanced):** Student takes initiative to exceed the standard; consistently produces excellent work and demonstrates an exceptional level of understanding, applying and transferring advanced skills and complex thinking into the district curriculum standard. Student is independent and self-directed in extending the learning process and usually exceeds assignment requirements.

3   **Meets the Standard (Proficient):** Student produces work that meets the standard; frequently produces work of high quality, successfully demonstrating mastery of the content (skills/concepts) in the district curriculum standard. Student regularly applies thinking skills and learning strategies and meets assignment expectations.

2   **Approaching the Standard (Basic):** Student demonstrates a basic working knowledge of the content (skills/concepts) in the district curriculum standard; produces satisfactory work and usually applies skills/concepts correctly. Progress is evident in applying thinking skills and learning strategies. Student inconsistently meets assignment expectations.

1   **Does Not Meet the Standard (Below Basic):** Student is performing below the district standard. With help, the student demonstrates partial understanding of the basic skills/concepts. There is limited progress in applying thinking skills and learning strategies. Student usually does not meet assignment expectations and seldom produces work of satisfactory quality.

21st Century Skills/Personal & Social Responsibility include one or more of the following: Self-Direction, Teamwork, Leadership, Critical & Creative Thinking, Cultural Competence, Systems Thinking, Communication, Class Participation, Work Completion/Effort, and Behavior.

Note to Parents/Guardians: Please keep in mind that some of the curriculum content is just being introduced during the early term. Students may not reach or exceed proficiency until later in the school year. Grades reflect progress for each trimester.

TERM	OVERALL GRADE			
	Q1	Q2	Q3	Q4
WRITING/LITERATURE				
Reading Fluency				
Word Analysis and Vocabulary				
Strategies to Guide and Monitor Comprehension				
Main Idea and Supporting Details				
Textual Relationships				
Text Structures, Elements, and Techniques				
Research				
Writing Process				
Writing Style				
Writing Applications and Formats				

(continued)

TERM	OVERALL GRADE			
	Q1	Q2	Q3	Q4
Language Conventions				
Interactive Communication: Visual and Writing Applications				
Interactive Communication: Speaking and Listening Applications				
21ST CENTURY SKILLS/PERSONAL & SOCIAL RESPONSIBILITY/TECHNOLOGY				
Self-Direction				
Systems Thinking				
Work Completion/Effort				

Teacher Comment:

TERM	OVERALL GRADE			
	Q1	Q2	Q3	Q4
SCIENCE				
Scientific Inquiry				
Interaction of Science and Society				
Systems Thinking				
Characteristics of Living Things				
Interdependence of Living Things and Their Environment				
Structure and Properties of Matter				
Interactions of Matter				
Conservation and Transformation of Energy				
Structure and Processes of the Earth				
Structure and Processes of Objects in Space				
21ST CENTURY SKILLS/PERSONAL & SOCIAL RESPONSIBILITY/TECHNOLOGY				
Teamwork				
Tech: Digital Citizenship				

Teacher Comment:

(continued)

TERM	OVERALL GRADE			
	Q1	Q2	Q3	Q4
MATHEMATICS				
Number Systems				
Numerical Relationships				
Addition and Subtraction				
Multiplication and Division				
Higher Order Operations				
Patterns				
Algebraic Concepts				
Geometric Properties and Figures				
Coordinate Geometry and Transformation				
Dimensional Measurement				
Measurement Systems				
Probability and Discrete Mathematics				
Data Organization and Interpretation				
Problem Solving				
Reasoning and Proof				
21ST CENTURY SKILLS/PERSONAL & SOCIAL RESPONSIBILITY/TECHNOLOGY				
Tech: Creativity and Innovation				
Class Participation				
Behavior/Conduct				

Teacher Comment:

TERM	OVERALL GRADE			
	Q1	Q2	Q3	Q4
ART				
Art Concepts, Processes, and Techniques				
Personal Involvement and Communication Through Original/Interpretive Work				
Universal Concepts/Themes and Connections to Culture and History				
Assessment of Characteristics/Merits of Own and Others' Work				
21ST CENTURY SKILLS/PERSONAL & SOCIAL RESPONSIBILITY/TECHNOLOGY				
Teamwork				
Self-Direction				

Teacher Comment:

Example Box 5.7   Envision Schools Portfolio Assessment/DLSAI

The College Success Portfolio Defense is a capstone activity that pulls *knowing, doing* and *reflecting* into one place, into one moment. It is the final inquiry, the final essential question, the final exhibition– a culmination of a 4-year project (or 2 years for sophomores). All students are expected to:

KNOW

- Master academic subjects that meet the University of California's A-G Requirements

DO

- Inquire, analyze, research, and express themselves creatively
- Use 21st Leadership Skills: Communicate Powerfully, Think Critically, Collaborate Productively, and Complete Projects Effectively
- Participate in at least one Workplace Learning Experience in which they do real work and complete a project that not only benefits their workplace, but demonstrates their ability to use leadership skills as well as inquire, analyze, research, and express themselves creatively in the workplace

REFLECT

- Recognize and acknowledge growth, accomplishments and successes as well as areas of future growth and development

- Revise work to proficiency based on feedback from teachers and peers

The Portfolio is organized by type of task not subject area:
A completed Graduation Portfolio has five deep pieces of work (artifacts) & a cover letter:

▓ Research Paper ▓ Textual Analysis ▓ Inquiry ▓ Creative Expression ▓ Workplace Learning Experience	**Students choose 3 or 4 of these artifacts to defend.**

Students must show proficiency in each type of task in order for their work to be certified. This usually means several revisions of their work.

Once students have reached proficiency on the tasks and the cover letter, they upload their certified artifacts onto the Digital Archive. Certified tasks are then available to all of Envision staff so they can share student work with each other as well as measure how well the process is working.

Finally, students prepare a Keynote presentation driven by their cover letter to organize and highlight the artifacts they're using in their portfolio defense.

---

defense is a central element of the performance. The student's public communication skills, along with the items in the portfolio being presented, are all assessed. Notably, a passing grade on the senior defense is required for graduation. This means that without any state policies requiring it, Envision has integrated critical thinking, communication, creativity and collaboration into a high stakes assessment (it doesn't get any more high stakes than high school graduation). A large majority of students are coached successfully through this performance, but those who do not are given multiple opportunities to refine their portfolios and present again as needed until they are able to meet the graduation requirement.

The Envision team is in the process of offering their portfolio system to any interested schools or districts. Called the Deeper Learning Student Assessment Initiative (DLSAI), it takes the most effective aspects of the portfolio system and makes it much more accessible to interested educators. DLSAI supports teachers in the use and development of rigorous standards aligned performance tasks, and the implementation and scoring of the tasks. It also helps school leaders in leading this work at the school and district level. It is aligned with the Common Core State Standards as well as the two assessment consortia (Smarter Balanced Assessment Consortium (SBAC) and Partnership for Assessment of Readiness for College and Careers (PARCC)). The DLSAI will also be supported by a new web-based technology platform—Show Evidence (www.showevidence.com) that will significantly reduce the time a teacher works on this type of assessment.

A key insight described by Bob Lenz, CEO of Envision Schools, is that one of the most impressive and necessary changes in a school that is committed to assessing students for what they know and can do is the nature of the school culture. The school culture (for both students and teachers) must be "driven by revision"—meaning a commitment to ongoing growth and development, honest reflection about growth areas, with supportive yet critical feedback that spawns a rigorous pursuit of mastery. The new assessments will only be as powerful as their ability to leverage changes in the everyday learning experience for students.

Action Step: Focus on Project Based Learning (PBL) Assessment Strategies

Although many educators value Project Based Learning (PBL) for its ability to better engage students with deeper learning, PBL is also a great way to assess a set of skills highly valued in both college and career. The New Tech Network's approach to PBL lends itself to innovative assessment practices. Its combination of PBL with technology-enabled assessment tools makes assessment of the 4Cs much easier and less time-consuming for teachers. At the end of each project, students use the New Tech Network's online system, Echo, to evaluate group members with a common school-wide rubric. Because the evaluations are anonymous to the student (but monitored by the teacher who also guides students in how to provide constructive feedback), each member of the team receives a detailed report on how their collaboration skills were demonstrated during the course of the project. In New Tech Network schools, this evaluation can happen one or more times a week. An example of the Echo feedback screen is shown in Figure 5.4.

Echo also serves as an electronic gradebook. All teachers utilize grading categories such as work ethic, content, collaboration, critical thinking, written communication, and public speaking. When scoring assignments, multiple criteria form a subtotal that is calculated for each category. This provides students and parents great visibility into individual strengths and areas for improvement. These types of innovations become part of the environmental change that allows teachers to more easily adopt new assessment practices, which, in turn, lead to changes in overall teaching and learning practices. A screen shot of the Echo gradebook is shown in Figure 5.5.

FIGURE 5.4 Echo Feedback Screen

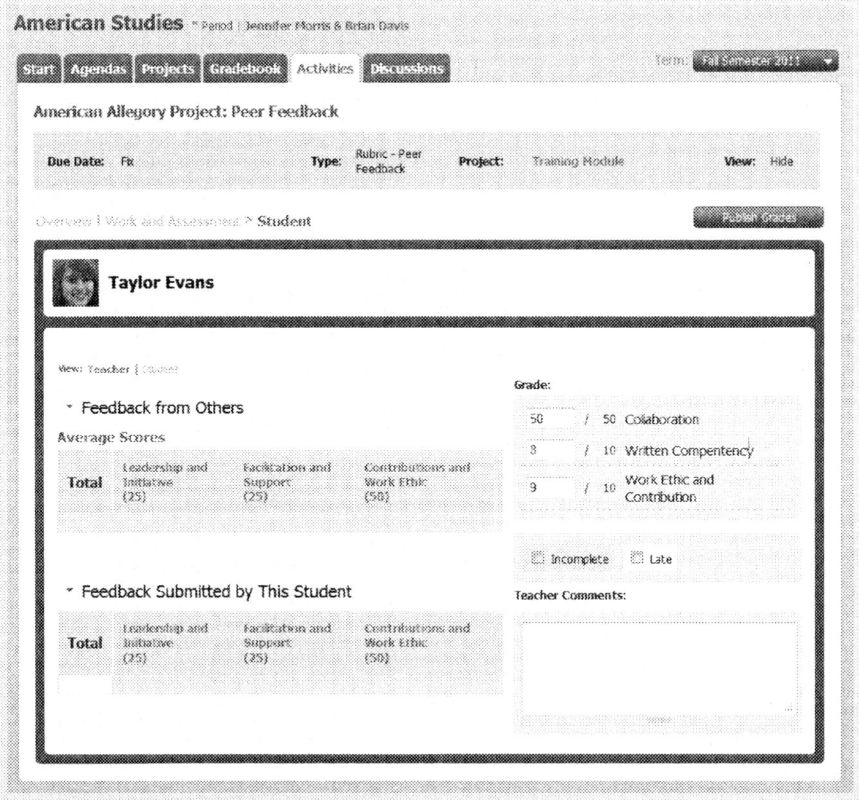

Action Step: Implement Capstone Projects

In most cases, capstone projects tend to take the form of culminating projects at the end of middle school and/or high school (such as a major project that is undertaken during the second semester of a student's senior year). Many capstone projects we have seen are accompanied by rubrics that are used by students and teachers to evaluate the work as it progresses. A typical project might require content mastery, critical thinking, communication skills, and self-direction. The student advisor and student use rubrics for these skills as well as others where applicable (e.g., collaboration, creativity, global competence, and/or financial literacy).

Since 2006, Upper Arlington City Schools (Ohio) has been implementing a senior capstone approach much like this. It is described in the Example Box 5.8.

FIGURE 5.5 Echo Gradebook

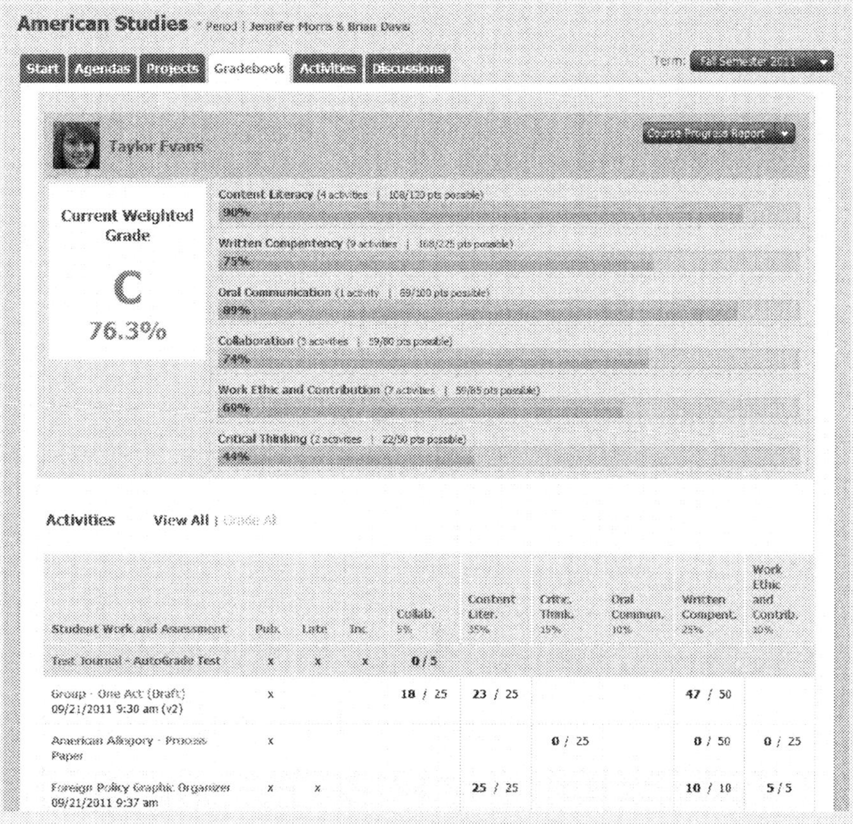

American Studies · Period | Jennifer Morris & Brian Davis

Start | Agendas | Projects | Gradebook | Activities | Discussions

Term: Fall Semester 2011

Taylor Evans

Course Progress Report

Current Weighted Grade

C

76.3%

Content Literacy (4 activities | 108/120 pts possible)
90%

Written Competency (9 activities | 168/225 pts possible)
75%

Oral Communication (1 activity | 89/100 pts possible)
89%

Collaboration (5 activities | 59/80 pts possible)
74%

Work Ethic and Contribution (7 activities | 59/85 pts possible)
69%

Critical Thinking (2 activities | 22/50 pts possible)
44%

Activities   View All | Grade All

Student Work and Assessment	Pub.	Late	Inc.	Collab. 5%	Content Liter. 35%	Critic. Think. 15%	Oral Commun. 10%	Written Compent. 25%	Work Ethic and Contrib. 10%
Test Journal – AutoGrade Test	x	x	x	0 / 5					
Group · One Act (Draft) 09/21/2011 9:30 am (v2)	x			18 / 25	23 / 25			47 / 50	
American Allegory · Process Paper	x					0 / 25		0 / 50	0 / 25
Foreign Policy Graphic Organizer 09/21/2011 9:37 am	x	x			25 / 25			10 / 10	5 / 5

Example Box 5.8   Upper Arlington Capstone Project

The Upper Arlington School District's senior capstone project is designed as a culminating piece of work required for high school graduation. Using Understanding by Design (UbD) principles, each student formulates an essential question about a community project he or she will pursue, creates a thesis question, and produces three distinct pieces of work: a research paper, a product related to his or her community project, and a presentation. The product related to the student's community project can take many forms; in one student's case, it was a video documentary of a school she was studying. In another case, it was an artistic scrapbook documenting the student's work with art immersion therapy.

Because the capstone project is a key component in the district's 21st century learning initiative, a rubric was developed to provide mid-year as well as summative evaluations of the student projects. The rubric focuses on the 4Cs along with self-direction and global citizenship (please see Appendix 12 for a copy of the full rubric). Students must meet all of the rubric's criteria in order to receive a passing grade.

One important aspect of the rubric design phase is that students were directly involved—for example, students participated in discussions about "how to define quality."

(continued)

Students were adamant about two things: that the rubrics needed to be easy to understand and that teachers would *actually use them* to assess student projects. Prior to the collaboration around rubric design, many students felt that grading was carried out too subjectively; the students immediately understood and appreciated the value of using rubrics to guide grading practices. Many teachers have reported that the rubrics' focus on 21st century outcomes helped them initiate more in-depth, formative discussions with students. And, over time, scoring of student projects has become much more consistent.

Upper Arlington education leaders noted that assessing capstone projects has been challenging for some teachers who like things to be "black and white." The rubrics were written, as a result, with very detailed descriptions. Teachers are also expected to meet with students throughout the year to gauge progress and guide the projects in the draft phases. This takes time and requires a shift in the role of the teacher to a coaching, mentoring role—which is much harder for teachers who prefer direct instruction. As the initiative has progressed, however, a better culture for teaching and learning is emerging throughout the district. The student presentations are evaluated by the entire faculty, which allows *all* staff to see the work that senior students are completing. This has encouraged a more open discussion among faculty about the strengths and weaknesses evident in student work. For example, one year several science teachers expressed concerns about the quality of research many students were presenting. These teachers offered additional resources and guidance to improve the research skills among all students (not just their own advisees).

What's on the Horizon?

While the action steps we have summarized are good places to start your work around assessing the 4Cs, they aren't enough. Nationally, we all need to demand a balanced and effective assessment system that emphasizes content mastery *and* the 4Cs. This must include performance-based elements not only in formative instruments but in summative ones as well. This long-term goal is shared by many leading thinkers and educators throughout the United States, but we are not yet there. There is, however, progress to report. In the next five years, more and more assessment tools will be released to support a more balanced assessment strategy.

As we mentioned earlier, the work being done by AP, PISA, and the U.S. Department of Education through its funding of the Common Core assessment consortia will mean new assessment tools that do a better job of measuring complex thinking skills than the tools we've had in the past. Starting in 2012, new AP exams will reinforce critical thinking. The PISA exam will issue a benchmark assessment for schools and districts in 2012. The new Common Core assessments are expected as soon as 2014. This means that states should be able to utilize their "college and work ready" standards for general state assessments shortly thereafter.

Two additional projects that future-oriented districts and schools might find interesting include:

- Assessment & Teaching of 21st Century Skills (http://atc21s.org): The ATC21S project, founded by Microsoft, Cisco, and Intel, is an innovative research project that aims to develop new forms of assessment and teaching approaches to meet the demands of the 21st century.

- Center for K12 Assessment & Performance Management, an initiative by ETS (http://k12center.org/index.html): This group has produced a number of events, papers, and presentations in order to disseminate the best thinking and research on the range of measurement issues facing national, state, and local decision makers.

Each of the projects mentioned here help illustrate the positive momentum toward assessing 21st century outcomes. The field of assessment is changing profoundly, and we are cautiously optimistic about the advances we hope will occur over the next five years. It is good news that so many wide-ranging projects are under way, demonstrating that it is, in fact, possible to assess the 4Cs and other 21st century outcomes.

FINAL THOUGHTS

As a way to conclude, we have developed a simple tool that might help you and your team members reflect on the curricula and assessment strategies currently in place in your district. In the left column, list the four to eight student outcomes that you decided upon in Step 1 as part of your 21st century vision. Then, for each outcome, answer the following questions:

1. Does the school or district have a widely adopted definition of this outcome?
2. Do existing curricula focus on these outcomes?
3. Do students and parents receive meaningful feedback on how students are performing against these outcomes?
4. Do teachers have assessment tools that help them evaluate student performance on these outcomes?
5. Do you and your board get feedback on how/whether the system is producing these outcomes?

This chart should help you clarify whether your curricular and assessment systems are aligned with your 21st century vision and if there are any gaps. What does this chart tell you about the curricula and assessments in your district? As you reflect on this chart, what do these results indicate to you?

Student Outcome	Are there definitions, and are they integrated into curricula?	Do students get feedback?	Do parents get feedback?	Do teachers get feedback on their instructional practices?	Is there tracking of school and district performance?
Core academic content					
Critical thinking					
Communication					
Collaboration					
Creativity					
Other					
Other					

In this step, you have been asked to carefully consider whether and how your curricula and assessment systems align with your overall vision for 21st century education. We have encouraged you to consider a range of questions and action steps. This is challenging and time-consuming work, as you know. Luckily, some of your most important allies are naturally motivated to help you solve these challenges. We'll talk about teachers in the next step, and how you can most effectively support them in teaching and assessing the 4Cs.

REFERENCES

Figure 5.1 Inspired in part by Curtis McKnight's model developed during the Second International Mathematics Study (SIMS) (1979), along with the work of Robert Marzano on curriculum and opportunity to learn, most specifically *What Works in Schools: Translating Research into Action*. Alexandria, VA: ASCD, 2003.

Bransford, John D., Ann L. Brown, and Rodney R. Cocking, eds. *How People Learn: Brain, Mind, Experience, and School*. Washington, DC: National Academy Press, 1999.

College and Work Readiness Assessment. Web. Jan. 2012. http://www.cae.org/content/pro_collegework.htm

Conery, Mary Jo. Personal interview. August 5, 2011.

PBL. *BIE Essentials of PBL*. Web. Jan. 2012. http://www.bie.org/about/what_is_pbl

Wiggins, Grant P., and Jay McTighe. *Understanding by Design*. Upper Saddle River, NJ: Pearson/Merrill Prentice Hall, 2006.

Support Your Teachers

THE 4CS FOCUS

When it comes to the "big intersections" between the 4Cs and the topic of supporting teachers, think about these ideas:

- Creativity: Rely on your own creative abilities to give teachers the freedom and flexibility to innovate without fear of repercussions. Reward experiments, and treat failures as learning and innovation opportunities.
- Collaboration: Schedule time for teachers to collaborate regularly through professional learning communities.
- Communication: Clearly define 4Cs student work and 4Cs instructional strategies, and communicate these regularly to all educators, students, and other stakeholders.
- Critical thinking: Carefully consider the unique challenges facing your school and district, and think critically about which teaching strategies will produce the best results.

Motivate Teachers

At this point in the book, we hope we've made your 21st century journey a little clearer when it comes to translating your vision into curricula and assessment systems. We've stressed the fundamental building blocks of 4Cs professional development, curricula, and assessments, all of which lead us to the conversation about supporting teachers in 4Cs instruction, where the rubber really meets the road. If there's a lesson to be learned in past education reform efforts, it is how hard it is to affect daily practice once the classroom door is closed (Tyack and Cuban). In our experience working with leaders, they agree. It can take years of consistent priority setting for the instructional culture of a school or district to embrace an "open door" classroom in which teachers actively collaborate around producing visible 21st century outcomes for all students. And most leaders we've spoken with say that while 4Cs curricula and assessment systems must be put in place, it is the buy-in of teachers and their passionate efforts that make the biggest difference for students.

In Step 6, we emphasize the importance of your leadership when it comes to supporting teachers in 4Cs instruction. This is not simply about crafting an effective professional development strategy for your teacher workforce. This is about creating a culture of learning among the professional educators in your system and motivating them to do the work that inspired them to become teachers in the first place. Step 6 focuses on how to create a 4Cs educational environment in which every teacher can implement 4Cs strategies in daily practice.

One of the most important responsibilities to assume as a leader is the role you can play in motivating teachers to do their best work. Inquiry-based instructional strategies are time- and labor-intensive, requiring sustained efforts by highly motivated teacher teams. Teachers need practical things, too—such as adequate time *out of class* to craft performance tasks and inquiry-based lessons, time to collaborate with their peers, time to work with 4Cs instructional coaches and interdisciplinary teams, and time to reflect on and refine their practices. And, as we detailed in Steps 3, 4 and 5, curricula, assessment, and PD approaches must be aligned with the 4Cs. But at the end of the day, most of these practical issues boil down to the issue of teacher motivation. Do teachers see the value of this work? Are teachers engaged, motivated, and supported? As a leader, you should care deeply about these questions if you hope your vision will become a reality for all students in your school or district.

One of the most distressing recent developments in the national conversation about education has been the relentless rise in criticism of U.S. teachers. From popular documentaries such as *Waiting for Superman*, to the push for value-added teacher performance data ("Grading the Teachers"), to failed experiments with merit-based pay (Sparks), to the *Newsweek* cover "Why We Must Fire Bad Teachers," along with some of the policies proposed by the U.S. Department of Education, it sometimes seems as if the entire country is attacking the current state of "teaching" and "teachers" specifically. Not surprisingly, most teachers we know feel beleaguered.

This situation is unfortunate and one you should consider thoughtfully. Teachers who are in a defensive crouch will not embrace innovation. They will not take risks; they will not collaborate effectively. And they will not begin focusing instruction around the 4Cs simply because they have been directed to do so by the central office.

This is not to say teachers don't share responsibility for improving our systems of education. Teacher accountability does matter. But your 21st century education initiative rests upon your ability to engage and support all teachers in their practices around the 4Cs. Even the most innovative curriculum and assessment system can be reduced to rote classroom instruction if teachers aren't on board and supported in this work. If instructional planning at the classroom level is viewed by teachers as a compliance exercise—walkthroughs that check simply for alignment with pacing guides and essential elements of instruction (EEI) checklists, for example—it can undermine all the goals of your leadership agenda.

Supporting teachers in 4Cs instruction means making sure teachers are supported in developing deep, rather than rote, understanding in students. And it means making it clear that all instruction should be geared toward students' ability to "learn how to learn" so they can, over time, become more independent, self-directed learners. Good educators are motivated by this kind of vision because it's often the reason they find satisfaction in their work. Most teachers work incredibly hard to reach the "aha!" moment with each and every student. "We want our students to own their learning," one middle school leader told us. "It's the difference between a bumper sticker that says 'I met my goal at my middle school' and 'I'm on the honor roll at my middle school.'"

Motivating teachers to embrace this work is a grand challenge—and it is often very difficult. Teachers must sense that the district or school leaders "get it." This means making sure that effective education practices are acknowledged, supported, and shared. It also means acknowledging and systematically removing barriers that can inhibit effective teaching such as lack of mentoring for new educators, inflexible scheduling, and/or rigid pacing guides. As Tyack and Cuban point out in their classic book *Tinkering toward Utopia*, experienced public school teachers that have survived many evolutions of education reform are understandably cautious about embracing new or different practices. This is even more true today. In the extreme, teachers actively resist and undermine new initiatives—and they can be quite effective in doing so. This is not news to anyone who has led a school or a district. It is also why focusing on the motivation of teachers around this work is so important.

As a leader of a district or school, you have a unique role to play in tapping into teachers' inherent desires to improve students' lives. We think Daniel Pink's 2010 book *Drive* is one of the most intelligent and helpful resources for education leaders on the issue of motivation. While Pink does not focus specifically on education, he uses decades of scientific research to point out some compelling truths about what really motivates people to excel or change or improve. Carrot-and-stick approaches can work in limited scenarios—such as when they are aimed at routine work. But when carrot-and-stick approaches are applied to more complex tasks—we'd say teaching fits this description perfectly—they do not work very well. Research shows that individuals are more highly motivated—and perform better over time—when they are paid fairly (but not excessively) and when they have high levels of autonomy, mastery, and purpose in their work. Think about what this means for issues like merit pay, for example. We encourage you to read and share Pink's book with your leadership teams and consider the following questions:

- As leaders, are we truly focused on motivating and supporting teachers in their 4Cs practices?
- Do we as leaders provide teachers with appropriate levels of autonomy, mastery, and purpose around 4Cs instruction? In other words:
  - Are we supporting teachers in 4Cs-focused professional learning communities (PLCs)?
  - Have we identified systemic barriers that undermine 4Cs instruction? For example, have we instituted adequate time during the school day for teachers to plan, collaborate, and improve? As leaders, are we giving teachers enough flexibility to engage students in project-based learning and multidisciplinary content? Do teachers have adequate access to technology and other collaborative tools?
  - Are our district and site leaders providing teachers with timely, constructive feedback about 4Cs instruction?

These questions should help you and your team think critically, collaborate, communicate, and be creative about how to motivate and support teachers in 4Cs practices.

Focus on Student Work

After you've thoughtfully considered the far-reaching issue of teacher engagement and motivation, we recommend working with your teachers on a tactical, seemingly straightforward question: What does 4Cs student work look like?

The typical way to respond—at least in our circles—is with a laundry list of instructional strategies like problem-based and project-based learning. (We'll cover these, too.)

But jumping straight to instructional strategies leaves out a lot of rich opportunities to collaborate with teachers.

In our experiences with educators, looking at real examples of student work and asking the question, "Does this work display any of the 4Cs?" is a compelling way to start talking about instruction. It forces us to think in concrete terms about what student performances we are trying to support. It makes us honestly grapple with tricky questions such as:

- Are we looking for signs of sheer excellence in the 4Cs? Or are we looking for signs that the student has grown in his or her work over time?
- When we see an excellent example of the 4Cs, how can we tell whether it is a reflection of the teacher's practices or simply a particular student's "natural" abilities? Does the distinction matter?

Education leaders in the Hewlett Foundation's Deeper Learning initiative have dedicated considerable time exploring these kinds of questions; we recommend familiarizing yourself with this project to learn more about what the 4Cs looks like in student work (http://www.hewlett.org/programs/education-program/deeper-learning). To make this approach a little more concrete, we'd like to share an example that is often cited by Ron Berger, Chief Program Officer of Expeditionary Learning and author of *An Ethic of Excellence: Building a Culture of Craftmanship with Students* (Berger is also a key leader in the Deeper Learning initiative). His work on the importance of student artifacts and creating school cultures that support the idea of "craftsmanship" is well respected and directly relevant to any discussion of instruction and the 4Cs. He often shares an example called "Austin's Butterfly" to illustrate the importance of quality student work in informing our understanding of high-quality instruction. In this example, Austin's first grade class was completing a unit on butterflies (see Figure 6.1). As a culminating activity, students were given the assignment of drawing a butterfly. A photograph (Assignment Photo) was provided as a guide. Austin's sketches (Draft 1 through Draft 5) were reviewed by his peers at each stage of the work. Five times, Austin's peers met as a group, compared his draft with the photo, and gave him feedback about how to improve his drawing. Note how the drafts become progressively more detailed—the antennae, the points of the wings, the butterfly's proportions, and its distinctive markings—and result in an absolutely beautiful piece of final work.

When Berger presents this piece of student work, he emphasizes the process of collaboration and communication among Austin's peers that helped Austin produce such a stunning final drawing. Berger notes that if you simply viewed Austin's final (and sixth) draft, the significance of the instructional setting would be overlooked. It would be tempting to assume this is the work of a child prodigy. However, when you examine the entire portfolio of Austin's work in this case, it is clear that the student is a fairly typical first grader. The stellar quality of the final piece is a result of a highly effective learning environment—an intentionally developed and thoughtfully implemented set of instructional strategies put in place and guided by a skilled teacher.

How might this kind of example help open a dialogue among your teachers about the 4Cs in pedagogy? We suggest organizing one or more professional development sessions around the sharing and discussion of 4Cs student work. Ask teachers to bring at least one example of student work that illustrates some aspect of 4Cs mastery. Then facilitate small- and large-group discussions around each example to consider questions such as:

- Does the student work illustrate mastery of at least one of the 4Cs? Why or why not?
- In cases where there is widespread agreement about the presence of the 4Cs in a piece of student work, what instructional practices appear to have helped support this outcome?

FIGURE 6.1 Austin's Butterfly

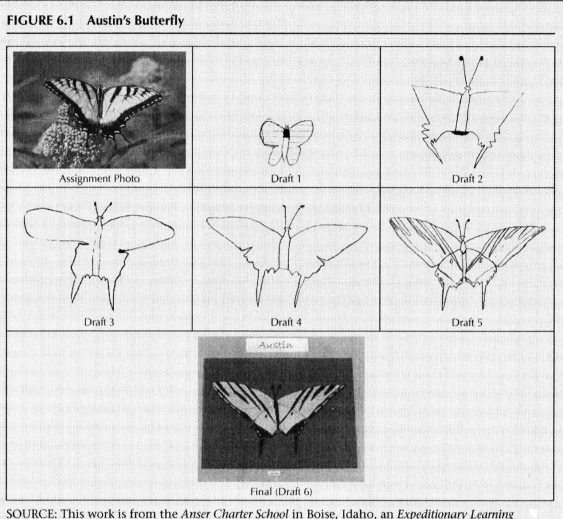

SOURCE: This work is from the *Anser Charter School* in Boise, Idaho, an *Expeditionary Learning* School. Austin was a first grader when he completed this project. Ron Berger led the critique session in which this work was created, with the critique (kind, specific and helpful) coming from the other first graders. Used with permission.

- What additional instructional strategies might have enhanced a particular piece of student work? Why?
- What similarities exist among 4Cs examples of student work, if any?
- What big differences exist among the student examples that are shared?

Engaging teachers in a discussion about instruction by sharing and discussing actual student work provides a powerful way to address the 4Cs in practice. The variety of student examples that will inevitably be shared is, in and of itself, a helpful reminder to teachers (and to education leaders) that there is no "one size fits all" approach to

21st century education. And, perhaps most helpfully, these kinds of shared experiences among teachers help foster a kind of collaborative professional learning that can lead to what Berger calls an "ethic of excellence" that also supports real improvements in practice and student outcomes.

Prioritize 4Cs Pedagogies

Once you and your teachers have a shared (and, hopefully, clearer) understanding of "what 4Cs student work looks like," it's much easier to begin talking about what instructional strategies best enable such outcomes.

Among the models we have seen, we believe teaching for understanding—an implementation method based on the principles of Understanding by Design (UbD)—offers a comprehensive framework for this kind of instructional practice. When implemented well, it includes a range of techniques including direct instruction and interdisciplinary and inquiry-based instructional design and practice. Grant Wiggins and Jay McTighe in *Understanding by Design* describe a range of teaching strategies that support student understanding (or, in our vocabulary, what we call 4Cs student outcomes); some of their most helpful points about teaching for understanding include the following (233–242):

- The textbook is *not* the syllabus. It is a resource.
- The specific teaching strategy depends on the purpose of the instructional moment; in other words, teaching for understanding is *not* about eliminating lectures or direct instruction. For example, they recommend the following approaches:
  - Use didactic or direct instruction when students need to grasp basic information through observation, listening, and answering.
  - Use constructivist (inquiry-based) methods when students need to construct, examine, and extend meaning.
  - Use coaching (feedback and guided practice) when students need to refine skills and deepen understandings.

Teaching for understanding is an incredibly deep and broad topic, the fine details of which extend far beyond the focus of this chapter. However, we'd like to share a few insights from one more resource on this topic. In her book *Powerful Learning: What We Know About Teaching for Understanding*, Linda Darling-Hammond uses a research-based lens to clarify what is effective when it comes to *instruction* that supports deep student understanding. Some of her recommendations that are helpful to a 4Cs approach to instruction include:

- Use carefully designed collaborative activities, where roles are clear and students are accountable to each other.
- Use *inquiry-based* lesson designs and teaching practices. Darling-Hammond identifies three primary categories:

  - Project-based learning, in which students complete complex tasks and present final work in the form of a product or presentation; the emphasis here is on building performance-based competencies that help students transfer their knowledge and skills to novel situations.
  - Problem-based learning, in which students encounter "good" problems that are realistic and complex; the emphasis here is on effective questioning, problem identification, and analysis. This is sometimes also referred to as Challenge-Based Learning.

- Design-based learning, in which students—often in the sciences—design and create an object or artifact using technical knowledge and systems thinking; the emphasis here is on creating, prototyping, and revising, as in robotics competitions or architecture projects.

Each of these approaches is worthy of exploration by you, your leadership team, and your teachers. Additional models that can support 4Cs pedagogy that are being used by district leaders we know are included in Figure 6.2.

FIGURE 6.2   Additional Models for School- and/or District-Wide Implementation

Model	Description	Relation to 4Cs Instruction
Habits of Mind (www.instituteforhabitsofmind.com)	Art Costa's framework focuses on student dispositions such as metacognition, persistence, communication, and thinking flexibly and creatively, among others.	The Habits of Mind framework, definitions, and implementation resources are directly supportive of 4Cs teaching and learning. A wide range of resources is available for leaders and teachers.
Accountable Talk (http://ifl.lrdc.pitt.edu/ifl)	Developed by Lauren Resnick of the University of Pittsburgh, accountable talk is a set of strategies employed by teachers to help students formulate responses to problems, interpret information, and go beyond rote knowledge.	The emphasis on active listening, collaborative dialogue, and reflection helps teachers deepen students' critical thinking, communication, and collaboration skills.
AVID (www.avid.org/index.html)	AVID, Advancement Via Individual Determination, is an elementary through postsecondary college readiness system that is designed to increase school-wide learning and performance. The curriculum focuses on average-performing students who are capable of more rigorous work.	The AVID model is a comprehensive model that includes a full curriculum. Its focus on writing, inquiry, collaboration, and reading is well aligned with 4Cs pedagogy.
Being a Writer (www.devstu.org/being-a-writer)	The Being a Writer program is a yearlong writing curriculum for grades K–6 that combines two decades of research in the areas of writing, motivation, and learning theory with social and ethical development.	Leaders interested in 4Cs teaching strategies for the K–6 range will find this program helpful.
Authentic Intellectual Work (http://centerforaiw.com)	AIW primarily supports teachers taking time to teach for in-depth understanding rather than superficial coverage of materials. It provides a common conception of student intellectual work that promotes professional community and equips students to address the complex intellectual challenges of work, civic participation, and managing personal affairs in the contemporary world.	AIW resources include rubrics, checklists, and criteria that help teachers plan and deliver authentic, performance-based instruction. The AIW resources dedicated to scoring student work are particularly rigorous and detailed.

When we went on a learning walk at Cooke Elementary, a Title I school in Virginia Beach City Public Schools, we witnessed some of these instructional strategies in action. Principal Barbara Sessoms has framed the school's curricula to support teaching for understanding principles by using Costa's Habits of Mind and Resnick's Accountable Talk as central instructional strategies. Evidence of these approaches was visible in every classroom we visited. One of the most impressive things we noticed was that it was hard to tell which classes were predominantly special needs students versus mainstream students. The description below is typical of what we saw that day. In this case, we have described a lesson in an English language arts third-grade classroom:

> Students assembled in pairs on a rug placed in one corner of the classroom, with the teacher sitting in a chair facing the group. The teacher showed the students a book and read the description on the book's cover. She did not read the book to them (that came later). She then asked the students an essential question about the day's topic, "genres of literature": "Based on what you've heard and seen so far, would you say this book is fiction or nonfiction?" She then directed the students to use evidence to support their points and to listen with understanding: "Remember, eye to eye, and knee to knee!" (Listening with understanding is a key disposition in Costa's Habits of Mind.) On this cue, each student turned to his or her partner, knee to knee, and made direct eye contact. One student would begin by stating his or her opinion about the genre of the book while the other student listened without interrupting, nodding and maintaining eye contact. (Maintaining eye contact and careful listening are key components of accountable talk strategies.) When the first student finished, the second student responded in the following way: "I hear what you're saying" (and the student would repeat what he or she heard). Then the student would go on to either agree or disagree with the first student's analysis. Then the first student would respond in turn, agreeing or disagreeing with his or her partner's points. The teacher allowed this accountable talk exercise to continue for approximately 10 minutes and then asked pairs of students to share what they learned from their discussions. Then she read the short book (which was nonfiction) and led the group in a discussion of why it was nonfiction and what additional elements of the story supported that conclusion. Throughout, students were engaged, raising their hands and asking insightful questions. By the end of the lesson, they had not only demonstrated understanding of the basic difference between fiction and nonfiction, they had also begun to debate the issue of authenticity and credibility of authorship!

This approach was repeated in class after class we visited in the school. We saw the same kinds of teacher–student engagement around an essential idea, using accountable talk instructional strategies, in every classroom we walked through. Principal Sessoms seemed a little surprised at how impressed we were. When we asked her to explain how she had achieved such consistent buy-in from her teachers, she just shrugged and said, "It's just the way teachers teach at Cooke Elementary. It's nothing revolutionary—this is just good instruction! Our teachers see how well it works for kids. That's all, really." Well said.

Strengthen the 4Cs Learning Environment

You might have already identified what changes you need the most to support your teachers in 21st century instructional practices. The following suggestions are worth considering as you decide where to take action and how to prioritize your activities.

Action Step: Institute Learning Walks

Let's say there is consensus among your teachers about what the 4Cs look like in student work and instruction and that you've eliminated barriers in the teaching environment to make 4Cs instruction a fact of life in the school or district. Teachers still need to understand how to reflect on their practices, refine them, and develop along clear paths to mastery of 4Cs pedagogy. As an education leader, you must help them establish such paths. Providing teachers with timely, effective feedback is a critical step in this process.

Classroom visitations are a commonly used method to support teachers and 4Cs instruction. These visits are not used as compliance exercises or performance reviews but instead are used to inform professional learning throughout the school or district. When used to support teachers, walk-throughs by peers and administrators can be extremely effective at providing specific feedback around 4Cs instruction. Richard Elmore's well-regarded work in this area is detailed in his book *Instructional Rounds in Education: A Network Approach to Improving Teaching and Learning*. The authors start with the basic premise that if you want to improve student learning, you have to improve teaching; specifically, they recommend the use of "instructional rounds," a technique modeled after medical rounds used in medical schools. Teams of education leaders visit classrooms and reflect—without passing judgment—on what they have seen in order to better understand what is actually happening in the interactions between teachers and students. In this approach, the emphasis must be on teaching, not the teacher. It is a kind of "observational learning" that can lead to improvements in how teachers are supported around initiatives such as the 4Cs.

The use of instructional rounds, or learning walks, as part of capacity building within a school or district is also addressed by many other prominent education researchers, including:

Elizabeth A. City, Richard F. Elmore, Sarah E. Fiarman, and Lee Teitel's book, *Instructional Rounds in Education: A Network Approach to Improving Teaching and Learning* (2009) focuses on what high-quality instruction looks like and the role of instructional rounds in supporting it.

Lauren Resnick, with the Institute for Learning at the University of Pittsburgh, has conducted research over many years on learning walks. Her methodologies center around learning walks as self-evaluation and school improvement tools. (http://ifl.lrdc.pitt.edu/ifl)

Carolyn J. Downey, professor emeritus of educational leadership at the College of Education at San Diego State University, is a leader in the area of classroom walk-throughs. Her book *The Three-Minute Classroom Walk-Through* is an often-cited resource for classroom visitation that supports teachers. (www.corwin.com/books/Book225980)

Robert Marzano has developed a research-based protocol for walk-throughs as part of his Art and Science of Teaching Framework. (www.iobservation.com)

Tony Wagner also emphasizes learning walks as part of a comprehensive change leadership strategy that emphasizes supportive relationships with teachers (45).

In each of these protocols, the emphasis is always on supporting teacher capacity through informative feedback rather than enforcing a strict compliance culture. It is imperative that these educational rounds, or walk-throughs, are conducted in a spirit of collaboration with and respect for teachers rather than in the context of a performance review. When learning walks are performed in ways to encourage growth and self-direction among teachers, they become invaluable tools in supporting teachers' paths to mastery of 4Cs instruction.

Action Step: Create Instructional Coaching Positions

Keeping teachers engaged as continually learning professionals is another important consideration for education leaders. We can't tell you how often we hear administrators describe the following scenario: A teacher becomes recognized for excellence in instruction and student outcomes. And the next thing that happens is that the teacher is recruited out of the classroom, often into an administrative position—becoming a principal, designing curricula, or managing professional development initiatives. While some teachers aspire to this kind of path, many high-achieving teachers actually would prefer alternatives that allow them to take a break from the classroom but return to it after a period of time. Being an administrator is a terrific and admirable educational career path, and there is always a need for excellent educators to fill these positions—don't get us wrong. However, as an education leader, we encourage you to consider whether your teachers have a diverse menu of career paths or whether teachers' choices are constrained to either classroom teaching or administration with no alternatives in between.

In Albemarle County Public Schools in Charlottesville, Virginia, budget cutbacks forced Superintendent Pam Moran's team to reconfigure all their instructional coaching positions. Previously, each school in the district was assigned an instructional coach who was a central office employee; these coaches were responsible for supporting teachers in their uses of technology and overall instructional improvement. In reality, the coaches had become the "go to" people directed by site leaders and teachers to attend to basic technology integration needs. The coaches had essentially become high-level gophers for teachers who had adopted a "learned helplessness" around technology integration in their classes. Common tasks carried out by the coaches included editing PowerPoints and fixing digital projectors. The positions were eliminated out of budget necessity, but in the process a new system was created. In the reconfigured system now in place, "21st century skills coaches" are recruited on a rotating basis among teachers in the district. This has become a highly competitive process with some of the most accomplished teachers seeking the positions. Each coach that is selected as a 21st century skills coach is assigned to a different school each year, for a maximum of three years. After three years, each coach returns to his or her classroom. Teachers are enthusiastic about the system because it provides an innovative alternative to the administrative career path. It allows them to develop relationships across the district and expand their knowledge of teaching and learning. Notably, the coaches are not given a specific set of tasks to perform when they arrive at their assigned schools. Their only guidance is to integrate themselves into the culture of the school—each of which is quite unique, thus the lack of explicit guidance—and support teachers in integrating 21st century learning into daily practice. Superintendent Moran describes it as an unqualified success. The rotating assignments mean that the coaches are constantly refining their approaches in new and diverse environments; each year, the coaches receive more positive feedback from the teachers they are helping. Not only does this program provide unique support for Superintendent Moran's 21st century vision around professional learning, it has also saved the district money.

We cannot emphasize enough the importance of providing such growth opportunities for teachers who prefer *to teach*. Rotating teachers through temporary assignments out of the classroom but supportive of your 4Cs efforts—for example, 21st century skills coaches, community and business partnerships, internships, PLC design and support—is worth considering.

Action Step: Make Teacher Evaluations Meaningful

Providing meaningful feedback to teachers is another action step we recommend. In the Odyssey School in Denver, Colorado (an Expeditionary Learning (EL) school), the school's director, Marcia Fulton, has launched an innovative approach to evaluating teacher performance. Two key factors influenced her decision to create the new system. First, she realized that if teachers were to adopt the kinds of practices that would enable 21st century outcomes among students, she—as the leader of the school—would need to model the same learning culture with the teachers. Second, Colorado's SB191, which goes into effect in 2014, will require 50 percent of a teacher's evaluation to include student achievement data; Fulton is focused on meeting this goal in a way that rewards excellent teaching that is consistent with her 21st century focus.

In response, Fulton and some of her EL colleagues and school designers met for several months and designed a framework for teacher evaluation that would reinforce their vision for 21st century education. They looked at leading practices around the country, taking into account EL core practices and created the approach that was then customized in each school. One of the first things Fulton did upon implementing this new framework was to develop an online evaluation tool so her teachers could collaborate with her throughout the evaluation process. Fulton recognized that if she were asking her teachers to use performance assessment techniques with students, she would need to use the same techniques with teachers. Accordingly, the online performance evaluation system is designed to collect and store multiple pieces of evidence for each teacher. Artifacts include Fulton's observations from class visits, Fulton's feedback based on rubric criteria, teacher comments, and teacher-provided evidence such as lesson plans. Fulton uses this system to provide feedback to teachers on an ongoing basis. It is also the primary vehicle through which she identifies "master" teachers who are then asked to take on leadership roles within their PLCs to improve 21st century teaching and learning practices.

Fulton's approach is a useful example because she has focused on creating an evaluation system that *treats teachers like learners*. Teachers experience the exact same structures and processes that they are being asked to implement with their students. This allows the teachers—most of whom were not exposed to this kind of learning environment when they were in school—to transfer their experiences to their work with students. It has transformed the experiences of both teachers and students.

Action Step: Support Teachers with the Right Infrastructure

We'd like to make a special comment about technology. We've both worked at the intersection of technology and education for more than a decade. We're duly impressed with its ability to transform the education landscape. So it might seem counterintuitive for us to say this, but we would like to be very clear about something: 4Cs instructional strategies *do not require technology.* Students can learn to think critically, communicate, collaborate, and create without ever using a single piece of technology! One of the biggest misconceptions about 21st century skills is that they are all about technology. They most certainly are not.

Instructional technology can be enormously helpful, however, *as long as it is thoughtfully aligned with your overall goals.* We encourage you to consider how instructional technologies can *best* assist with your 21st century education initiative by making sure of two key things:

- Ensure that instructional technology offerings are aligned with, and add real value to, your 4Cs efforts.

- Have a clear way of determining what works and what doesn't, in terms of ROI on instructional technology and the 4Cs.

In light of these points, we thought it would be helpful to highlight three technology uses that we believe are worth the investment because they provide valuable support for 4Cs instruction:

- **Collaboration technology.** Evaluate whether your teachers have adequate technology tools to help them facilitate student collaboration. It is very difficult and time-consuming to design and plan effective inquiry-based group work. The right technology tools can streamline some of the tasks (assigning and monitoring groups), freeing the teacher to focus more intently on designing and facilitating better collaboration among students. And, of course, these technologies have another important effect: They can engage students more fully in collaborative learning. Asynchronous communication tools, file sharing, and mind-mapping/ideation tools can give students new opportunities to connect, share, and learn from and with each other and in ways that reflect the digitally connected lives they lead outside of school.
- **Digital portfolio and assessment tools.** Consider whether digital portfolio technologies would benefit your teachers and students. These tools provide powerful ways for teachers and students to create, manage, evaluate, and refine portfolios of their digital work over time. The best uses of portfolios we have seen allow students, with some level of facilitation from teachers, to collect their best work, organize it, add comments and context, and selectively share it with others as desired. Because the portfolios are digital, portable, and easy to maintain over time, students build an intimate understanding of their own learning progress over the course of several years, not just a class or semester. This allows teachers to help students "own" their learning by teaching them to reflect on, manage, curate, and present their best work.
- **Digital content management.** Technology tools that help teachers access, create, organize, assign, and track digital resources are often referred to as learning management or course management systems. The most innovative educators have always mixed and matched resources in their lessons from a wide range of sources: textbooks, self-created modules, district-published resources, videos, free and fee-based websites, student-created items, and so on. It is very time-consuming for even the most energetic and dedicated teachers to manage such a broad array of items into a coherent set of assignments for their students, unit after unit, year after year, using a mix of random online management tools. We know teachers, for example, that maintain their bookmarks on one website, have videos on their hard drive, and have their lesson plans on a wiki. This is especially burdensome in cases where the 4Cs are being integrated into core academic subjects because 4Cs-oriented instruction tends to be highly customized. Technology solutions that reduce the administrative and creative burden on teachers, allowing them to re-mix and re-use their digital content in unlimited combinations with groups and subgroups of students in a single management interface/environment, are a powerful way to support your leading teachers.

Beyond technology, we also recommend evaluating the physical infrastructure needs in your school and district. Are there adequate physical spaces for teachers to collaborate with other teachers and for students to work in groups on projects that take weeks to complete? A science teacher we know nods appreciatively when we talk about inquiry-based projects. But he is always quick to point out that a lot of teachers—him included—teach in classrooms they share with other educators. He can't leave project materials out because another teacher uses his lab right after his class ends.

We visited a Tucson middle school where the 4Cs are often integrated thoroughly into core academic courses, yet the principal was shaking her head at the lack of consistent Internet access in the school. She has teachers who love to integrate technology tools into their practices, but at least three times a week the network goes down. She described how difficult it was to keep her best teachers energized about such practices when the basic technology infrastructure could not be counted upon.

Matching your vision for 21st century education with the nuts and bolts of supporting teachers is incredibly important—more than any other partners in your system, teachers need to have the right tools and the right infrastructure available to them when they actually need them. Otherwise, classroom innovation will be infrequent and the cultural shifts you are trying to enact will be much harder to accomplish. When teachers are supported with the tools and infrastructure they need, your work with teachers will be much more successful. (For two helpful resources on the topic of school design, see the National Summit on School Design Report published by KnowledgeWorks and the American Architecture Foundation (AFF) http://www.ncef.org/pubs/nationalsummit.pdf and the P21 white paper on Learning Environments at http://p21.org/storage/documents/le_white_paper-1.pdf.)

FINAL THOUGHTS

We hope we have helped reinforce the importance of supporting teachers in your work. They should be your most effective partners. As an education leader, you are in a unique position to help them clarify what the 4Cs look like in student work, establish backward-design approaches such as UbD, and strengthen all aspects of the learning environment with an eye for 4Cs teaching. It is an exciting step, in our opinion, because if you can truly engage teachers in this work, the 4Cs will become a visible, regular element of learning for all students in your school or district.

REFLECTION

To support your teachers in 4Cs instruction, consider questions such as these:

- Is our system truly aligned around the 4Cs?
- Are teachers supported with appropriate professional learning opportunities to guide their work in 4Cs instruction?
- Are we allowing teachers enough autonomy in lesson planning and instruction? For example, are we providing teachers with the flexibility and autonomy to experiment in their practices? Do we encourage teachers to use their best judgments and learn from their failures, or are teachers penalized for things that don't work?
- Are we giving teachers enough flexible time for instruction and planning? For example, does the master schedule provide common planning time for horizontal and vertical teacher teams? Are specialists being used strategically to allow this kind of time/space for professional learning communities to thrive? Can teachers create project-based lessons that span several weeks of instructional time?
- Do teachers have appropriate physical spaces for collaborative student projects?

- Are design decisions about the physical spaces of the school being made with consideration for 4Cs instruction?
- Do teachers have access to meaningful education partners outside the physical walls of the school? For example, are there opportunities for teachers to extend student instruction through partnerships with museums, after-school programs, businesses, and/or other informal learning partners?
- Do teachers have access to education technology tools that enhance 4Cs student outcomes?

EXERCISE

The 4Cs and Teachers	Reflection	Next Step
Critical Thinking	What critical thinking approaches will you use to influence your support of teachers?	
Communication	How do/will/should you communicate with your teachers about the support systems you are considering?	
Collaboration	How will you engage with your teacher workforce and co-create the needed supports to accomplish your 21st century education vision?	
Creativity	How will your support of teachers enable creativity and innovation in pedagogy?	

REFERENCES

Blanding, Michael. "Treating the 'Instructional Core': Education Rounds." Harvard Graduate School of Education. http://www.gse.harvard.edu/news-impact/2009/05/ treating-the-instructional-core-education-rounds.

City, Elizabeth A., Richard F. Elmore, Sarah E. Fiarman, and Lee Teitel. *Instructional Rounds in Education: A Network Approach to Improving Teaching and Learning.* Cambridge: Harvard Education Press, 2009.

Darling-Hammond, Linda, et al. *Powerful Learning: What We Know About Teaching for Understanding.* San Francisco: Jossey-Bass, 2008.

"Grading the Teachers: Value-Added Analysis." *Los Angeles Times.* http://www .latimes.com/news/local/teachers-investigation.

Partnership for 21st Century Skills. *21st Century Learning.* Web. Jan. 2012. http:// p21.org/storage/documents/le_white_paper-1.pdf

Pink, Daniel. *Drive: The Surprising Truth About What Motivates Us.* New York: Riverhead, 2009.

Sparks, Sarah D. "Study Leads to End of New York City Merit-Pay Program." *Education Week.* http://blogs.edweek.org/edweek/inside-school-research/2011/07/a_new_study_by_the.html.

Tyack, David, and Larry Cuban. *Tinkering toward Utopia: A Century of Public School Reform.* Cambridge: Harvard University Press, 1995.

Wagner, Tony, and Robert Kegan. *Change Leadership.* San Francisco: Jossey-Bass, 2006.

"Why We Must Fire Bad Teachers." *The Daily Beast.* http://www.newsweek.com/2010/03/05/why-we-must-fire-bad-teachers.html.

Wiggins, Grant P., and Jay McTighe. *Understanding by Design.* Upper Saddle River, NJ: Pearson/Merrill Prentice Hall, 2006.

STEP 7

Improve and Innovate

THE 4CS FOCUS

Here is how the 4Cs operate within Step 7:

- Critical thinking: Critical thinking is required to develop continuous improvement processes and solutions so the 4Cs are effectively embedded into teaching, learning, and the operation of your school or district organization.
- Communication: Leaders must effectively communicate and model the need for a continuous improvement culture for classrooms, PLCs, and their leadership team.
- Collaboration: Continuous improvement should not be a strategy for isolated students, teachers, and administrators but should be developed in the context of professional learning communities.
- Creativity and innovation: Continuous improvement will only thrive and be effective in an environment in which creative experimentation is embraced and in which out-of-the-box ideas are valued and tested.

Creating A "Step 7" Organization

Like us, you must be excited to get to Step 7. Somehow it always feels good to get to the end of something. But in the 21st century, the end is never the end. It is actually the beginning of the next phase. These seven steps are no different. The goal isn't to complete them—but to get better and better at them.

Here's a good reality check. Are you happy to be at Step 7 because you are almost done? Or are you happy to be at Step 7 because you can go back and start to refine the other steps—in effect start all over again? If you are happy simply to get to the finish line, you are still stuck in the 20th century. If you are excited about the prospect of making a long-term commitment to revise and refine this work . . . welcome to 21st century education.

Step 7 might be the last of the steps in this book, but it also takes you back to the beginning of your journey. As you get to Step 7, you'll review the cycle you've been through to determine how you might improve it.

Catalina Foothills School District is clearly a "Step 7" district. As soon as they got to Step 7, they began revising Step 1. In their original vision, they had identified 12 student outcomes. But after seven years and lots of feedback from educators and stakeholders, they refined their list to seven outcomes. That's continuous improvement at work! Their revised model is showcased in Step 1 on pages 20–21.

From our perspective, you need to aspire to become an organization that is constantly trying to improve on your past and current work. Being satisfied with your past successes rarely yields sustainable improvements over time. The constant pursuit of excellence is what marks a truly high-performing 21st century organization—a "Step 7" organization.

Over the past 20 years, there have been several different approaches to continuous improvement in the private sector. Many of you are familiar with and have studied these processes. You should draw on this expertise as you proceed with Step 7.

We have been fortunate to have witnessed firsthand many examples of continuous improvement, particularly in the high-tech arena. In 1993 as part of his work with the computer industry in Washington, D.C., Ken visited the National Center for Supercomputing Applications (NCSA) in Champaign-Urbana, Illinois. During the course of the several-day tour, there was a special emphasis on the internet and its impact on research. Researchers demonstrated how projects from around the world could be accessed based on algorithms they had memorized to access and use the internet. The research tools being demonstrated were not for the average "non-techie."

The highlight of the tour was when Ken met three undergraduate students who were working on various research projects. One of them showed the group a relatively simple experiment that he was working on. He was trying to see if he could take the complicated algorithms that created access to the internet and have them be replaced by a simple "click" of a mouse. He demonstrated his approach and the delegation of "non-techies" immediately comprehended its significance. It was obvious that this was a game-changing innovation in technology—the internet didn't have to remain only in the domain of information technology researchers. Non-technical people would be able to leverage the internet for a variety of purposes, many of them well outside the realm of research.

The undergraduate student Ken met happened to be Marc Andreessen. He had been demonstrating "Mosaic." He went on the following year to become a founder of the company Netscape, which dramatically improved and then popularized the web browser.

Andreesen had asked a relatively simple question: "Can I take the current internet algorithms and replace them with a much simpler and more efficient interface so that the internet can be more widely accessible to non-researchers?" Andreesen was focused on how he might improve the internet to make it fundamentally more accessible to a wider audience. And he went on to refine and improve this idea in the private sector. It's fair to say that his relatively "simple" improvement has had enormous effects on all of our lives.

We understand that using examples of simplicity and improvement isn't always welcomed by those in the education sector. We believe that, when it comes to continuous improvement, the private sector offers a number of high-value examples and models for educators. In the corporate world, these process approaches have a variety of names: total quality management, six sigma, lean manufacturing, continuous improvement, and productivity and process improvement.

Some of the attempts to migrate these business concepts into K–12 education have been quite successful. For example, the well-regarded Baldrige Award is now given in education. A number of districts have pursued the Baldrige performance excellence program (www.nist.gov/baldrige). In almost every state, you can now find a district has participated in or won a Baldrige Award. Leaders in these districts might be a good source of information and counseling for you; consider engaging a retired district leader who has experience with these processes.

In addition, the Broad Foundation has awarded superintendents who have relentlessly pursued ever-increasing student performance (see www.broadfoundation.org). Broad winners are excellent examples of districts that are "high-performing organizations." Additionally, the American Productivity and Quality Center (APQC), which focuses on productivity and quality in the business sector, has created a program called the North Star Project (http://www.apqceducation.org/what-we-do/north-star-vision.html). It is designed to bring the principles of process improvement to school districts. APQC also has an excellent track record. These projects in the education sector have often focused on district processes such as maintenance and repair schedules, master scheduling, food services, and transportation services. A few have focused on academic strategies such as graduation rates and processes to launch online academies.

One of your most important tasks as an education leader is to harness the continuous improvement strategies that work best in support of your 21st century education vision. Use the power of Step 7 to fully realize the vision you developed in Steps 1 and 2.

RECOMMENDED READING

As you think about continuous improvement, we suggest the following books that help set a broad context for ongoing change and innovation. While these texts are not specifically focused on continuous improvement per se, we think they provide useful insights for any leader contemplating this work.

- Milton Chen, *Education Nation*
- Clayton Christensen, *Disrupting Class*
- Michael Fullan, *All Systems Go*
- Yong Zhao, *Catching Up or Leading the Way: American Education in the Age of Globalization*

Create a Culture That Supports Continuous Improvement

Before you can focus on the substance of continuous improvement, you will need a culture that supports it. When you walk into a "Step 7" school or district, the "feel" you get is noticeable. It just seems different. There is an energy of collaboration and excitement that, to us, represents a culture of improvement.

We've seen this energy in classrooms in New Tech Network (NTN) schools. In every NTN school we have visited we have noticed teachers in the hallway, or in the cyber café, discussing their latest projects, asking each other how to make the work more engaging for students and more in line with the NTN model. This kind of teamwork among New Tech teachers is common. It's no surprise, then, to see their students actively engaged in challenging work.

When you walk into High Tech High in San Diego, the feeling is also palpable. Administrators and teachers have created a culture of cooperation and experimentation throughout the school. Ben Daley, the chief academic officer, attributes their success at creating a continuous improvement culture to the use of rigorous protocols. They use several to guide work around specific issues; for example, the most popular ones include the "dilemma consultancy" protocol, the "project tuning" protocol and the "looking at student work" protocol. Such protocols require facilitators to focus on constructive comments and potential improvements in every interaction. The protocols help depersonalize dialogue so that participants can focus on improvement. The norms are described as "hard on the content, soft on the people," "be kind, helpful, and specific," and "share the air (or step up, step back)." We really like one of their favorite phrases they use to describe their continuous work: "Everyone is about to be doing better work."

Each protocol divides a 40-minute period into six sections, including what Daley considers a critical five-minute "debrief" at the end. Daley explains that these norms and the tactics of the protocols are pivotal in creating an improvement-oriented discussion. Teachers and administrators have become very effective at leading groups of educators through the protocols, and this has enabled the continuous improvement culture. One of the protocols is included in Appendix 13.

The importance of establishing solid ground rules for an improvement-related discussion was underscored to us recently in a session with educators in a district we were visiting. The 21st century coaches in the district were concerned that critical thinking strategies were being implemented unevenly across the district's elementary schools. They were reluctant to raise the issue in the regularly scheduled leadership meetings, fearing that they might damage their relationships with the principals of the schools that were struggling. With the coaches' permission, we spoke with the principals in question. One of the principals immediately suggested a group meeting with the coaches to review everyone's progress to date and share best practices. This principal demonstrated a continuous improvement mindset, suggesting that a healthy culture existed that supported continuous improvement. However, while we were impressed with the principals' reactions and suggestions for improvement, the reluctance of the coaches was problematic. Protocols such as the ones we saw at High Tech High might have helped the coaches in this district establish a more constructive, non-threatening platform for initiating such delicate conversations.

This same district experienced another challenge in its work on critical thinking. The 21st century skill coaches were assigned to help the district improve pedagogy around critical thinking. But after a year on this work they found that they were "competing" with other instructional coaches who were focused on other things (such as math and International Baccalaureate (I.B.). In some cases, the coaches were competing for the attention and time of principals, department heads, and/or teachers. In other cases—often without being aware of it—they were undercutting each other's efforts.

At some point, they finally recognized that working in such isolation made no sense. They initiated a group meeting among all the coaches. Together, they organized the disparate aspects of the work under a single theme ("Implementing Standards for the 21st Century Learner"). This has helped all the coaches—whether they are focused on I.B., science inquiry, or critical thinking—work together to accomplish a unified goal. They are able to collaborate more effectively and have established a common vocabulary for reviewing collective progress over time.

These conversations about district processes are very important, but it is also critical to establish an environment that encourages an improvement mindset among individual teachers. One indicator for this is how your educators react to new ideas. Here we can offer an example to consider. We both live in Tucson, Arizona, where the tragic shootings on January 8, 2011, caused many like us to focus on the issue of civility in political discourse. We helped initiate a project in which classrooms of students from around the city and country could focus on civility in the context of political campaigns. The students would develop a rubric for civility and use it to rank the level of civil discourse they witnessed in debates, television ads, and other political events. The students could then write articles, post results on the Web, and encourage further community dialogue on the civility of the campaigns. As we began sharing this idea with leaders around the country, most responded very positively. A few, however, noted that the teachers in their districts would be overwhelmed at the prospect and would likely dismiss it immediately unless it was mandated.

How do you think your educators would respond to a new proposal like this one? Would they consider it with an open mind, or would they wait to see if their participation was required? Would they tend to pull a group together to brainstorm around it or ignore it and hope it disappears? The answers to these questions might give you some sense of how close you are to having a "Step 7" culture in your school or district and what obstacles exist to moving in that direction. In some cases, it might be as simple as resistance to change; in our experience, however, the obstacles have a lot to do with environmental factors such as lack of common planning time or ineffective professional development.

Consider, then, how you might support teachers in nurturing an improvement mindset among students. Ken likes to tell the story of his younger son, Braden (now a graduate student), who, in the third grade, was given a very interesting assignment. He was told to go home and find something in the house that he could improve. As a fledgling cook, Braden focused on his inability to easily hold utensils in the kitchen. He also had observed that his grandmother, who had severe arthritis, also had trouble holding utensils. So Braden went out to the garage and removed the handlebars from his bicycle. He filled them with putty and then stuck a vegetable peeler in one and a knife in the other. He found that he and his grandmother had a much easier time grasping the utensils. He brought his utensils to school and was told by the teacher that his invention was not a very creative improvement. He was very disappointed.

About a year later, Ken was shopping and noticed the first set of utensils marketed by "Oxo," which included items such as a vegetable peeler, paring knife, and pizza cutter using Braden's design of super-grips. It was clear that Braden's idea for utensils was, in fact, a significant innovation. It was a subtle and simple solution, much like the 'click of the mouse' Marc Andreessen used to revolutionize access to the internet. And Braden's instinct that he had found a "worthwhile" improvement for utensils has been borne out by a robust market for the product that continues to this day. Most importantly, however, the teacher had made Braden feel a sense of failure about a real innovation, something Braden recalls affecting him for years afterward.

Students don't develop an improvement mindset in a vacuum. They need a culture in which this kind of thought process is nurtured and rewarded. It is no different for teachers. As a leader, your role in creating an improvement culture is incredibly important.

In your desire to continuously improve, don't forget the perspective of your students. They must be an essential element of your culture of continuous improvement. As you get ideas for improvement, you and your teachers can test them out on students. Your students themselves are capable of designing major elements of improvement.

You, your teachers, and your leadership team need to consistently have your pulse on your students' perspective. Do they feel part of a culture of continuous improvement? In Step 2, we described the importance of student outreach and pointed you to Appendix 10, the student outreach toolkit. In that context, we were primarily suggesting you use it to help you do outreach to your students about your vision for 21st century education. We suggest revisiting that toolkit (see Appendix 10) from a broader context. Are your students' perspectives fully represented in the culture and organization of your school or district? Do students have seats at the appropriate tables? Are students viewed as co-creators of your continuous improvement culture?

Focus Your Continuous Improvement on 4Cs Teaching and Learning

Once the culture is in good shape, you can begin to focus your attention on the substance of what you want to accomplish—supporting the 4Cs. Consider how to expand any existing continuous improvement activities to your 4Cs implementation work. In the Springfield Public School District in Springfield, Missouri, education leaders have long used continuous improvement processes to strengthen their day-to-day operations such as facilities and transportation. However, they have expanded their continuous improvement approaches to include their 21st century education work (which is focused on critical thinking, communication and collaboration). The leaders in Springfield are using the APQC North Star project model to improve implementation of their teaching and learning transformation work. The project teams completed four days of training with APQC and continue to receive ongoing virtual coaching via the North Star project. The project teams have also designed and implemented a process flowchart to refine the scope and sequence for continuous improvement work through 2015–16.

We also recommend integrating continuous improvement practices into the protocols for your PLCs. In our view, the function of the PLCs is where the rubber meets the road. As we've traveled the country, we have noticed that more and more districts are embracing the notion of PLCs. We are particularly encouraged when we see PLCs serving as vehicles of real transformation—this, in our opinion, is the "right work" for PLCs. This doesn't happen in every school or district, but the trend is growing.

We have collaborated with Rick DuFour on how best to integrate strong PLC practices with 21st century learning outcomes as a way to guide school and district transformation. As DuFour has shared with us, a key requirement is to "focus on the right work." Continuous improvement has a role to play in helping PLCs get clear on the focus of the work. If the PLCs are focused only on core academic subject mastery, your vision for 21st century student outcomes is unlikely to be achieved. Consider how to establish structures, protocols, and expectations for the PLCs to focus on both content and 21st century outcomes. Then you might encourage the PLCs to track their progress using metrics and data. Measuring success on common indicators will help all educators understand whether their students are mastering the 4Cs.

Imagine a continuous cycle that works something like this:

- Common vision
- Shared outcomes
- Shared measures of success
- Take action
- Measure progress
- Reflect on progress
- Revise action
- Repeat

For real progress to occur, a "culture of action and improvement" must be present in PLC work. Ideally, PLCs can propose improvements, teachers can test them and then return to the PLC. The PLCs can discuss successes and failures, determine solutions, and then start the process over again to keep refining solutions that work and produce real results for students. PLCs that focus on continuous improvement can be a vibrant source of innovation in your school or district with the potential to produce real gains for all students.

Expand Your 4Cs Continuous Improvement Strategy to Other Key Parts of Your Organization

Continuous improvement has real value in many other parts of your school or district organization as well. Here's a suggestion. Sit down with your leadership team and ask them the following question:

> If we improved just one organizational process in our school or district that could have the most impact on the 4Cs among students, what would it be?

Ask each member of your leadership team to share an answer. Discuss all the responses, and prioritize them as a group. Once you've done that, you will have developed a robust list of options for your leadership team's continuous improvement agenda. One common area that leadership teams often identify in this exercise is human resources. The reasoning goes, if we want teachers and leaders who can critically think, communicate, collaborate, and be creative, we should promote those features in everything our human resources department does.

What does it look like to apply continuous improvement processes to support a 4Cs human resources agenda? We think about it this way: What if from this point forward for *every* new teacher, administrator, and staff person hired in the district, the job description included the 4Cs and a commitment to continuous improvement? Consider all the places in the hiring process that the 4Cs and continuous improvement can fit. Consider adding the 4Cs to job descriptions and questionnaires for applicants. Incorporating the 4Cs in this way sends a strong signal about the district's commitment to these skills for every educator (not just the students).

A 4Cs human resource strategy should not be limited to teachers. If we want leaders to lead toward the 4Cs, we need administrators and staff who can model the 4Cs. If the 4Cs and continuous improvement are truly a component of your overall vision, it is worthwhile to consider how these skills relate to the job requirements for every position in the district—or, at the very least, consider which of the 4Cs are particularly appropriate for each hire. This includes "classified" employees who can and should be challenged to embed critical thinking, collaboration, communication, creativity, and continuous improvement strategies into daily practices. We have seen this approach applied for employees in departments as various as finance, HR, operations, food service, and facilities.

Additionally, consider how the 4Cs can play a role in the evaluation of all employees. Performance evaluations can be a powerful component of your 21st century implementation work. The Catalina Foothills School District has embraced this approach. After establishing its 21st century outcomes, it embedded 21st century outcomes in its evaluation tools used with teachers, administrators, and staff. Every employee is judged on his or her own critical thinking, communication, collaboration, and creativity skills. Catalina Foothills has also tied 21st century outcomes with compensation. In some districts, this tactic could present a daunting challenge, but it is the logical outcome of a 4Cs continuous improvement strategy. If in Step 2 you built consensus with your teachers' union, this improvement ought to be a viable option.

Our hope is that we have raised some constructive ideas for how you might go about effectively embedding the 4Cs and continuous improvement into the operational aspects of your school or district. We have highlighted human resources here, but this is just one common example among many that can advance your 4Cs teaching and learning vision. We hope you and your team will be able to implement similar strategies in additional parts of your system where the 4Cs and continuous improvement can be helpfully embedded.

These suggestions are meant to help you begin a series of conversations with your leadership team about how to model and drive the 4Cs along with a culture of continuous improvement. As a reminder, please look again at the MILE Guide (discussed in Step 3). The far right column of the guide is labeled "Continuous Improvement/Strategic Planning." It might help you define what you and your team believe is most important when it comes to 21st century continuous improvement.

FINAL THOUGHTS ON CONTINUOUS IMPROVEMENT

We hope that these suggestions on continuous improvement will help you set the bar high in your school or district. It will be difficult to sustain the work you are doing in Steps 1–6 without pursuing Step 7 diligently. If you commit to continuous improvement around the 4Cs and your 21st century vision, then you will leave your school or district with a sustainable legacy of improvement for all students.

As you consider Step 7, it will be helpful for you and your team to reflect on these questions:

- Do you and your district aspire to be a "high-performing" organization?
- Have you adopted a continuous improvement strategy in your school or district?
- Do your students have a culture of continuous improvement?
- Does your school or district have a culture that supports continuous improvement of teachers and leaders?
- Are your teachers organized in PLCs that are focused on 4Cs continuous improvement?
- Does your leadership team have an agenda of 4Cs continuous improvement for your organization?
- What are the ways you can shift your learning culture so that there is a spirit of continuous improvement by students in every classroom? By teachers in every PLC?

CONCLUSION

Thank you for taking this part of your 21st century education journey with us. We would like to end this phase of our work with you much as we began: focused on the 4Cs. We offer our 4Cs hopes for you as you continue on your 21st century education journey.

First, continue to critically think and focus on the 4Cs outcomes and the others you might have adopted. This is one of the most important lessons we have learned in our 21st century journey. The student learning outcomes are a critical part of this work. One of the major contributions we hope we have made to your ongoing work is to have you keep your focus on the 4Cs as a central component of your role as a 21st century leader.

Your students, today's students, need to be ready for:

- Ten to 15 jobs in their lifetime.
- Complex problems that require complex and creative problem solving.

- A highly networked world that requires complex and interactive communications skills.
- Massive amounts of information that require the ability to analyze, synthesize, leverage, and create new and old information.
- A society in constant flux that requires the need to continuously improve.

These were not the needs of the society when we were in school in the 1950s and 1970s. They were not the primary, intentional, and purposeful focus of the education system of that era. The vision and model you are creating need to be the purposeful and intentional work of yourself, your leadership team, your teachers, and your students. Don't lose that focus. Don't stop critically thinking about those outcomes for your students.

Second, don't stop communicating with your stakeholders. While we haven't focused on effective communication since Step 2, your success depends on ongoing communication with your internal and external stakeholders throughout the process. A unique part of our seven-step model is that we combine stakeholder outreach and consensus building with the work of curriculum, instruction, professional development, and assessment. Keep coming back to Steps 1 and 2 over and over again. Check in on your vision on consensus building with your students, your parents, your business leaders, your community leaders, and your teachers. The power of this work is that if you do it right you will have your community strongly behind you to support your efforts. But you also need to ensure they stay engaged and committed.

Third, create a culture that supports creative and innovative continuous improvement. Become a "Step 7" organization. Don't be a school or district that is satisfied with teachers who say, "We do that already." Become a school or district that embraces the question, "How can we do that better?"

Finally, don't stop collaborating. Yes, you need to continue collaborating with your teachers and your leadership team. But don't isolate yourself from other leaders. Find the support you need from other leaders with a similar vision. We hope you will consider joining our professional learning community of leaders committed to 21st century education.

Most importantly, we hope you will continue your 21st century education journey. Go to our website at www.edleader21.com to learn more about implementing this work. Step 7 isn't the end of the journey, and we hope this book isn't the end of yours—just the beginning.

REFERENCE

Daley, Ben. Personal interview and communication. Jan. 12, 2012

APPENDICES

117

APPENDIX 1

P21 Framework Definitions

To help practitioners integrate skills into the teaching of core academic subjects, the Partnership has developed a unified, collective vision for learning known as the Framework for 21st Century Learning. This Framework describes the skills, knowledge, and expertise students must master to succeed in work and life; it is a blend of content knowledge, specific skills, expertise, and literacies.

Every 21st century skills implementation requires the development of core academic subject knowledge and understanding among all students. Those who can think critically and communicate effectively must build on a base of core academic subject knowledge.

Within the context of core knowledge instruction, **students must also learn the essential skills for success in today's world, such as critical thinking, problem solving, communication, and collaboration.**

When a school or district builds on this foundation, combining the entire Framework with the necessary support systems—standards, assessments, curriculum and instruction, professional development, and learning environments—students are more engaged in the learning process and graduate better prepared to thrive in today's global economy.

While the graphic represents each element distinctly for descriptive purposes, the Partnership views all the components as fully interconnected in the process of 21st century teaching and learning.

21st Century Student Outcomes and Support Systems

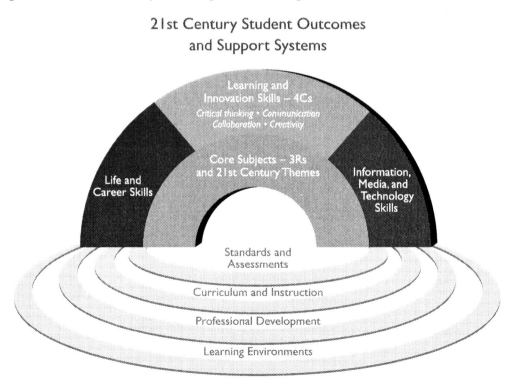

119

21st Century Student Outcomes

The elements described in this section as "21st century student outcomes" are the knowledge, skills, and expertise students should master to succeed in work and life in the 21st century.

Core Subjects and 21st Century Themes

Mastery of **core subjects and 21st century themes** is essential for all students in the 21st century. Core subjects include:

- English, reading, or language arts
- World languages
- Arts
- Mathematics
- Economics
- Science
- Geography
- History
- Government and civics

In addition to these subjects, we believe schools must move not only to include a focus on mastery of core subjects, but also to promote understanding of academic content at much higher levels by weaving **21st century interdisciplinary themes** into core subjects:

Global Awareness

- Using 21st century skills to understand and address global issues
- Learning from and working collaboratively with individuals representing diverse cultures, religions, and lifestyles in a spirit of mutual respect and open dialogue in personal, work, and community contexts
- Understanding other nations and cultures, including the use of non-English languages

Financial, Economic, Business, and Entrepreneurial Literacy

- Knowing how to make appropriate personal economic choices
- Understanding the role of the economy in society
- Using entrepreneurial skills to enhance workplace productivity and career options

Civic Literacy

- Participating effectively in civic life through knowing how to stay informed and understanding governmental processes
- Exercising the rights and obligations of citizenship at local, state, national, and global levels
- Understanding the local and global implications of civic decisions

Health Literacy

- Obtaining, interpreting, and understanding basic health information and services and using such information and services in ways that enhance health

- Understanding preventive physical and mental health measures, including proper diet, nutrition, exercise, risk avoidance, and stress reduction
- Using available information to make appropriate health-related decisions
- Establishing and monitoring personal and family health goals
- Understanding national and international public health and safety issues

Environmental Literacy

- Demonstrate knowledge and understanding of the environment and the circumstances and conditions affecting it, particularly as relates to air, climate, land, food, energy, water, and ecosystems
- Demonstrate knowledge and understanding of society's impact on the natural world (for example, population growth, population development, resource consumption rate, and so on)
- Investigate and analyze environmental issues, and make accurate conclusions about effective solutions
- Take individual and collective action towards addressing environmental challenges (for example, participating in global actions, designing solutions that inspire action on environmental issues)

Learning and Innovation Skills

Learning and innovation skills increasingly are being recognized as those that separate students who are prepared for more and more complex life and work environments in the 21st century and those who are not. A focus on creativity, critical thinking, communication, and collaboration is essential to prepare students for the future.

Creativity and Innovation

Think Creatively
- Use a wide range of idea creation techniques (such as brainstorming)
- Create new and worthwhile ideas (both incremental and radical concepts)
- Elaborate, refine, analyze, and evaluate their own ideas in order to improve and maximize creative efforts

Work Creatively with Others
- Develop, implement, and communicate new ideas to others effectively
- Be open and responsive to new and diverse perspectives; incorporate group input and feedback into the work
- Demonstrate originality and inventiveness in work, and understand the real world limits to adopting new ideas
- View failure as an opportunity to learn; understand that creativity and innovation are long-term, cyclical processes of small successes and frequent mistakes

Implement Innovations
- Act on creative ideas to make a tangible and useful contribution to the field in which the innovation will occur

Critical Thinking and Problem Solving

Reason Effectively
- Use various types of reasoning (inductive, deductive, and so on) as appropriate to the situation

Use Systems Thinking
- Analyze how parts of a whole interact with each other to produce overall outcomes in complex systems

Make Judgments and Decisions
- Effectively analyze and evaluate evidence, arguments, claims, and beliefs
- Analyze and evaluate major alternative points of view
- Synthesize and make connections between information and arguments
- Interpret information and draw conclusions based on the best analysis
- Reflect critically on learning experiences and processes

Solve Problems
- Solve different kinds of non-familiar problems in both conventional and innovative ways
- Identify and ask significant questions that clarify various points of view and lead to better solutions

Communication and Collaboration

Communicate Clearly
- Articulate thoughts and ideas effectively using oral, written, and nonverbal communication skills in a variety of forms and contexts
- Listen effectively to decipher meaning, including knowledge, values, attitudes, and intentions
- Use communication for a range of purposes (for example, to inform, instruct, motivate, and persuade)
- Utilize multiple media and technologies, and know how to judge their effectiveness *a priori* as well as assess their impact
- Communicate effectively in diverse environments (including multilingual)

Collaborate with Others
- Demonstrate ability to work effectively and respectfully with diverse teams
- Exercise flexibility and willingness to be helpful in making necessary compromises to accomplish a common goal
- Assume shared responsibility for collaborative work, and value the individual contributions made by each team member

Information, Media and Technology Skills

People in the 21st century live in a technology- and media-suffused environment, marked by various characteristics, including: (1) access to an abundance of information, (2) rapid changes in technology tools, and (3) the ability to collaborate and make individual contributions on an unprecedented scale. To be effective in the 21st century, citizens and workers must be able to exhibit a range of functional and critical thinking skills related to information, media, and technology.

Information Literacy

Access and Evaluate Information
- Access information efficiently (time) and effectively (sources)
- Evaluate information critically and competently

Use and Manage Information
- Use information accurately and creatively for the issue or problem at hand
- Manage the flow of information from a wide variety of sources
- Apply a fundamental understanding of the ethical/legal issues surrounding the access and use of information

Media Literacy

Analyze Media
- Understand both how and why media messages are constructed and for what purposes
- Examine how individuals interpret messages differently, how values and points of view are included or excluded, and how media can influence beliefs and behaviors
- Apply a fundamental understanding of the ethical/legal issues surrounding the access and use of media

Create Media Products
- Understand and utilize the most appropriate media creation tools, characteristics, and conventions
- Understand and effectively utilize the most appropriate expressions and interpretations in diverse, multicultural environments

ICT (Information, Communications, and Technology) Literacy

Apply Technology Effectively
- Use technology as a tool to research, organize, evaluate, and communicate information
- Use digital technologies (computers, PDAs, media players, GPS, and so on), communication/networking tools, and social networks appropriately to access, manage, integrate, evaluate, and create information to successfully function in a knowledge economy
- Apply a fundamental understanding of the ethical/legal issues surrounding the access and use of information technologies

Life and Career Skills

Today's life and work environments require far more than thinking skills and content knowledge. The ability to navigate the complex life and work environments in the globally competitive information age requires students to pay rigorous attention to developing adequate life and career skills.

Flexibility and Adaptability

Adapt to Change
- Adapt to varied roles, job responsibilities, schedules, and contexts
- Work effectively in a climate of ambiguity and changing priorities

Be Flexible
- Incorporate feedback effectively
- Deal positively with praise, setbacks, and criticism
- Understand, negotiate, and balance diverse views and beliefs to reach workable solutions, particularly in multicultural environments

Initiative and Self-Direction

Manage Goals and Time
- Set goals with tangible and intangible success criteria
- Balance tactical (short-term) and strategic (long-term) goals
- Utilize time and manage workload efficiently

Work Independently
- Monitor, define, prioritize, and complete tasks without direct oversight

Be Self-Directed Learners
- Go beyond basic mastery of skills and/or curriculum to explore and expand one's own learning and opportunities to gain expertise
- Demonstrate initiative to advance skill levels toward a professional level
- Demonstrate commitment to learning as a lifelong process
- Reflect critically on past experiences in order to inform future progress

Social and Cross-Cultural Skills

Interact Effectively with Others
- Know when it is appropriate to listen and when to speak
- Conduct oneself in a respectable, professional manner

Work Effectively in Diverse Teams
- Respect cultural differences and work effectively with people from a range of social and cultural backgrounds
- Respond open-mindedly to different ideas and values
- Leverage social and cultural differences to create new ideas and increase both innovation and quality of work

Productivity and Accountability

Manage Projects
- Set and meet goals, even in the face of obstacles and competing pressures
- Prioritize, plan, and manage work to achieve the intended result

124

Produce Results
- Demonstrate additional attributes associated with producing high-quality products, including the abilities to:
  - Work positively and ethically
  - Manage time and projects effectively
  - Multi-task
  - Participate actively as well as be reliable and punctual
  - Present oneself professionally and with proper etiquette
  - Collaborate and cooperate effectively with teams
  - Respect and appreciate team diversity
  - Be accountable for results

Leadership and Responsibility

Guide and Lead Others
- Use interpersonal and problem-solving skills to influence and guide others toward a goal
- Leverage strengths of others to accomplish a common goal
- Inspire others to reach their very best via example and selflessness
- Demonstrate integrity and ethical behavior in using influence and power

Be Responsible to Others
- Act responsibly with the interests of the larger community in mind

21st Century Support Systems

The elements described below are the critical systems necessary to ensure student mastery of 21st century skills. Twenty-first century standards, assessments, curriculum, instruction, professional development, and learning environments must be aligned to produce a support system that produces 21st century outcomes for today's students.

21st Century Standards

- Focus on 21st century skills, content knowledge, and expertise
- Build understanding across and among core subjects as well as 21st century interdisciplinary themes
- Emphasize deep understanding rather than shallow knowledge
- Engage students with the real-world data, tools, and experts they will encounter in college, on the job, and in life; students learn best when actively engaged in solving meaningful problems
- Allow for multiple measures of mastery

Assessment of 21st Century Skills

- Supports a balance of assessments, including high-quality standardized testing along with effective formative and summative classroom assessments
- Emphasizes useful feedback on student performance that is embedded into everyday learning
- Requires a balance of technology-enhanced, formative, and summative assessments that measure student mastery of 21st century skills

- Enables development of portfolios of student work that demonstrate mastery of 21st century skills to educators and prospective employers
- Enables a balanced portfolio of measures to assess the educational system's effectiveness in reaching high levels of student competency in 21st century skills

21st Century Curriculum and Instruction

- Teaches 21st century skills discretely in the context of core subjects and 21st century interdisciplinary themes
- Focuses on providing opportunities for applying 21st century skills across content areas and for a competency-based approach to learning
- Enables innovative learning methods that integrate the use of supportive technologies, inquiry- and problem-based approaches, and higher-order thinking skills
- Encourages the integration of community resources beyond school walls

21st Century Professional Development

- Highlights ways teachers can seize opportunities for integrating 21st century skills, tools, and teaching strategies into their classroom practice, and helps them identify what activities they can replace/de-emphasize
- Balances direct instruction with project-oriented teaching methods
- Illustrates how a deeper understanding of subject matter can actually enhance problem solving, critical thinking, and other 21st century skills
- Enables 21st century professional learning communities for teachers that model the kinds of classroom learning that best promotes 21st century skills for students
- Cultivates teachers' ability to identify students' particular learning styles, intelligences, strengths, and weaknesses
- Helps teachers develop their abilities to use various strategies (such as formative assessments) to reach diverse students and create environments that support differentiated teaching and learning
- Supports the continuous evaluation of students' 21st century skills development
- Encourages knowledge sharing among communities of practitioners, using face-to-face, virtual and blended communications
- Uses a scalable and sustainable model of professional development

21st Century Learning Environments

- Create learning practices, human support, and physical environments that will support the teaching and learning of 21st century skill outcomes
- Support professional learning communities that enable educators to collaborate, share best practices, and integrate 21st century skills into classroom practice
- Enable students to learn in relevant, real-world 21st century contexts (for example, through project-based or other applied work)
- Allow equitable access to quality learning tools, technologies, and resources
- Provide 21st century architectural and interior designs for group, team, and individual learning
- Support expanded community and international involvement in learning, both face to face and online

About the Partnership for 21st Century Skills

The Partnership for 21st Century Skills is a national organization that advocates for the integration of skills such as critical thinking, problem solving, and communication into the teaching of core academic subjects such as English, reading, or language arts, world languages, arts, mathematics, economics, science, geography, history, government, and civics.

The Partnership and our member organizations provide tools and resources that help facilitate and drive this necessary change.

Learn more and get involved at www.p21.org.

APPENDIX 2

21st Century Skills Maps

These resources have been created by P21 in conjunction with the major U.S. content associations in the subjects of

- Mathematics
- English
- Science
- The Arts
- World Languages
- Social Studies
- Geography

They are available for free download here:
http://p21.org/tools-and-resources/publications/1017-educators#SkillsMaps

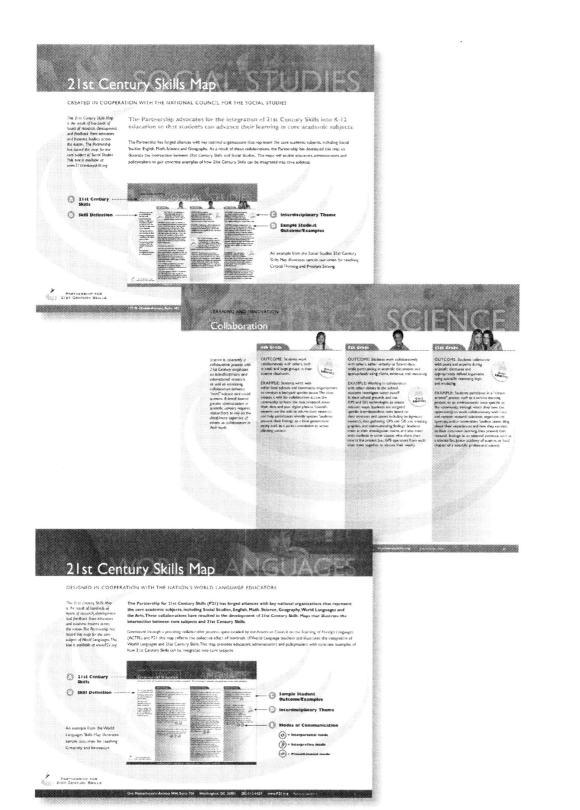

APPENDIX 3

Critical Thinking Resource Document

Skill Definition

Below we share some definitional language you might wish to consider in your implementation efforts. This definition of critical thinking is derived originally from the P21 version, with additions from EdLeader21 members.

Reason Effectively

- Use various types of reasoning (such as inductive and deductive) appropriate to the situation.
- Evaluate the strength of conclusions, differentiating reasoning based on facts from reasoning based on opinions.

Use Systems Thinking

- Analyze how parts of a whole interact with each other to produce overall outcomes in complex systems and how systems effectively interact with each other.
- Apply tools of systems thinking (iceberg, ladder of inference, systems archetypes, reinforcing/balancing feedback loops, systems archetypes, behavior-over-time graphs) to understand complexity, interdependence, change, and leverage.
- Practice personal mastery, shared visioning, and team learning.
- Examine mental models.

Make Judgments and Decisions

- Effectively identify, analyze, and evaluate evidence, arguments, claims, beliefs, and alternate points of view.
- Synthesize and make connections between information and arguments.
- Interpret information and draw conclusions based on the best analysis.
- Propose defensible conclusions that address multiple and diverse perspectives.
- Reflect critically on learning experiences and processes.

Identify, define, and solve authentic problems and essential questions

- Formulate essential questions; identify and ask significant questions that clarify various points of view and lead to better solutions.
- Identify and define authentic problems clearly and precisely.
- Solve different kinds of unfamiliar problems in conventional and innovative ways.

Collect, assess, and analyze relevant information

- Collect multiple and diverse sources of credible evidence.
- Identify and assess information relative to the essential question.
- Analyze information by identifying a relationship and/or pattern among components based on evidence or data.

- Organize information effectively.
- Gather, question, and evaluate the quality of information from multiple primary and secondary sources.

Reflect critically on learning experiences, processes, and solutions

- Reflect with candor and depth on the learning experiences (what I did and what I learned) and processes (how and why I did it).
- Evaluate and refine solutions and determine next steps.

Critical Thinking Resources

Following are general resources dedicated to critical thinking.

Organizations/Projects

Creative Learning Exchange (www.clexchange.org)
The Creative Learning Exchange encourages an active, learner-centered process of discovery in K–12 education that challenges preconceptions, deepens conceptual understanding, and engages in meaningful, real-world problem solving through the mastery of systems thinking and system dynamics modeling.

The Foundation for Critical Thinking (www.criticalthinking.org)
The foundation and its related entities aim to improve education in all subjects at every level by providing information, research, and resources on critical thinking. This site provides excellent background resources on the subject of critical thinking.

International Center for Leadership in Education Rigor/Relevance Framework (www.leadered.com/rrr.html and www.leadered.com/pdf/ R&Rframework.pdf)
The Rigor/Relevance Framework is a tool to examine curriculum, instruction, and assessment. The Rigor/Relevance Framework is based on two dimensions of higher standards and student achievement. Having teachers instruct in the framework's "Quadrant D" enables students to work collaboratively to solve real-world, unpredictable problems.

Project Zero at Harvard University: Visible Thinking Routines (http:// pzweb.harvard.edu/vt/VisibleThinking_html_files/VisibleThinking1.html)
This project focuses on research-based approaches to integrating the development of students' thinking with content learning across subjects. A number of in-depth, helpful resources focused on visible thinking are available on this site and are highly recommended by EdLeader21 members.

Waters Foundation (www.watersfoundation.org)
The Waters Foundation resources are designed to increase the capacity of educators to utilize systems thinking concepts, habits, and tools in classroom instruction and school improvement. The sample systems thinking rubrics can be accessed here: www.watersfoundation.org/index.cfm?fuseaction=content.display&id=252, and sample lessons by subject can be found here: www.watersfoundation.org/index.cfm?fuseaction= stdm.classinstruction. The best practices section of the website contains helpful resources as well; most EdLeader21 members recommend the Waters Foundation as a crucial resource when developing strategies for critical thinking in school systems.

School and Classroom Resources

CAE's Collegiate Learning Assessment (CLA) and College and Work Readiness Assessment (CWRA)

These assessments by the Council for Aid to Education measure analytic thinking, critical thinking, problem solving, and written communication skills. The CWRA is available for high school use. Scoring rubric: http://bit.ly/fly3AJ and general information: www.cae.org/content/pro_collegework.htm.

Catalina Foothills Critical Thinking Rubric (http://bit.ly/4n677D)

Catalina Foothills School District created a series of rubrics to assess student critical thinking skills. They measure critical thinking skills such as comparing, classifying, inductive and deductive reasoning, error analysis, and decision making.

Critical Thinking Lesson Plans—UNC (http://bit.ly/dOmrsa)

These lesson plans integrate critical thinking into core academic subjects such as science, English language arts, social studies, geography, and others.

First Lego League Rubrics (http://tinyurl.com/88wajev)

The FIRST LEGO League (FLL) robotics program not only focuses on STEM but also stresses teamwork and collaboration, communication skills, creativity, and innovation and critical thinking. There are several rubrics here that help measure the 4Cs.

Isaksen and Treffinger's model for critical and creative thinking

Scott Isaksen and Donald Treffinger developed a six-stage critical and creative thinking model that is outlined in their book *Creative Problem Solving: The Basic Course* (1985).

Muhammad Kamarul Kabilan, Creative and Critical Thinking in Language Classrooms (http://bit.ly/hnnL5k)

This paper addresses issues of "creative" and "critical" language learners, including questions around what teachers need in order to develop creative and critical language learners and how to achieve such learning. Sample activities are provided.

National Council of Teachers of Mathematics (NCTM): Mathematics and Reasoning Resources (http://bit.ly/VtCDr)

NCTM's resources on reasoning and sense making in mathematics curriculum and instruction help make the connection to critical thinking more visible.

Onondaga-Cortland-Madison BOCES 21st Century Skills Resources (www.ocmboces.org/teacherpage.cfm?teacher=1221)

This is an excellent list of links to resources that assist with assessment of 21st century skills such as critical thinking.

Social Studies and Critical Thinking (http://bit.ly/eq14T6)

Article published by the Ohio Department of Education that discusses the evidence base for critical thinking in social studies.

UK A-Level Critical Thinking Examination Guide (www.criticalthinking.org.uk)

This overview of the A-Level critical thinking examination for United Kingdom students provides an interesting glance at another country's approach to critical thinking. Links and resources are included that address the four areas of the exam: Credibility of Evidence, Assessing and Developing Argument, Resolution of Dilemmas, and Critical Reasoning.

**Inés Valdez, *Using Language as an Instrument for Critical Thinking*
(http://bit.ly/gvxO4x)**
This brief overview provides some interesting ideas for how to use non-English languages for critical thinking.

Virginia Beach City Public Schools Resources
- VBCPS Continuum for 21st Century Skills (http://www.vbschools.com/compass/pdfs/VBCPSContinuum.pdf)
- Critical thinking "look-fors": VBCPS has developed a list of critical thinking "look-fors" describing student behaviors that demonstrate critical thinking. Many of the "look-fors" have a basis in "Quadrant D" of the Rigor and Relevance framework (http://www.leadered.com/rrr.html). The "look-fors" list was developed as a collaborative effort between a group of expert teachers and administrators. The purpose of this list is to guide teachers as they plan learning that requires students to think critically. (http://bit.ly/g85MG3)
- The school division's *Compass to 2015* strategic plan defines the skills necessary for students to be 21st century learners, workers, and citizens. Definitions here: www.vbschools.com/compass/skillsGlossary.asp

Books

James Bellanca: *Enriched Learning Projects: A Practical Pathway to 21st Century Skills*
This book draws from the 21st Century Enriched Learning School model designed to meet standards and develop skills in communication, collaboration, critical thinking, creativity, and global and cross-cultural awareness. (http://amzn.to/e6vzDL)

James Bellanca and Ron Brandt, Editors: *21st Century Skills: Rethinking How Students Learn*
This volume explores three overarching questions: (1) Why are the skills listed in the Framework for 21st Century Learning needed for learning in the future? (2) Which skills are most important? (3) What can be done to help schools include these skills in their repertoire so that 21st century learning results? (http://amzn.to/g56hYY)

Susan Brookhart: *How to Assess Higher Order Thinking Skills*
This book focuses on developing and using test questions and other assessments to reveal how well students can analyze, reason, solve problems, and think creatively. (http://bit.ly/eriCEd)

Arthur Costa and Bena Kallick: *Habits of Mind Across the Curriculum: Practical and Creative Strategies for Teachers*
Compilation by teachers that details how "habits of mind" are developed most effectively in specific subjects. (http://bit.ly/eB74ey)

Charles Fadel and Bernie Trilling: *21st Century Skills: Learning for Life in Our Times*
This book explores the three main categories of 21st century skills as defined by P21: learning and innovations skills; digital literacy skills; and life and career skills. It includes a DVD with numerous video examples from classrooms where 21st century teaching is taking place. (http://amzn.to/clwMNv)

Robert Marzano and Debra Pickering: *The Highly Engaged Classroom*
Designed as a self-study text, this book provides a practical guide for how to generate high levels of student attention and engagement. It summarizes key research and translates it into recommendations for classroom practice. (http://bit.ly/e6xkix)

Betsy Moore and Todd Stanley: *Critical Thinking and Formative Assessments: Increasing Rigor in Your Classroom*
Building from a careful explanation of Bloom's Taxonomy, this 2010 title provides many practical classroom applications to help teachers promote critical thinking in a variety of subject areas. Found throughout are strategies that can be immediately put to use in the classroom. (http://amzn.to/dGelbI)

David N. Perkins, Heidi Goodrich, Shari Tishman, and Jill Mirman Owen: *Thinking Connections: Learning to Think and Thinking to Learn*
This title from Harvard's Project Zero research group includes step-by-step instructions and practical suggestions for teaching critical thinking strategies. (http://pzpublications.com/31.html)

Peter Senge, et al.: *Schools That Learn: A Fifth Discipline Fieldbook for Educators, Parents, and Everyone Who Cares About Education*
Senge and his fellow authors present a useful set of concepts and practices to help educators and education stakeholders lead more effective learning environments. (http://amzn.to/amKANO)

Allison Zmuda: *Breaking Free from Myths About Teaching and Learning: Innovation as an Engine for Student Success*
Zmuda suggests that we need to break free from myths about learning and teaching in order to meet the demands of the 21st century. She offers concrete suggestions for transforming schools into engaging, relevant, and meaningful places. (http://ascd.org/publications/books/109041.aspx)

Other Resources

ASCD: *Learning to Think . . . Thinking to Learn*
PD activities designed for large-group workshops, small study groups, and individual study that help teachers promote three major types of thinking skills: information processing skills, critical thinking skills, and complex thinking strategies, with lessons from elementary, middle, and high school classrooms. Includes user guide. (http://shop.ascd.org/productdisplay.cfm?productid=607087)

Edutopia Project Based Learning Videos
Edutopia's website features a number of project based learning video resources that demonstrate how skills like critical thinking can be enabled in classrooms. The videos here include a focus on STEM, science design, and architectural design. (www.edutopia.org/project-based-learning)

ITC Publications: *The TeacherPD Video Series*
This Australian company has produced 20 excellent short videos of teachers demonstrating proven classroom techniques and activities that promote students' critical thinking skills. ITC also publishes teacher diaries and posters that provide critical thinking exercises and strategies. (**www.itcpublications.com.au**)

Microsoft, in association with ISTE: *Developing Critical Thinking Through Web Research Skills*
Lesson plans include prerequisites, rationale, essential concepts, and descriptions of related National Educational Technology Standards (NETS) and are designed for beginner, intermediate, or advanced levels, and are aimed at middle school and secondary students. (http://tinyurl.com/6mgmvoy)

Regional Training Center: Encouraging Skillful, Critical and Creative Thinking—PD Course

Based on recent brain research and learner-centered principles, this is a practical experiential course on how to teach for, of, and about thinking. Topics include the thoughtful and respectful classroom, specific thinking skills and processes, questioning frameworks and methods, metacognition and reflection, graphic organizers, and cooperative learning to enhance thinking. These courses are held on the east coast, but instructor guides may be available for purchase. See course list for details. (www.thertc.net/main.php)

APPENDIX 4

Communication Resource Document

Introduction

Communication is a foundational skill taught throughout K–12 education, most directly in subjects such as English language arts. With the common core standards in ELA, new attention is now being given to literacies across the curriculum (for example, reading/writing in science and nonfiction/technical texts). There has also been a growing body of work relating to the use of technology in communicating effectively. Communication in subjects like mathematics and science is an important topic as well.

Communication is collaborative by nature—which is why some definitions of communication (see P21, for example) specifically tie communication to collaboration and highlight the interactive aspects of communication.

Definitions

Communication skills have been defined by a broad number of organizations and initiatives. Following are a few common ones for consideration:

P21

Communicate Clearly

- Articulate thoughts and ideas effectively using oral, written, and nonverbal communication skills in a variety of forms and contexts
- Listen effectively to decipher meaning, including knowledge, values, attitudes, and intentions
- Use communication for a range of purposes (for example, to inform, instruct, motivate, and persuade)
- Utilize multiple media and technologies, and know how to judge their effectiveness *a priori* as well as assess their impact
- Communicate effectively in diverse environments (including multilingual)

SCANS

"Communication" is represented in the following *three* components of the SCANS Framework:

Writing
Communicates thoughts, ideas, information, and messages in writing; records information completely and accurately; composes and creates documents such as letters, directions, manuals, reports, proposals, graphs, flow charts; uses language, style, organization, and format appropriate to the subject matter, purpose, and audience.

Listening
Receives, attends to, interprets, and responds to verbal messages and other cues such as body language in ways that are appropriate to the purpose.

Speaking

Organizes ideas and communicates oral messages appropriate to listeners and situations; participates in conversation, discussion, and group presentations; selects an appropriate medium for conveying a message; uses verbal language and other cues such as body language; speaks clearly and communicates a message.

"Communication" as defined by EFF Content Standards for Adult Literacy:

Speak So Others Can Understand

Determine the purpose for communicating; organize and relay information to effectively serve the purpose, context, and listener; pay attention to conventions of oral English communication, including grammar, word choice, register, pace, and gesture in order to minimize barriers to listener's comprehension; use multiple strategies to monitor the effectiveness of the communication.

Listen Actively

Attend to oral information; clarify purpose for listening and use listening strategies appropriate to that purpose; monitor comprehension, adjusting listening strategies to overcome barriers to comprehension; integrate information from listening with prior knowledge to address listening purpose.

Convey Ideas in Writing

Determine the purpose for communicating; organize and present information to serve the purpose, context, and audience; pay attention to conventions of English language usage, including grammar, spelling, and sentence structure, to minimize barriers to reader's comprehension; seek feedback and revise to enhance the effectiveness of the communication.

General Reading

NCTE's 21st Century Curriculum and Assessment Framework

Twenty-first century readers and writers need to:

- Develop proficiency with the tools of technology
- Build relationships with others to pose and solve problems collaboratively and cross-culturally
- Design and share information for global communities to meet a variety of purposes
- Manage, analyze, and synthesize multiple streams of simultaneous information
- Create, critique, analyze, and evaluate multimedia texts
- Attend to the ethical responsibilities required by these complex environments

(www.ncte.org/positions/statements/21stcentframework)

New Literacies Research Lab

Lisa Zawilinski, Donald Leu, and members of the New Literacies Research Lab share additional thoughts on 21st century literacies. Good insights on how digital texts and information are affecting reading, writing, and communication skills. (www.ncte.org/magazine/extended)

Classroom Talk/Accountable Talk

Chapter Five: Procedures for Classroom Talk, **Content-Area Conversations** *by Douglas Fisher, Nancy Frey, and Carol Rothenberg*

This chapter includes focus on English language learners, discusses the types of classroom talk that can be enhanced (including accountable talk), and includes discussion of how to structure effective collaborative discussions and groups with emphasis on communication. (www.ascd.org/publications/books/108035/chapters/Procedures-for-Classroom-Talk.aspx)

Institute for Learning: Accountable Talk Resources

The Institute for Learning at the University of Pittsburgh was founded by Lauren Resnick in 1995. Resnick, an internationally renowned cognitive psychologist, Senior Scientist at the Learning Research and Development Center of the University of Pittsburgh, and leader in the standards movement, was asked by leading practitioners to help them achieve the goals of the standards movement—giving all students the opportunity to reach or exceed world-class standards.

The Institute's website has numerous resources on Accountable Talk, pioneered by Resnick. She describes Accountable Talk as "talk that is orchestrated by teachers so that students learn to formulate responses to problems, interpretations of text that are correct in disciplinary terms and go beyond what was actually written there . . . The basic idea is that the more you manipulate the pieces of knowledge, the better you understand them, the better you remember them, the more complex your memories become and the smarter you get." (http://ifl.lrdc.pitt.edu/ifl)

Video of Resnick Describing Accountable Talk

(http://ifl.lrdc.pitt.edu/ifl/index.php/resources/ask_the_educator/lauren_resnick)

Accountable Talk Sourcebook for Classroom Conversation That Works

Sarah Michaels, Clark University, Mary Catherine O'Connor, Boston University, Megan Williams Hall, University of Pittsburgh with Lauren B. Resnick University of Pittsburgh (http://ifl.lrdc.pitt.edu/ifl/index.php/download/ats)

Accountable Talk: General Overview

This clear, concise overview is focused on fourth to sixth graders. (http://www.scholastic.ca/education/movingupwithliteracyplace/tiparchivepdfs/tip-0311.html)

ICT Literacy

General resources related to information, communications, and technology literacy (ICT literacy):

- P21 ICT Literacy Maps (http://bit.ly/mLS0hA)
- ETS Report on ICT Literacy (http://bit.ly/mk7enm)
- Digital Literacy Portal (www.ictliteracy.info)
- National Center for Technology Literacy (www.mos.org/nctl)
- Teacher Tools on ICT Literacy (http://bit.ly/kdtPLJ)

Teacher Tools

The Reading and Writing Project

K–8 writing samples (http://tc.readingandwritingproject.com/resources/student-writing/
kindergarten)

Creative Communication Skills Activities for High School Students

(www.essortment.com/teaching-good-communication-skills-classroom-36140.html)

Rubrics

Edutopia Analytical Writing Rubric

(http://tinyurl.com/6tdujyo)

K–8 Continuum for Assessing Narrative Writing

(http://tc.readingandwritingproject.com/public/themes/rwproject/resources/assessments/
writing/narrative_writing_continuum.pdf)

Science Communication Rubric

(www.scienceforall.com/BWLP/PlanVisit/rubric.pdf)

Written and Oral Communications Skills Rubric (Marzano 2000)

(www.uen.org/Rubric/rubric.cgi?rubric_id=1226)

From Higher Ed Institutions (adaptable for K–12)

Higher Education Rubrics: Scroll down to see communication rubrics (focused on
higher education). (http://business.fullerton.edu/centers/CollegeAssessmentCenter/
RubricDirectory/other_rubrics.htm)

Team Oral Presentation (www.cse.ohio-state.edu/~neelam/abet/DIRASSMNT/
oralTeamPresRubric.html)

Individual Oral Presentation (www.cse.ohio-state.edu/~neelam/abet/DIRASSMNT/
oralPresRubric.html)

21st Century Communication Rubric, Amphitheater District, Tucson, AZ

Education leaders use this rubric to measure students' communications skills. It offers
strategies for clearly and easily evaluating oral and written communications, as well
as the usage of presentation tools and technology. (www.p21.org/route21/index.
php?option=com_jlibrary&view=details&id=849&Itemid=179)

Writing to Persuade Rubric

(www.intercom.net/local/school/sdms/mspap/wkidpers.html)

Utah Department of Education Writing Rubric

This scoring guide includes the categories of "voice," "ideas and content," and "sentence fluency." (www.schools.utah.gov/eval/DOCUMENTS/UBSCT_WRITING_SCORING_RUBRIC.pdf)

Books

***Teaching Communication Skills to Students with Severe Disabilities, Second Edition* by June E. Downing, Ph.D., with invited contributors**
(www.brookespublishing.com/store/books/downing-7551/index.htm)

***Powerful Conversations: How High Impact Leaders Communicate* by Phil Harkins**
Powerful Conversations is aimed at maximizing the impact of your communications. Specific guidelines show you how to personalize Harkins' program to your own unique style and situation. Examples of Powerful Conversation techniques in action, case studies, and self-tests help you analyze your own conversational style.(http://amzn.to/ipNNna)

***The Fifth Discipline Fieldbook: Strategies and Tools for Building a Learning Organization* by Peter M. Senge et al.**
This book is a compendium of articles, case studies, and exercises for developing a learning organization. Key to the creation and maintenance of a learning organization is interpersonal communication skills, which are highlighted throughout the book.(http://amzn.to/ktgxh3)

***Difficult Conversations: How to Discuss What Matters Most* by Douglas Stone, Bruce Patton, Sheila Heen, and Roger Fisher**
This book was developed from 10 years of work at the Harvard Negotiation Project. Written to help professionals, parents, teachers, government officials, corporations, and communities, Difficult Conversations offers a concrete, step-by-step approach to preparing for and conducting your most challenging conversations. (http://amzn.to/lraLUE)

Organizations/Initiatives/Professional Development

The New Literacies Research Lab

The New Literacies Research Lab at the University of Connecticut is the most widely recognized center in the world for conducting research on the new reading comprehension and learning skills required by the Internet and other emerging information and communication technologies. Our work develops research-based evidence to prepare students for their literacy and learning future. (www.newliteracies.uconn.edu/index.html)

National Writing Project

Unique in breadth and scale, the NWP is a network of sites anchored at colleges and universities and serving teachers across disciplines and at all levels, early childhood through university. We provide professional development, develop resources, generate research, and act on knowledge to improve the teaching of writing and learning in schools and communities. (www.nwp.org)

Miscellaneous Resources/Links

Building Effective Interpersonal Communication Skills: Self-Assessment Exercise

(http://spot.pcc.edu/~rjacobs/career/effective_communication_skills.htm)

ESL and Communication Skills

Teaching Social Communication Skills to ESL Kids (www.suite101.com/content/teaching-social-communication-skills-to-kids-a147871)

Teaching Listening Skills (www.abax.co.jp/listen/index.html)

Activities for ELL Students (www.pcieducation.com/store/default.aspx?DepartmentId=48&CategoryId=5)

Everything I Know About Presentations I Learned in Theatre School

Engaging list of how to create engaging oral presentations (www.darrenbarefoot.com/archives/2007/09/everything-i-know-about-presentations-i-learned-in-theatre-school.html)

How Good Are Your Communication Skills? Self-Test

(www.mindtools.com/pages/article/newCS_99.htm)

Thinkfinity

Verizon Thinkfinity offers comprehensive teaching and learning resources in each academic subject and literacy. The easy-to-navigate K–12 resources are grade-specific and are aligned with state standards. (www.thinkfinity.org) (www.thinkfinity.org/21st-century-skills)

Vocational Information Center List of Communication Resources

(www.khake.com/page66.html)

APPENDIX 5

Collaboration Resource Document

Introduction

Integrating collaboration into teaching and learning for every student requires a serious re-think of the entire learning enterprise. That's because doing this work well requires a cooperative culture of practice throughout the school and district. Teachers must move beyond traditional, isolated practices and work more often in teams if they are to model the collaboration skills they expect of students. District leaders must also model these skills and create policies that support teachers in this work (for example, common planning time).

When discussing the issue of collaboration skills, it is also important to distinguish between the *student outcomes* (a student's ability to collaborate effectively) and the *supportive methods and structures that enable these outcomes* (something that is often referred to in education literature as "cooperative learning"). This document details some commonly available resources to help education leaders identify best practices in cooperative learning with the goal of improving collaboration skills among all students.

A quick note about technology and collaboration: Collaborative technologies play a transformational role in cooperative learning. The capacity for educators and students to collaborate in extraordinary ways using digital tools, regardless of time or place, is improving at a rapid pace. However, technology tools will not be very useful if they are simply "add-ons"—the ability to coordinate, communicate, and work in teams using digital tools promotes powerful learning only when the underlying structures of the education system actually prioritize and support cooperative learning at every level.

So, as you begin to think about collaboration, we invite you to consider the following questions.

1. Are you modeling effective collaboration skills for your students?
2. Do your learning environments support collaboration skills?
3. Do your students have numerous, high-quality opportunities to work in diverse teams?
4. Are classroom teachers and specialists being supported in improving their practices for collaborative, cooperative learning?

Definition

How do we define "collaboration skills"? There are several ways to think about the definition of collaboration when it comes to teaching and learning environments. Three basic ones include:

Students

A student-centered definition of collaboration skills, from P21, is as follows:

Collaborate with Others

- Demonstrate ability to work effectively and respectfully with diverse teams
- Exercise flexibility and willingness to be helpful in making necessary compromises to accomplish a common goal
- Assume shared responsibility for collaborative work, and value the individual contributions made by each team member

Professional Staff Capacity

A teacher-focused standard for collaboration skills (from Learning Forward/NSDC) is:

Staff development that improves the learning of all students [and] provides educators with the knowledge and skills to collaborate.

Education Leaders

A commonly cited framework for *cooperative learning*, a primary support system for enabling collaboration skills among students and educators, is from David Johnson and Roger Johnson (http://www.co-operation.org/):

Cooperative learning is the instructional use of small groups so that students work together to maximize their own and each other's learning. It may be contrasted with competitive (students work against each other to achieve an academic goal such as a grade of "A" that only one or a few students can attain) and individualistic (students work by themselves to accomplish learning goals unrelated to those of the other students) learning.

Johnson and Johnson highlight five key elements of cooperative learning:

- Individual accountability
- Positive interdependence
- Face-to-face promotive interaction
- Group processing
- Interpersonal skills and small-group skills

Resources

All Things PLC

The All Things PLC website provides research, articles, data, and tools to educators who seek information about Professional Learning Communities at Work™. This information is provided so schools and districts have relevant, practical knowledge and tools as they create and sustain their professional learning communities.

- Teamwork and collaboration research articles (www.allthingsplc.info/articles/articles .php#10)
- PLC Tools and Resources: (www.allthingsplc.info/tools/print.php#13)
- Making Time for Collaboration (planning tool): (www.allthingsplc.info/pdf/tools/ makingtimeforcollaboration.pdf)

143

Assessing the Common Core Standards: Collaboration (Andrew Miller)

This blog discusses the presence of collaboration in the common core state standards and how it might be assessed: "One on the most striking and pleasant surprises that I encountered in the Common Core Standards was the prevalence of Collaboration. This alone says that we are on the right track with common core. What is a needed 21st Century Skill? Collaboration." (http://www.andrewkmiller.com/tag/common-core-standards/page/2/)

Buck Institute for Education (BIE)

BIE is one of the leading nonprofit organizations focusing on project-based learning in schools. Its website includes excellent materials related to PBL research, professional development, curricula, and assessments. Its PBL Starter Kit is a widely used and cited resource in the field. (www.bie.org) (www.bie.org/research) (www.bie.org/tools/freebies) (www.bie.org/store/item/pbl_handbook)

Classroom Instruction that Works (Robert J. Marzano, Debra J. Pickering, and Jane E. Pollock)

This highly regarded book includes an excellent section on cooperative learning. (www.amazon.com/Classroom-Instruction-That-Works-Research-Based/dp/0871205041)

Classroom Management that Works (Robert J. Marzano, Jana S. Marzano, and Debra J. Pickering)

Book description from Amazon: "How does classroom management affect student achievement? What techniques do teachers find most effective? How important are schoolwide policies and practices in setting the tone for individual classroom management? In this follow-up to *What Works in Schools,* Robert J. Marzano analyzes research from more than 100 studies on classroom management to discover the answers to these questions and more. He then applies these findings to a series of 'Action Steps'—specific strategies that educators can use." (http://amzn.to/lT7Dov)

Coral: Collaborative Online Research and Learning

CORAL is a multidisciplinary collaborative task force composed of members at various universities who have been dedicated to creating and testing a model for the integration of technology with collaborative teaching and learning. The **CORAL** group believes classrooms should provide places where students have the opportunity to be learners actively working together on a specific learning objective, a goal endorsed by the Forum on Technology in Education. Therefore, the model developed by the **CORAL** project has used the Internet as a collaborative tool connecting university-level students in varied disciplines and at distant sites in an effort to complete a joint project. (http://coral.wcupa.edu)

Collaborative Group Techniques

UMass Scientific Reasoning Research Institute

This is an accessible yet comprehensive overview of various types of cooperative learning structures and teaching methods. (http://srri.umass.edu/topics/collaborative-group-techniques)

Commonly Asked Questions about Teaching Collaborative Activities

Schreyer Institute for Teaching Excellence—Penn State

This is an excellent Q&A focused on higher education that is also applicable to K–12 (particularly high school) educators. Topics include dealing with conflict in groups and assessing collaborative work. (http://bit.ly/eNVcGc)

Cooperative Learning Institute and Interaction Book Company

The organization founded by David Johnson and Roger Johnson offers a wide range of helpful resources and background materials on cooperative learning. (www.co-operation.org/?page_id=65)

Cooperative Learning—ASCD Education Leadership Issue Jan 1990

In this issue, articles by noted cooperative learning experts are freely available online. (www.ascd.org/publications/educational-leadership/dec89/vol47/num04/toc.aspx)

Creating Online Professional Learning Communities and How to Translate Practices to the Virtual Classroom

This resource details what professional learning communities in schools are, who joins them, and how they work. (www.elearnmag.org/subpage.cfm?section=articles&article=122-1)

Developing Student Collaboration Skills with Google Docs

This presentation covers why the ability to collaborate effectively is a critical skill, what student collaboration looks like in a personalized learning environment, and how to facilitate student collaboration through Google Docs. (www.edtechteam.com/workshops/2010-10-27-bell)

Department of Education: Teacher's Guide to International Collaboration on the Internet

A list of resources for cross-cultural interaction and project work; compiled by the Department of Education. (www2.ed.gov/teachers/how/tech/international/guide_pg2.html)

DuFour: Resources on PLCs

Richard and Becky DuFour have led exemplary work around professional learning communities and collaboration for decades. Selected resources:

- *Learning by Doing: A Handbook for Professional Communities at Work* (http://amzn.to/jwiLdK)
- *Getting Started: Reculturing Schools to Become Professional Learning Communities* (http://amzn.to/j6eDEY)
- *Work Together but Only If You Want To:* In this Phi Delta Kappa article from February 2011, DuFour argues that collaboration should not be voluntary in schools: "In order to establish schools in which interdependence and collaboration are the new norm, we must create the structures and cultures that embed collaboration in the routine practice of our schools, ensure that the collaborative efforts focus on the right work, and support educators as they build their capacity to work together rather than alone." (http://allthingsplc.info/articles/KapanMagazineRickDuFour2011.pdf)

- NSDC's compilation of columns on community and cooperative learning in schools (www.learningforward.org/news/authors/dufour.cfm)

The GLOBE Program

The Global Learning and Observations to Benefit the Environment (GLOBE) program is a worldwide, hands-on, primary and secondary school-based science and education program. GLOBE's vision promotes and supports students, teachers, and scientists to collaborate on inquiry-based investigations of the environment and the Earth system working in close partnership with NASA, NOAA, and NSF Earth System Science Projects (ESSPs) in study and research about the dynamics of Earth's environment. (http://globe .gov/about)

Dr. Spencer Kagan

Kagan's work on cooperative learning spans decades and is widely cited and used. Several highlights include:

- *Kagan Cooperative Learning*: The book written by Dr. Spencer Kagan and Miguel Kagan, updated (http://bit.ly/9yWWNI)
- Kagan Publishing & Professional Development—workshops, tools and resources: (www .kaganonline.com)
- Kagan catalog of additional reading (excellent list of publications related to cooperative learning at all grade levels) (http://bit.ly/jWCaVe)
- Simple, brief summary of Kagan Structures (http://bit.ly/kTIDzD)

Peter Noonan on "Common Language, Common Definitions"

Be Inkandescent magazine, May 2010
In this article, Peter Noonan of Fairfax County Public Schools discusses the importance of student-centered, cooperative, and collaborative learning environments. Other educators are also featured. (http://bit.ly/iWMEY2)

Meta Collab

A discussion of Wikiversity and other collaboration efforts—the wiki on collaboration. (http://collaboration.wikia.com/wiki/Category:Education)

NoodleTools: Curriculum Collaboration Toolkit

Very helpful Q&A for teachers that provides you with links to various documents and suggestions on collaboration. (www.noodletools.com/debbie/consult/collab)

Rubrics

- BIE collaboration rubric (www.bie.org/images/uploads/useful_stuff/PBL_St_Kit_rubrics .pdf)
- The New Tech collaboration rubric (www.p21.org/route21/index.php?option= com_jlibrary&view=details&task=download&id=382)
- SCORE collaboration rubric (www.sdcoe.net/score/actbank/collaborub.html)
- SDSU collaboration rubric (http://edweb.sdsu.edu/triton/tidepoolunit/rubrics/ collrubric.html)

Teachnology Cooperative Learning Resources

Good, accessible overview of cooperative learning with summaries of major authors, researchers, and best practices in the field. Summaries of Kagan, Johnson and Johnson, Slavin, and others. (www.teach-nology.com/litined/cooperative_learning)

Using Groups Effectively: 10 Principles

Kevin Washburn, Edurati Review

This is a useful list of 10 principles for teaching collaboration effectively in classrooms. Answers questions such as: When are groups effective as means of learning? What tasks are better accomplished collaboratively than individually? How do you structure groups for optimal effectiveness and results? (http://eduratireview.com/2011/01/using-groups-effectively-10-principles)

APPENDIX 6

Creativity Resource Document

Definition

Following is the definition for creativity (in this case, including innovation) as established by the Partnership for 21st Century Skills. We welcome your suggestions for additional indicators.

Think Creatively

- Use a wide range of idea creation techniques (such as brainstorming)
- Create new and worthwhile ideas (both incremental and radical concepts)
- Elaborate, refine, analyze, and evaluate their own ideas in order to improve and maximize creative efforts

Work Creatively with Others

- Develop, implement, and communicate new ideas to others effectively
- Be open and responsive to new and diverse perspectives; incorporate group input and feedback into the work
- Demonstrate originality and inventiveness in work and understand the real world limits to adopting new ideas
- View failure as an opportunity to learn; understand that creativity and innovation is a long-term, cyclical process of small successes and frequent mistakes

Implement Innovations

- Act on creative ideas to make a tangible and useful contribution to the field in which the innovation will occur

Food for Thought/Briefs/Background

Can imagination be taught?

Article by Mike Antonucci for Stanford Magazine that details the "innovation hothouse" approach used by the d.school (formally, the Hasso Plattner Institute of Design at Stanford) and how it is "changing the way people think." (http://bit.ly/fmZ1qh)

The Creativity Crisis

This *Newsweek* article by Po Bronson and Ashley Merryman is an excellent background document for strategic conversations around creativity in education. It covers some of the historical and global context of creativity in the classroom and its importance in the 21st century economy. The piece also details emerging research on cognition and neuroscience and how these new findings are changing how we think about creativity. (http://www.thedailybeast.com/newsweek/2010/07/10/the-creativity-crisis.html)

148

Cultivating the Imagination

This short piece by John Seely Brown and Douglas Thomas discusses the critical difference between imagination and creativity: "Creativity and imagination are each important tools for the growth and development of learning in the 21st century, but it is critical that we understand how each operates in order to better use our resources to understand, build, create and play in the knowledge economies and environments of the digital world." (http://tinyurl.com/46oy8wd)

How Nonsense Sharpens the Intellect

This piece by Benedict Carey in the *New York Times* is excellent. A snippet: "New research supports what many experimental artists, habitual travelers and other novel seekers have always insisted: at least some of the time, disorientation begets creative thinking." (http://nyti.ms/dZmcxn)

How—and why—to teach innovation in our schools

This eSchool News article by Alexander Hiam discusses the "five Is": Imagination, Inquiry, Invention, Implementation, and Initiative. (http://bit.ly/hPCiUv)

It's Time to Get Serious About Creativity in the Classroom

Jim Moulton's Edutopia blog post discusses "freedom within a structure"—in other words, making the assignment clear and focused, but allowing real freedom in how the tasks will be accomplished: "Let's say we bring a group of kids into the art room and tell them they can do whatever they want. Will they become creative? I always thought the answer to this was yes, but turns out the answer is no." (www.edutopia.org/freedom-structure-balance-classroom)

Music and the Brain Podcasts

The Library of Congress resources on Music and the Brain project offer lectures, conversations, and symposia about the explosion of new research at the intersection of cognitive neuroscience and music. Project chair Kay Redfield Jamison convenes scientists and scholars, composers, performers, theorists, physicians, psychologists, and other experts at the Library for a compelling two-year series. (www.loc.gov/podcasts/musicandthebrain/index.html)

Neuroscience Sheds New Light on Creativity

This Fast Company article by Gregory Berns discusses what neuroscience reveals about how to come up with new ideas: "In order to think creatively, you must develop new neural pathways and break out of the cycle of experience-dependent categorization. As Mark Twain said, 'Education consists mainly in what we have unlearned.' For most people, this does not come naturally. Often, the harder you try to think differently, the more rigid the categories become." (www.fastcompany.com/magazine/129/rewiring-the-creative-mind.html)

On the Psychology of Creativity (Book Chapter)

Book Chapter (2009) by Joachim Funke that provides an overview about creativity from a psychological point of view is given (http://bit.ly/gocMwa)

Sir Ken Robinson on Schools that Kill Creativity (TED talk—video)

Sir Ken Robinson makes an entertaining and profoundly moving case for creating an education system that nurtures (rather than undermines) creativity. (www.ted.com/talks/ken_robinson_says_schools_kill_creativity.html)

Think Again Video (meeting opener/conversation starter—video)

Think Again is a humorous and inspiring look at some of history's most famous innovations and at how some very smart and successful people initially dismissed them as impossible. (www.youtube.com/watch?v=3NPL2f0WVEM&feature=youtube_gdata)

Professional Development

The following resources help teachers understand how to promote the creativity and innovation skills of their students.

ASCD: Promoting Creativity and Innovation in the Classroom

Drawing from what innovative Fortune 500 companies do to promote creativity and innovation in the workplace, this video shows real-world strategies for classroom curricula and instruction. Additional tools are also available. (http://shop.ascd.org/productdisplay.cfm?categoryid=books&productid=609096)

Creativity Workshop

The Creativity Workshop (founded in 1993) is dedicated to helping educators develop and nurture their creativity and that of their students. The Creativity Workshop has developed a unique series of simple and effective exercises aimed at keeping the creative juices flowing both in the classroom and personally. The Creativity Workshop is a professional development opportunity that includes learning, travel, available credits, and association with peers from all over the world. (http://creativityworkshop.com/index.html)

Creativity in the Classroom: What Research Says to the Teacher (Paul Torrance)

This booklet discusses this creativity and explores the evidences of change in educational objectives, teaching methods, curriculum and instructional materials, procedures for identifying creative talent, and the assessment of creative achievement. (http://1.usa.gov/f3cMI9)

CyberSmart: Authentic Learning and Creativity

This online workshop provides educators with hands-on practice in engaging students in real-world tasks that require the use of technology and in exploring ways of developing students' creative thinking. (http://cybersmart.org/workshops/smart/learningcreativity)

Professional Development: Supporting Creativity in the Classroom

This article by Alice Sterling Honig underscores the importance of creative thinking in your educational program, especially in getting children to think "outside the box." (www2.scholastic.com/browse/article.jsp?id=10583)

Project Zero

This research center located at Harvard Graduate School of Education publishes a number of titles on creativity, with a special focus on how teachers can promote it in their classrooms. (http://pzpublications.com/creativity.html)

School and Classroom Tools

Arts Edge—The Kennedy Center

This rich website features lessons, activities, projects, and curriculum guidelines for educators to use to promote creativity in the arts, history, literature, and other humanities disciplines. In addition, there are a wealth of multimedia resources and ideas for encouraging the use of technology as a creative educational tool. (http://artsedge.kennedy-center.org/educators.aspx)

Critical and Creative Thinking—Bloom's Taxonomy

This site addresses key questions such as: What are critical thinking and creative thinking? What's Bloom's taxonomy, and how is it helpful in project planning? How are the domains of learning reflected in technology-rich projects? (http://eduscapes.com/tap/topic69.htm)

Dan Pink's Right Brain Discussion Guide for Educators

This basic discussion guide encourages educators to consider how their education systems are incorporating "right brain" (creative) approaches to teaching and learning. The guide draws from Pink's book *A Whole New Mind*. (www.danpink.com/PDF/AWNMforeducators.pdf)

Habits of Mind in Math (Blog Post)

This blog post contains a thoughtful list of ideas that touch on the issue of creativity/ "tinkering" (see items #5 and #6) in mathematics. The ideas here, as well as the comments section, might prove thought-provoking ones for educators who are interested in exploring inquiry-based approaches to mathematics instruction (a subject that can be challenging when it comes to creativity). (http://mathteacherorstudent.blogspot.com/2010/09/habits-of-mind.html)

Intel: Visual Ranking, Seeing Reason, and Showing Evidence Tools

These free online tools are effective ways of bringing idea creation techniques into the classroom. Tutorials, project examples, and instructional strategies are also provided. (www.intel.com/education/teachers)

Mathematics and the Arts

The theme of this issue of the Notices of the American Mathematical Society is "Mathematics and the Arts." These four articles showcase different aspects of mathematics and art. (www.ams.org/notices/201001)

Teaching Creativity

Written by an art teacher, this article covers pedagogical approaches to teaching creativity in the classroom: "I write this as an art teacher for other art teachers. However, I think teachers in every area need to reflect on what they are doing that tends to foster or

151

hinder the creative critical thinking that is so essential as a survival and success skill in today's world." (www2.goshen.edu/~marvinpb/arted/tc.html)

The Creative Wisconsin Guide for Local Community Action Planning: A Toolkit for Communities Seeking to Advance the Arts and Creativity in Education

This guidebook provides valuable tools and processes for local teams—composed of representatives from area businesses, schools, community groups, and cultural arts organizations—to improve arts and creativity in education in their communities. (www.creative.wisconsin.gov)

The Marshmallow Challenge

The Marshmallow Challenge is a remarkably fun and instructive design exercise that encourages teams to experience simple but profound lessons in collaboration, innovation, and creativity. (www.marshmallowchallenge.com/Welcome.html)

For a fascinating take on who does this challenge best, see this TED talk: (www.ted.com/talks/lang/eng/tom_wujec_build_a_tower.html)

Route 21

Route 21, a P21 online database, houses dozens of articles, chapters, classroom tools, and other items related to creativity. We have highlighted a few below, but we encourage you to visit the site and type "creativity" in the search box to browse the full range of materials. (www.p21.org/route21) keyword "creativity"

- *Identifying and Developing Creative Giftedness* by Robert Sternberg
- Chapter from "The Cambridge handbook of thinking and reasoning" by Robert Sternberg, Todd Lubart, James Kaufman, and Jean Pretz discussing creativity.
- *Creativity: Developmental and Cross-Cultural Issues* by Todd Lubart

STEM to STEAM

The issue of creativity in STEM subjects is a topic unto itself; we have included several pieces below that address the addition of the "arts" to STEM (aka "STEAM").

ArtStem

An ongoing initiative of the Thomas S. Kenan Institute for the Arts at the University of North Carolina School of the Arts (UNCSA), in Winston Salem. Inspired by artists and scholars who efface the lines between "the arts" and the "STEM" disciplines, the project brought together academic and arts faculty members from UNCSA with an interdisciplinary team of public school educators for an academic summer seminar about teaching and learning at the intersection of the arts and STEM disciplines, followed by a year of creative teaching collaborations and programming. (www.artstem.org)

Bridging STEM to STE(A)M: Developing New Frameworks for ART/SCIENCE Pedagogy

Artists, scientists, researchers, educators, and leaders in information and creative technology gathered at this NSF-funded workshop held at the Rhode Island School of Design, January 21–22, 2011, to explore the questions: What do you consider the greatest potential of your field of research, work, or teaching? How might you see the value of your work benefiting from interaction with other disciplines? (www.stemtosteam.org)

Innovation, Education, and the Maker Movement

This report covers the "Proceedings from the Maker Faire Workshop at the New York Hall of Science" held September 26–27, 2010. (www.nysci.org/media/file/MakerFaireReportFinal122310.pdf)

On Meaningful Observation

This piece by John Maeda, President of Rhode Island School of Design (RISD), discusses the notion of adding art and design to science education—often referred to as "STEAM" rather than "STEM" education. It's a nice context piece for talking about creativity and art in education. (http://seedmagazine.com/content/article/on_meaningful_observation1)

Assessment

EdSteps: Creativity Assessment Project

EdSteps aims to understand the complexities of creativity and how to promote creativity in the classroom. EdSteps defines creativity as the valued uses and outcomes of originality driven by imagination, invention, and curiosity. The EdSteps tool aims to measure the originality and impact of creativity within and across all disciplines. (http://bit.ly/fJ5TIX)

Rubrics for Creativity

- Catalina Foothills School District (http://bit.ly/focKV8)
- Intel Teach Elements Rubric (http://filesocial.com/7sy660f)
- Creative Thinking Skills (from state of Kansas) (www.adifferentplace.org/creativethinking.htm)
- Dance through Poetry Rubric (http://gcuonline.georgian.edu/wootton_l/dancing_through_poetry_rubric.htm)
- Metiri (http://akron4.metiri.wikispaces.net/Creativity+Rubrics)
- VALUE Rubric (www.aacu.org/value/rubrics/pdf/CreativeThinking.pdf)

Torrance Tests of Creative Thinking, Torrance Center

The Torrance Center for Creativity & Talent Development is a service, research, and instructional center concerned with the identification and development of creative potential and with gifted and future studies. Its goals are to investigate, implement, and evaluate techniques for enhancing creative thinking and to facilitate national and international systems that support creative development.

- Overview of the test (www.indiana.edu/~bobweb/Handout/d3.ttct.htm)
- The center's website (www.coe.uga.edu/torrance)

Books

Coloring Outside the Lines by René Díaz-Lefebvre

Explores the application of Howard Gardner's theory of Multiple Intelligences in developing a community college curriculum that enhances an educator's ability to teach students based upon their dominant intelligences, such as verbal/linguistic or musical/rhythmic. (http://1.usa.gov/dLqqKA)

The Rise of the Creative Class by Richard Florida

Florida's book focuses on the context of the creative economy and how cities and people relate to this 21st century shift. (www.amazon.com/Rise-Creative-Class-Transforming-Community/dp/0465024769) (www.creativeclass.com)

Unscripted Learning: Using Improv Activities Across the K–8 Curriculum by Carrie Lobman

Improvisation is recognized internationally as an exciting tool to jumpstart learning. In this practical book, teachers will discover how to use improv throughout the K–8 curriculum to boost creativity and to develop a class into a finely tuned learning ensemble. Readers will learn how to use this revolutionary tool to teach literacy, math, social studies, and science. (http://amzn.to/h6kAP8)

Creating a Digitally Rich Classroom: Teaching and Learning in a Web 2.0 World by Meg Ormiston

This book provides a research base and practical strategies for using Web 2.0 tools to create engaging lessons that transform and enrich content. (http://bit.ly/fOoTvw)

A Whole New Mind by Daniel Pink

The era of "left brain" dominance and the Information Age that it engendered are giving way to a new world in which "right brain" qualities—inventiveness, empathy, meaning—predominate. That's the argument at the center of this provocative and original book, which uses the two sides of our brains as a metaphor for understanding the contours of our times. (www.danpink.com/whole-new-mind)

The Power of the Creative Classroom: An Educator's Guide for Exploring Creative Teaching and Learning (The Creative Classroom Series, Volume 2) by Ron Ritchhart and Tina Blythe

(www.amazon.com/Power-Creative-Classroom-Educators-Exploring/dp/B000OBDMVO)

Out of Our Minds: Learning to Be Creative (new edition 2011) by Sir Ken Robinson

This book focuses on how to reach true creative potential by thinking differently. (www.amazon.com/Out-Our-Minds-Learning-Creative/dp/1907312471/ref=sr_1_1?ie=UTF8&s=books&qid=1301422133&sr=8-1) Also see his website (http://sirkenrobinson.com/skr)

Sparks of Genius: the 13 Thinking Tools of the World's Most Creative People by Robert and Michéle Root-Bernstein

Exercise your imagination and set off sparks of genius. Explore the "thinking tools" of extraordinary people, from Albert Einstein and Jane Goodall to Amadeus Mozart and Virginia Woolf, and learn how you can practice the same imaginative skills to become your creative best. (http://amzn.to/hNd9Up)

The Creative Habit by Twyla Tharp

This book by famed choreographer Twyla Tharp is a good resource. She argues that creativity is not just for artists and provides exercises that challenge common creative assumptions. (http://amzn.to/dXyYNw)

APPENDIX 7

Community Groups Outreach Toolkit

EdLeader21 Community Groups Outreach Toolkit

Members have recently requested a toolkit to focus on outreach to the broader community beyond just the business community. We welcome the opportunity to create this "Community Groups Outreach" toolkit. It is offered as a starting point and we encourage you to customize it for your needs.

This toolkit includes:

- An outreach letter to community groups.
- An agenda for a meeting with community groups.
- A set of "engagement questions" to use with community groups.
- A set of "engagement questions" to use with the higher education community.
- A resource page on videos and books you can utilize in this outreach work.
- A draft PowerPoint to use with community groups.

We hope these tools provide you with a helpful starting point for your interaction with community groups.

Background

When it comes to engaging stakeholders and building consensus, it isn't enough just to reach out to the business community. The broader community needs to be cultivated as well. Community and state organizations focused on workforce development and economic development can be helpful allies. Local workforce development boards, for example, understand the need to promote critical thinking, communication, collaboration, and creativity as essential requirements of the 21st century workforce. Once you begin reaching out to these kinds of organizations, it becomes possible to imagine your work fitting within a regional economic development initiative. Some regional projects are already using the 4Cs as a theme for organizing their communities around 21st century economic success. Such regional initiatives have started in Cleveland, Cincinnati, and Northwest Indiana.

Leaders in youth development and informal education are another group to consider for outreach. There are innovative youth development programs all over the country that already recognize the importance of the 4Cs. Such groups are using innovative strategies to prepare at-risk youth for the challenges of the workforce. One such example is the Year Up program in Boston. Companies in Boston fund scholarships for individuals to participate in the Year Up preparation program and make a commitment to hire the individual when the program is completed. It makes great sense for traditional K–12 districts to align themselves with programs like these. The 4Cs vision provides an excellent platform for such partnerships.

Informal education providers are also important partners. After-school programs, youth programs, summer school programs, museums, and public libraries all fall into this category. In some cases, these programs have integrated 21st century skills into their strategies more quickly and more intentionally than their K–12 counterparts. Students who participate in after-school programs—Boy Scouts, Girl Scouts, Little League Soccer, YMCA,

YWCA, 4-H, and so on—are all honing their critical thinking, communication, collaboration, and creativity skills.

The North Salem Central School District in New York is in the midst of a 21st century education initiative focused on creative problem solving. They have been pleasantly surprised to find that the youth development programs in their area have been very enthusiastic and feel very well-aligned with the district's new initiative.

Also, many public library and museum leaders have begun focusing more intently on their roles in supporting 21st century skills in their communities. An initiative of the Institute for Museum and Library Services (IMLS), "21st Century Skills, Museums, and Libraries," can provide a very effective kick-start for a conversation around how leaders in K–12 education, public libraries and museums can work together more closely to foster the development of the 4Cs in your community. (For more information, please see (http://www.imls.gov/about/21st_century_skills_home.aspx)

You might also consider approaching adult education programs. In some communities, you as a K–12 leader might have jurisdiction over those programs. In many communities, they are separate. In any event, many adult education experts have found the 21st century framework relevant and helpful. One notable example is Comprehensive Adult Student Assessment Systems (CASAS). CASAS works with state and local programs to assist youth and adults to improve basic skills, earn a nationally recognized high school diploma (the National External Diploma Program), and develop essential skills to ensure success in the 21st century workplace.

Finally, we encourage you to reach out to the higher education community. The most obvious connection is with colleges of education. Engage them around your vision for the future of education in your district. After all, it is likely that you will be recruiting their graduates who, ideally, should be able to teach and assess the 4Cs. Also, forward-thinking colleges of education can be a resource for you in providing professional development for your teachers around critical aspects of 21st century education. The Partnership for 21st Century Skills and AACTE published *21st Century Knowledge and Skills in Educator Preparation,* a helpful resource on this very topic and can be a helpful resource as you reach out to these partners (see publications at the P21 site, www.p21.org). And NCATE, the accreditation entity for colleges of education has also prepared a new vision that embraces 21st century education strategies for colleges of education. In California, K–12 and higher education leaders worked together to develop the California Early Assessment Program, which has done a remarkable job of improving college readiness among high school graduates (www.calstate.edu/eap/index.shtml).

We also suggest that you engage with the higher education community more broadly. In the draft agenda for the community groups meeting (in this document), we have included sample questions that might be helpful in your dialogues with higher education leaders.

Goals of Community Outreach

The goal of this toolkit is to help you engage in a community dialogue on 21st century education with a diverse set of community members. We suggest you consider inviting representatives from:

- The business community
- After-school programs
- Summer programs
- Youth development programs
- Public libraries
- Museums
- Higher education
- Civic groups

You will be able to add a few categories that make sense in your community. The goal is to energize community representatives around your 21st century education initiative and consider how they can:

- Put such an initiative in place in their institutions.
- Complement your initiative with programs in their institutions.
- Partner with you on joint initiatives to help both of your programs.
- Develop a community-wide approach to 21st century education.

The toolkit will give you the specific tools you need to run an initial outreach session with a broad base of community groups.

Conclusion

Too many educators consider their K–12 strategy to be an internal exercise within their school or district. We are excited that the work of EdLeader21 from the beginning has been framed as *both* external and internal. We believe it is powerful to engage in a dialogue with your community around 21st century education. The potential is not only to build support for a K–12 focused 21st century education initiative, but to also create a broader community response in which *all* of the potential players are working together on a common set of 21st century outcomes for *all* of the learners within the community. We hope this toolkit can help take you in that direction.

Draft Letter to Community Groups

Dear _____,

As you know, our school district has been very committed to helping each of our students prepare for 21st century life, citizenship, and work. We have undertaken an initiative to identify the skills our young people need to be effective citizens and workers.

We very much would like to get your input and hear your suggestions on how we can improve this initiative.

However, we also recognize that this is a conversation that potentially affects our entire community.

- As a community, do we want to consider working collectively on the challenges of 21st century citizenship?
- As a community, do we want to consider working collectively on the challenges of the 21st century workforce?

We would like to invite you to a community dialogue where we will consider questions such as:

- Has your organization identified 21st century outcomes for youth or another key community constituency?
- What work is currently being done in our respective organizations to address some of these outcomes?
- How might the community benefit from a more collaborative approach to addressing some of these competencies?

Your perspective on these questions will help us continue to improve the quality of education in our school or district. It will also help determine whether we would all benefit from some more collaborative or even community-wide approaches to the challenges facing our community's children in the 21st century. An agenda for the meeting is attached.

We hope you will be able to join us.

Most appreciatively,

[insert signature]

Date: _____

Time: _____

Location: _____

Contact: _____

Draft Agenda

[Insert Date/Time/Location/Contact]

Community Conversations on 21st Century Education

  I. Introduction to meeting

 II. Introduction to participants

III. Presentation on 21st Century Education (PowerPoint)

IV. Discussion on 21st century citizenship and 21st century work in our community. Each participant come prepared to discuss:
  a. What work is your organization currently pursuing relative to these challenges?
  b. What might the community do to work more collaboratively on these challenges?

  V. Potential next steps

Note:
Attachment A, Engagement Questions for Dialogue with Community Groups
Attachment B, Engagement Questions for Dialogue with Higher Education Community on 21st Century Education
Attachment C, EdLeader21 Resource Guide—Videos and Books

Engagement Questions for Dialogue with Community Groups on 21st Century Education

Please consider the following questions:

- How can all of you help us better understand the economic and workforce capabilities that our students will need to possess?
- How can all of you help us to better understand the civic capabilities that our students will need to possess?
- How can we in K–12 education better prepare our young people for the challenges of 21st century citizenship?
- How can we in K–12 education better prepare our young people for the challenges of life in the 21st century?

- How can we in K–12 education better align our work with the workforce and economic development needs of our community?
- How can we better align the work of formal with informal education in our community?
- How could we work together to develop a common nomenclature that K–12 educators and the broader community could use in working together to produce students more prepared for the civic and economic needs of the community?
- Can we develop strategies more intentionally purposeful with one another to produce a better set of 21st century education strategies for our young people?
- How could we potentially work together to create community-wide strategies to prepare all of our people for 21st century citizenship and work?

Engagement Questions for Dialogue with the Higher Education Community on 21st Century Education

Please consider the following questions:

- What attributes are you looking for from our students when they graduate from high school?
- What kinds of students is higher education really looking for?
- How do higher education leaders think about the 4Cs?
- What do higher education leaders think about the other student outcomes our school or district is considering focusing on?
- Are there additional competencies that higher education leaders would recommend we focus on, to better prepare our students for college success?
- How do you expect higher education admissions policies to change over the next five to 10 years?
- What work is being done currently in higher education to deliver 21st century skills to college students? What can K–12 education leaders learn from this?
- What changes in pedagogy and assessment are likely to occur in higher education over the next five to 10 years?
- What are the most optimal partnerships between higher education, K–12 schools and districts and the broader community around 21st century citizenship and work?

EdLeader21 Resource Guide: Videos and Books

Specific 21st Century Education Videos

Above and Beyond
An animated video produced by the Partnership for 21st Century Skills and Fablevision that "brings to life" the importance of the 4Cs. This video can be used as an effective discussion starter with educators, parents, students, and community members. (www.p21.org/4Cs)

The Role of 21st Century Leaders in Education
This is a video produced by EdLeader21 and the Pearson Foundation that features several EdLeader21 superintendents. This may be helpful for any meetings that focus on leadership and 21st century education. (www .youtube.com/watch?v=Vsan9hjWSPg)

Video Libraries on 21st Century Skills

BIE: Videos on Project-Based Learning
A great repository of videos on project-based learning produced by BIE. (www.bie.org/videos)

Teach 21
An excellent library of videos of classroom projects produced by the West Virginia Department of Education. The site features videos of the classroom and explanations of the pedagogy by the classroom teacher. (http://wvde.state.wv.us/teach21)

Video 21
This is a very good library of videos on 21st century education maintained by the Partnership for 21st Century Skills. (www.thepartnershipfor21stcenturyskills238 .eduvision.tv)

Books

21st Century Skills: Rethinking How Students Learn edited by James Bellanca and Ron Brandt, foreword by Ken Kay (Solution Tree Press, 2010)
This is an excellent compendium of articles by real luminaries in the field of 21st century education. It is a good "reader" for educators on a variety of aspects of 21st century education.

21st Century Skills: Learning for Life in Our Times by Bernie Trilling and Charles Fadel (Jossey-Bass, 2009)
This is an excellent book on the Partnership for 21st Century Skills Framework for 21st Century Learning. It is written by two former board members of the Partnership.

The *Global Achievement Gap* by Tony Wagner (Basic Books, 2008)
This is an excellent book on the need for 21st century model of education. It would be particularly useful for a book group involving members of both the education and business communities.

APPENDIX 8

Business Community Outreach Toolkit

EdLeader21 Business Outreach Toolkit

Many of our EdLeader21 members have asked us to provide a toolkit to use for outreach to business leaders, concerning 21st century education.

The toolkit includes:

- Outreach letter to business community
- Draft agenda for meeting with business community
- Sample interactive exercise
- List of ways business community can contribute to 21st century education initiative
- Draft PowerPoint to use with business leaders (see separate PPT on the EdLeader21 community site)

We hope these tools provide you with a helpful starting point for your interaction with your business community.

Draft Letter to Business Community

Dear _____,

As you know, our school district has been very committed to helping each of our students prepare for 21st century life, citizenship, and work. Most recently, we have been engaged in strategic planning to identify the knowledge and skills each of our students should possess before they graduate so they can successfully confront challenges they are likely to face and even those that none of us can yet predict.

One element of this work is to better understand your needs as leaders in the workforce. We are asking members of the business community to help us better understand the knowledge and skills our young people need to succeed in current and future careers.

Specifically, we would like you to join us for a community conversation on the 21st century workforce. We'd like your input as we discuss the needs of today's businesses—we'll be considering questions such as:

- What skills are most important to you when you consider prospective employees?
- Which competencies do you most value in your current workforce?
- What competencies do you evaluate among current employees?
- What competencies do you see growing in importance over the next five years?

Your perspective on these questions will help us as we continue to improve the quality of education in our district to meet the demands of the 21st century. We also think you will enjoy engaging with us and other leaders who are interested in improving education in the [district/school]. An agenda for the meeting is attached.

We hope you will be able to join us.

Most appreciatively,

[signature]

Date: _____

Time: _____

Location: _____

Contact: _____

Draft Agenda

[Insert Date/Time/Location/Contact]

Business Community Input on 21st Century Education

I. Introductory remarks on [district/school] 21st century education initiative (insert speaker name)

II. Interactive exercise

III. PowerPoint Presentation—21st Century Education

IV. Q&A

V. Brainstorm—Business Involvement

VI. Next Steps

Interactive Exercise

Questions:

Q: What are the two to three biggest changes in society in the past 25 to 30 years?

A:

Q: List two to three skills that your students need to address the changes in society you described above.

A:

Q: In your view, how intentional and purposeful is our school district or other school districts you are familiar with about these outcomes?

A:

Involving the Business Community: Brainstorm

Following are models of business community involvement in local 21st century education initiatives. Use this list as a starting point for a brainstorm with meeting participants:

- In Tucson, one business—Raytheon—brings math and science teachers into the company for the summer to work on real company projects. Teachers are paid market rates for eight weeks and develop a deeper understanding of the challenges their students will be facing when they enter the workforce. One teacher observed after the eight-week stint: "It totally changed my perspective on the way I should teach math. I now want my students to have math challenges related to real world problems."

- The San Miguel High School (www.sanmiguelhigh.com) model in Chicago, Portland, and Tucson is a good example. At San Miguel, students attend class four days per week and spend one day a week employed by a local business in an internship setting. This strategy helps defray the operating costs of the school, but it also serves local businesses. Business owners, school leaders, and students all attest to how effective this model is at reinforcing academic knowledge and skills, as well as workforce preparedness.

- At the Met School in Providence, Rhode Island, every student is required to work in a business (although a few of the businesses are actually run by the school itself). The students spend half their week in jobs and the other half of the week in academic settings to help them meet their workplace obligations.

- The CORE Federal Credit Union in East Syracuse, New York, has partnered with the East Syracuse Minoa School District to operate a student run credit union in the high school. A drug company in the same district partnered to create a science course for junior and seniors on how to develop and get approved by the FDA a life-saving drug.

- A number of companies are able to financially contribute to innovative school district efforts. Some schools and districts have created foundations that businesses can contribute to and the money can be focused on targeted efforts like "mini-grants" to teachers who propose innovative ideas to advance 21st century education in their classroom or in the district.

APPENDIX 9

School Board Memo—Stakeholder Outreach

NOTE: This document is designed for your use as a district or school leader to communicate with your school board.

To: _____ Board of Education

From: _____, Superintendent

Re: District 21st Century Education Strategy

As you know, our district has been pursuing a 21st century education strategy. As we begin a new year, I thought it would be helpful to underscore our commitment to that strategy and to put it in context with other national and state education trends.

Current Accountability Trends

For the past decade, our system has operated in the context of traditional accountability systems fostered by No Child Left Behind, A.Y.P., and traditional assessment tools. This emphasis has been fueled by an understandable attempt to identify and to address low-performing students, schools, and districts.

This district has not shied away from such metrics. I am pleased that we have viewed them as a floor for performance, rather than a ceiling. In other words, while they are helpful at identifying a minimum level of performance, they do not define the true vision we have for student achievement.

21st Century Education

Our goal as educators, policymakers, and community members has been to prepare all our students for success in 21st century life, college, and work. This requires us to go beyond the minimum expectations established by our current systems of accountability.

What does this mean, exactly? In our district, we continue to value a rigorous academic curriculum, but we have also prioritized what we call the 4Cs [*insert your own definition/ vision here*] as a necessary set of competencies for 21st century students. They are:

- Critical thinking
- Communication
- Collaboration
- Creativity

(Add other skills your district has identified)

We are working to integrate these skills into all aspects of teaching and learning in the district. To date, we have taken the following steps to move this agenda forward:

- ***(insert actions districts have taken to date)***

- _____

- _____

National and State Developments

In light of major national trends affecting K–12 education, we are confident that the steps we have taken will position our district well. The Common Core State Standards represent a significant development in creating comparable state standards that are focused on college and career readiness. To date, standards have been developed for Mathematics and English Language Arts. These emphasize many 21st century competences such as critical thinking, communication, and collaboration.

Currently, we expect our state to *(insert the specific status of the Common Core State Standards in your state)*.

On a parallel path, two large assessment consortia are designing new assessments that intend to measure skills such as critical thinking and communication in addition to core academic content knowledge. These new assessments are expected to be in use by 2014–2015.

We also expect new federal policy developments as the Elementary and Secondary Education Act (ESEA) and the new NCLB come up for reauthorization. This legislation is likely to refine the nation's K–12 system to further boost its focus on college and career readiness.

We believe all of these trends suggest that the work we have begun in our district will position our students and our district for the changes we are likely to see in the next two to five years.

EdLeader21 *(NOTE: we offer this paragraph for your use in case you are a current EdLeader21 member)*

In order to stay ahead of the curve and align ourselves with the districts most committed to 21st century education, we have recently joined with a group of 20 districts whose leaders have committed to working together on these initiatives. EdLeader21 is a professional learning community created by superintendents and education leaders to be mutually supportive of this 21st century education work.

EdLeader21 was started by Ken Kay, the co-founder and past president of the *Partnership for 21st Century Skills*. He and his staff have spent the past eight years working on 21st century education policy, and they are now turning their attention to support 21st century districts like ours.

Our participation in the EdLeader21 PLC will provide us with:

- Access to resources and advice directly from the leaders of *21st Century Readiness*;
- Connections to other districts across the country similarly dedicated to the 21st century readiness of their students;
- Best practices in 21st century curriculum, instruction, and assessment;
- Networking with district leaders.

We are excited by our participation in this new initiative and will keep you updated on progress of the group. If you have any questions, please don't hesitate to ask.

Our District's Future Plans

The year 2011 will be a major year for advancing our plans for 21st century education in our district. Specifically, we plan to:

- *(insert plans for 2011)*
- _____
- _____

We are particularly pleased that our school board has taken such an active interest in our 21st century education work. We appreciate your support as we make the changes necessary to prepare our students for the very real challenges they will have ahead of them in college, work, and life. We look forward to our collaboration with you and the rest of the school community as we continue to move our vision for 21st century education forward.

APPENDIX 10

Student Outreach Toolkit

How to Use This Toolkit

We recommend adapting this toolkit for the following uses:

- Use as a discussion guide with specialized leadership teams—for example, equity discussions, dropout prevention, and so on
- Share it as background reading for general strategic planning sessions with your leadership team(s)
- Use as a planning tool with students to establish (or refine) the student role in your 21st century initiative

Introduction

As you lead your 21st century education initiative, students are the focus. Student success in 21st century life, work and career is the common denominator around which the work—curricula, assessments, instruction—is organized.

But the *role* of students in this work is also very important. This toolkit asks you **to consider whether and how students are involved in your efforts** and concludes with a tool to help you lead a series of in-depth planning sessions with students.

To help set the frame for thinking about student involvement, we recommend reading the *My Voice 6–12 Student National Report 2010*. It contains excellent data from the MyVoice survey on student aspirations, which was completed by more than 19,000 sixth to 12th graders nationally. Focusing on student self-confidence, desire to achieve and perceptions of school, the survey asked students to answer questions in categories such as belonging, sense of accomplishment, curiosity and creativity, leadership and responsibility, and confidence to take action.

While there are some positive trends noted in the survey, here are a few of the more concerning highlights for 21st century education leaders:

- Less than half of students think their teachers care about their problems and feelings, feel they are a valued member of the school community, or are proud of their school.
- Less than half of students enjoy being at school.
- Only slightly above one-third think their teachers make school an exciting place to learn. Roughly half think school is boring. At the same time, seven in 10 believe learning can be fun.
- Barely four in 10 feel their classes help them understand what is happening in their everyday lives.
- Approximately 25 percent of students are afraid to challenge themselves because they are afraid they might fail.
- Two-thirds of students reported confidence in their own leadership skills, but less than half feel they have a voice in decision making at school or believe that teachers are willing to learn from students.

The report can be found here: (http://www.qisa.org/publications/reports.jsp)

167

If even some of these attitudes are reflected in your school or district, the student's role in your 21st century initiative will be critical for your success. Below we provide some food for thought related to involving students in each of the seven steps.

Step 1: Your Vision and Students

We spend a lot of time in EdLeader21 discussing the importance of establishing your personal vision around 21st century education student outcomes, one that includes the 4Cs (critical thinking, communication, collaboration, and creativity). Without a personal commitment to this student-centered vision, it will be difficult to lead.

Students are not merely the recipients of your 21st century vision, however. They should help craft and implement it. If they are involved in authentic ways, they can be some of your most powerful implementation partners.

As you think about involving students in helping to refine your vision, it is important to understand where they are today. What are their attitudes about learning? How do they perceive their teachers, their classes, and their school environments? What are their expectations about what they need and want to learn? Do they see the school as a place that supports their aspirations for learning?

Engaging students around such questions is a logical step in the process of refining your vision. Also, consider these questions:

- Have you talked directly with students about 21st century education?
- How have the perceptions and attitudes of your students influenced your vision for 21st century education?
- Do students believe they play an active role in decision making in the school/district?
- Do all students perceive themselves as fellow implementers of the 21st century education initiative?

Step 2: Outreach with Students

We have included a student outreach tool in this document that can be customized and used for a series of in-depth discussion and planning sessions.

In general, we recommend reaching out to students consistently about your 21st century education initiative. Have them help define what "seat(s)" they want at the table, how they can help and what challenges they see.

As you consider how to reach out to your student population, reflect on these questions:

- In what ways are education leaders and students currently discussing and/or working together to implement 21st century education initiatives?
- What regular forums are in place to allow students to reflect on and participate in the transformation work you are pursuing?
- What barriers exist between students and education leaders that make such collaboration a challenge?
- Is your outreach strategy focused on all students, or a specific subset of students? (If it is a subset, such as the student council, is there a strategy for reaching out to the full student population?)

Step 3: Alignment and Students

Aligning your system to your 21st century education vision is a continual process. It is also one that is well-suited to student involvement.

Consider using specific columns from the MILE Guide tool (see the foldout included in this book and also downloadable from www.p21.org) in a collaborative activity with your students (see Part 2 in the tool below)—you might start by focusing on columns devoted to learning environments, student outcomes, partnering, or continuous improvement.

You can also work with your leadership team to analyze each column in the MILE Guide for opportunities to involve students. For each column, consider these questions:

- Have we provided students with meaningful opportunities for input on this area of our work?
- Do we know whether students share our perceptions about our progress in a particular area of work (for example, student outcomes, assessment, partnering)?

Step 4: Capacity Building and Students

There are two areas we recommend related to capacity building and the focus on students:

- Think about what capacity building makes sense for teachers around issues such as student engagement, student motivation, and student voice. It is perhaps an obvious point, but it is worth stating anyway: Students who are disengaged, who don't go to class, who drop out, or who perceive that educators are not responsive to their needs are not going to master the 4Cs. At the same time, all capacity building with teachers around these issues must be aligned with your 21st century education initiative; the goal should not be to simply reduce absentee or dropout rates (although these metrics are meaningful)—the goal is to engage students in mastering the knowledge and skills they need to succeed in the 21st century and to eliminate barriers to learning where they exist for student engagement.
- Consider involving students in professional development activities for teachers. Some districts, for example, ask students to lead PD sessions around new technologies. Students can also provide timely feedback on how well they think specific teaching practices are working. Involving students in professional learning communities might also be a targeted way to not only engage students but enhance capacity throughout the school or district.

Step 5: Students and 4Cs Curricula and Assessments

In Step 5, there are a number of opportunities to involve students. Consider each of these options (making sure they are aligned to your 21st century education vision):

- Portfolios: Using portfolios as a way to record and report student progress is an excellent way to involve students in evaluating and reflecting on the quality of their own work.
- Student-led conferences: Students understand quite a lot about what they know and need to know. It follows that giving them opportunities to lead conversations about their own progress will engage them more directly in the process of learning. For more information, this is a good overview: http://www.amle.org/Publications/WebExclusive/Portfolio/tabid/650/Default.aspx
- Student exhibitions and performances: There are many variations of this approach such as public exhibitions (to parents and the broader community), capstone projects, graduation portfolios/performances, and so on.
- Student expeditions: Students can be involved in selecting and planning expeditionary learning experiences that tie their classroom work to an authentic investigation.
- Student involvement in curricula and assessment design: Particularly when using backward-design processes (such as PBL or Understanding by Design), students can be directly involved in designing their own learning experiences, where appropriate.

Guiding students in curricula and assessment design can support student understanding of (and attention to) the 4Cs. Students can draft their own objectives for a 4Cs-focused activity or create their own essential questions to guide a lesson that integrates the 4Cs. Students can be asked to reflect on and revise assessments to make them more meaningful, rigorous, and reflective of 4Cs mastery.

Step 6: Students Supporting Teachers

When it comes to supporting the work of teachers in 4Cs instruction, students are natural allies. We tend to think about this step a little differently from Step 4, Build Professional Capacity. Here we ask you to consider the following:

- What roles and responsibilities can students assume for the day-to-day operations of a class, facility, or project? In East Syracuse-Minoa, students run a credit union in the school. They provide real time feedback to their teachers about the kinds of math and other instruction that would be most relevant to their work.
- Many EdLeader21 districts and schools have upper level students help instruct lower level students. The student-led instruction strengthens relationships across the school and supports deeper understanding (as well as communication and presentation skills).

Step 7: Students and Continuous Improvement and Innovation

Continuous improvement and innovation around 21st century education is a natural place to involve students. Students can assume meaningful roles alongside teachers and administrators to identify areas for improvement, innovation and progress tracking. As an education leader, consider:

- Do students model a continuous improvement and innovation mindset when it comes to their own work? In other words, are they comfortable receiving constructive criticism, making multiple revisions and pursuing innovative solutions in their work?
- Are students involved in supporting the continuous improvement and innovation work of educators?
- Do students perceive that their involvement matters when it comes to improvement and innovation in the school or district?
- How are student perceptions about improvement and innovation (in their own work and also the work of the school/district) being gathered and tracked?

Student Involvement Tool

This set of four activities can be produced as individual meetings on different days or as a single half-day summit with your students. These activities are designed to involve students in your work as a 21st century education leader.

For each session, invite as many students as you can comfortably facilitate in a group conversation. You might want to have your leadership team help you repeat these activities with different segments of students so that you can reach a larger percentage of your student population.

Audience
- These activities work best with high school students and upper-level middle school students.
- With some modifications, Parts 1 and 3 could be appropriate for younger students.

Objectives

- Strengthen student understanding of and involvement in the 21st century education initiative
- Create consensus among students about high-priority learning outcomes and implementation activities

Outcomes

- Part 1: List of the learning outcomes students believe are high priorities
- Part 2: Collect student feedback on their learning environments
- Part 3: Gather student input on the integration of the 4Cs in specific lessons/assignments
- Part 4: Collect student recommendations for improvement and innovation

Time/Format

- Four one-hour sessions or one half-day meeting
- We suggest 1–3 education leaders per 35 to 70 students

Part 1

Description

- [10 minutes] Provide some introductory remarks about the district's vision for 21st century education (10 minutes); avoid discussing specific skills, if possible.
- [15 minutes] Conduct the "three question" exercise. Ask each question one at a time and allow students to respond to each one before moving on to the next:
  1. What three skills do you consider to be most important to your future success in 21st century life and work? (Have students call out their responses; write these on a flip chart or project them on a screen.)
  2. What do you see about the requirements of life and work today that make these skills so important? (Have students share their thoughts—prompt them to share what they know about jobs/careers among peers and parents.)
  3. Are you presented with opportunities to learn these skills in your classes? Do you think the school/district is helping you learn these skills? (Ask for show of hands for "yes," "sometimes," and "no.")
- [15 minutes] Ask students to share examples of learning experiences they have had (in a class or outside school) that have struck them as valuable learning experiences. Ask them to describe what made the experience helpful to them. If possible, make links to practices that are present in the school/district that appear to be working well (for example, hands-on, fun, relevant, and so on).
- [15 minutes] Ask students to identify the top three (or five) skills that they would prioritize for their school or district. In addition, have them identify which of these skills they want to focus on improving for themselves (as individuals). Explain that this list will be considered as part of your vision process for 21st century education in the school/district.
- [5 minutes] Synthesize what you have heard. Explain how this discussion relates to next steps in reaching out to students (see next activity).

Part 2: Learning Environments/MILE Guide Discussion

Description

- Prior to this session, review the "Learning Environments" column in the MILE Guide (insert link). Develop a one-page list of learning environment changes you think would be valuable to your 21st century education initiative.

- [15 minutes] Start the session by asking students what they think about their current learning environment and how it helps (or hinders) 21st century learning. Use questions that are appropriate for your students, but consider ones such as these (write down student responses):
  - When you enjoy learning something new, what are you doing? What are your surroundings like, who are you with and where are you?
  - Describe the actual setting: Is it inside? Outside? Noisy? Quiet?
  - Is there a place in the school where you learn most comfortably? What makes that place different from other places?
  - Are there places in the school where you feel it is very difficult to focus on learning? Describe/discuss.
- [10 minutes] Share your thoughts as an education leader on the learning environment challenges in the school/district you are hoping to address over a period of time (for example, more time and space for project-based learning, more space for collaborative teams to work together, technology improvements for assignments, grades, and so on).
- [30 minutes] Share your list of possible improvements to the learning environment with students. Ask students to work in small groups to:
  - Document their reactions to the list (Do they agree with the list? Disagree with anything?)
  - Review and rank the list in priority order.
  - Add new suggestions to the list.
- [15 minutes] Small groups report out to the larger group. Document their responses.
- [5 minutes] Synthesize what you have heard. Explain how this discussion relates to next steps in reaching out to students (see next activity).

Part 3: Student Design Activity

Description

- Prior to this session, work with your leadership team to identify two to three current performance tasks or lessons slated for revision/refinement in the coming year, with associated samples of student work produced if possible. Recruit teachers to help facilitate who can present the lessons and describe the associated student work samples.
- [5 minutes] Introduce the exercise as a design activity where students can share what they think about the 4Cs in daily academic work.
- [15 minutes] Have a teacher explain the lesson, how it was presented and how the student work was produced. Ideally, the teacher will also discuss his/her perception of whether the 4Cs were integrated in the lesson's design and/or the student work sample.
- [30 minutes] Have teachers help facilitate small group discussions among the students, where they are considering questions such as:
  - Where do I see the 4Cs in this lesson plan and/or student work?
  - If I could change anything about the lesson to make sure the 4Cs were more of a focus, what would I change?
- [10 minutes] Small groups report to large group; facilitate discussion around responses; offer final thoughts and synthesis.

Part 4: Innovation and Improvement with Students

Description

- Organize students into four groups focused on each of the 4Cs: critical thinking, communication, collaboration, and creativity.
- [10 minutes] Briefly review your current understanding of how each of the 4Cs is being integrated into the school or district's systems of education. Explain that today's session

will involve students in this work by making their own recommendations for improvement and innovation.

- [30 minutes] Ask participants in each small group to brainstorm ideas for improving the integration of their "C" throughout the school or district (for example, have them consider questions such as "If our school were a better collaborative environment, what might that look like?") For each area of improvement identified, ask students to list any challenges/barriers along with innovations that might address these challenges.
- [15 minutes] Small groups report to large group.
- [5 minutes] Synthesize what you have heard and describe what next steps will follow as part of your 21st century education initiative.

APPENDIX 11

21st Century Problem Solving Task (PST)

NORTH SALEM CENTRAL SCHOOL DISTRICT SCIENCE
5/16/11

Course(s): Middle School Science

Teacher(s): Hugh Main

NY Science, Technology, Math, Education Learning Standards:

Standard 1: Analysis, Inquiry, and Design

Students will use mathematical analysis, scientific inquiry, and engineering design, as appropriate, to pose questions, seek answers, and develop solutions.

Standard 4: Science

Students will understand and apply scientific concepts, principles, and theories pertaining to the physical setting and living environment and recognize the historical development of ideas in science.

Standard 5: Technology

Students will apply technological knowledge and skills to design, construct, use, and evaluate products and systems to satisfy human and environmental needs.

NY English/Language Arts Learning Standards:

Standard 1: Language for Information and Understanding

Students will listen, speak, read, and write for information and understanding. As listeners and readers, students will collect data, facts, and ideas; discover relationships, concepts, and generalizations; and use knowledge generated from oral, written, and electronically produced texts. As speakers and writers, they will use oral and written language that follows the accepted conventions of the English language to acquire, interpret, apply, and transmit information.

Title of This Problem Solving Task (PST):

CREATURE CAPTURE

Unit Questions Relevant to This Task:

How do the external structures of an organism help it find, get, and consume food in its home habitat?

How does a scientist design a tool or apparatus to do a specific job in a scientific investigation?

Contact Information: Mike Hibbard, Assistant Superintendent, North Salem Central School District, North Salem, NY 10560 hibbardm@northsalem.k12.ny.us

Step 1 of the Cycle of Learning: Task, Audience, and Purpose

Your Role: You are a scientist finding new species of animals, catching them for study, and then releasing them unharmed back into their home habitat.

The Task: You will imagine and create a newly discovered creature and its planet earth home habitat and invent a way to catch it for humane, scientific study. Then you will create a three-minute video presenting your creature, your invention to catch it, and what you plan to learn about that creature. (The creature may have been discovered in a terrestrial habitat, a water habitat, or a combination of the two.)

Your Audience: Viewers of a "YouTube-like" video clip about your adventures in finding, catching, studying, and releasing your "creature."

(These flip videos will be posted on our class's collaborative software.)

How You Intend to Affect Your Audience: You intend to teach your viewers about the creature and how a scientist works humanely to study living organisms.

Background for this Project: There are many areas of the earth on land and in the water that have not been explored. When a new area of the earth is explored, scientists often find organisms that have never been seen or scientifically studied. The adventure of these explorations and the findings of humane, scientific investigations are often made available to the public on TV and the Internet.

Assessment of Your Work: Review the rubric that will be used by you and your teacher to assess your work, and pay attention to any goals you have set for yourself to improve your work. (See note about the rubric at the end of this Problem Solving Task.)

Step 2 of the Cycle of Learning: Accessing and Acquiring Information
You may use your science notebook and textbooks.

INDIVIDUAL WORK

Imagine a terrestrial or water habitat on planet Earth that has never been explored. Use all of your senses to imagine what it looks like, smells like, feels like, sounds like, and so on. (creative thinking)

Make **sketches** of this habitat. (creative thinking)

Make notes on the sketch **explaining** this habitat. (critical thinking)

Use your imagination to create a creature that lives in this habitat. **Draw** this creature in the habitat you have sketched and show the following about the creature: (creative thinking)

- Details of the external structures of this creature's body to show how the creature finds, gets, and consumes food—label your drawing
- Details of the external structures of this creature's body to show how it defends itself and escapes from enemies and predators—label your drawing
- Other details of the external structures of this creature's body to show how it is adapted to survive and flourish in this habitat—label your drawing
- Include dimensions to show the size of the creature and its parts

Use your imagination to improve your drawing of the habitat to include the following: (creative and critical thinking)

- Details about what the creature eats—label your drawing
- Details about what eats the creature—label your drawing
- Details about the non-living parts of the creature's habitat—label your drawing

GROUP WORK

Share and discuss the drawing of your creature and its habitat with two other students. (critical thinking)

Ask each other questions to help each person improve their creatures and habitats. (critical thinking)

INDIVIDUAL WORK

Make improvements to your drawings of the creature and its habitat. (critical thinking)

Due: _____

Step 3 of the Cycle of Learning: Processing Information

Answer these questions about your creature: (critical thinking)

- How do you know where the creature is on the food web in the habitat you created?
- How are the external body structures of your creature well suited for finding, getting, and consuming its food? What is that food?
- How are the external body structures of your creature well suited for defending itself and escaping from its predators and enemies? What are the creature's predators and enemies?
- How are the other external body structures of your creature well suited for surviving and flourishing in its habitat?

Sketch an invention to humanely catch this creature. Your invention must show the following: (creative thinking)

- The use of at least three simple machines (pulley, ramp, lever, wheel and axle, screw, wedge)
- How the invention is designed to work in the creature's habitat
- What materials are used to make the invention
- How the invention works to catch the creature in a way so it will not be injured
- The dimensions of the whole invention and its important parts

Make a list of at least seven things you want to find out about the creature when you catch it. Explain why you want to learn these seven things about the creature. You must respect the creature and treat it humanely. (creative thinking)

Due: _____

Step 4 of the Cycle of Learning: Producing Product

INDIVIDUAL WORK

Make a plan for a three-minute video clip that will present the following: (critical thinking)

- Your description of your creature and how its external body structures help it to survive and flourish in its habitat—you may use your drawings to support your verbal descriptions.
- Your description of your invention to catch the creature and how this invention is designed to catch this particular creature in its home habitat.
- What you want to find out about the creature when you catch it. Remember that you cannot harm the creature in any way and must release it back into its home habitat.

GROUP WORK

Work with a partner to use a video camera to make a three-minute video for each of you. (critical thinking)

Due: _____

Step 5 of the Cycle of Learning: Disseminating Product

Post your video clip on the class's collaborative software. (critical thinking)

Review and comment on at least three other videos made by your classmates. (critical thinking)

Due: _____

Steps 6, 7, and 8 of the Cycle of Learning: Self-Assessment, Self-Evaluation, and Self-Regulation (goal setting)

At the conclusion of your work on this task, write a reflection of your work according to the following:

INDIVIDUAL WORK

Assess your work using the rubric. (critical thinking)

Identify your specific strengths and weaknesses on this task. (critical thinking)

Think about how you used creative thinking process during your work on this task. How were these creative thinking processes important to your work on this task? (critical thinking)

Take an overall view of your work and list three goals that you should consider setting for yourself so that you will improve. (creative thinking)

Now, **select** one "doable" goal for yourself and **create** a simple action plan that you will pay attention to so that your work improves. (critical and creative thinking)

Due: _____

CREATURE CAPTURE
Problem Solving Task (PST).

A form of this analytic rubric will be used to assess all PSTs in all subjects and grade levels so that we can collect longitudinal, student-level data on skills and concepts.

APPENDIX 12

Upper Arlington City School District Capstone Project Rubric

21st Century Skills Criterion	Beginning 2–3	Approaching 4–5	Meeting 6–7	Succeeding 8–9
COMPLEX THINKING The learner:				
Identifies an essential question.	The learner identifies an essential question that is unclear or does not have a question at all.	The learner identifies an essential question that requires minimal personal, academic, or community exploration.	The learner identifies a precise essential question that requires personal, academic, or community exploration.	The learner identifies a precise essential question that requires personal, academic, and community exploration.
Proposes and develops a project that explores the essential question.	The learner is unable to propose, or develop a project.	The learner is able to propose and develop a project, but the project lacks exploration of the essential question.	The learner is able to propose and develop a project that explores the essential question.	The learner is able to propose and develop a project that deeply explores the essential question or explores the essential question in multiple ways.
Collects, assesses, and analyzes relevant information that is incorporated into the project.	The learner collects minimal information.	The learner collects information that is not relevant to the essential question or does not include enough information in the project.	The learner collects and analyzes information that is relevant to the essential question and incorporates it into the project. Data may be analyzed from sources such as academic research and field experiences.	The learner collects and analyzes diverse and extensive information that is relevant to the essential question and incorporates it seamlessly into the project. Data may be analyzed from sources such as academic research and field experiences.
Reflects critically on the learning experience. (Final Project Reflection)	The learner reflects on the learning experiences (includes only restatement of steps).	The learner reflects on the learning experiences, but reflection does not fully address strengths and weaknesses of the learner's process and project.	The learner reflects on the learning experiences and addresses strengths and weaknesses of the learner's process and project.	The learner reflects on the learning experiences realistically and with rich detail. Fully addresses the strengths and weaknesses of the learner's process and project.
CREATIVE THINKING AND INNOVATION The learner:				
Demonstrates creative thinking and/or innovation within the Capstone project.	The project may demonstrate imagination, but fails to create an idea, service, or product.	The project creates an idea, service, or product.	The project creates an idea, service, or product.	The project creates an idea, service, and/or product that reflects imagination, a fresh perspective, or a new approach.

(continued)

21st Century Skills Criterion	Beginning 2–3	Approaching 4–5	Meeting 6–7	Succeeding 8–9
Takes risks and pushes beyond his/her comfort level through her or his Capstone project.	The project is not challenging and doesn't require the learner to take a risk.	The project does not demonstrate the learner's willingness to engage in unfamiliar situations or tackle challenging problems.	The project demonstrates the learner's willingness to engage in unfamiliar situations or tackle challenging problems without obvious solutions.	The project demonstrates the learner's willingness to engage in unfamiliar situations or tackle challenging problems without obvious solutions.
Demonstrates willingness to adapt and benefit from errors and setbacks.	The learner becomes hindered by setbacks and/or errors in process or is unwilling to address them.	The learner acknowledges setbacks and/or errors in process.	The learner addresses setbacks and/or errors and shows how he/she corrected them.	The learner articulates setbacks and/or errors in process or planning, and uses it as a learning opportunity.
GLOBAL CITIZENSHIP **The learner:**				
Identifies and acts upon a connection between the essential question and a community need.	The learner identifies a connection between the essential question and a community need but does not follow through with the service component.	The learner identifies and acts upon a connection between the essential question and a community need.	The learner identifies and acts upon a purposeful connection between the essential question and a community need.	The learner identifies and acts upon a purposeful and closely aligned connection between the essential question and a community need.
Uses time, and/or talent to incorporate service into the Capstone project to make a positive difference in the community.	The learner demonstrates minimal involvement to facilitate change or student does not demonstrate an awareness of personal responsibility to community.	The learner demonstrates involvement to facilitate change but changes affect a situation without urgent or pressing needs.	The learner demonstrates involvement to facilitate change; new and unique benefits are realized; however, the learner's actions did not address the urgency or scope of a community need.	The learner demonstrates active and ongoing involvement to facilitate change, help alleviate a suffering, solve a problem, meet a need, or address an issue that addresses the urgency or scope of a community need.
SELF-DIRECTION **The learner:**				
Shows evidence of goal-setting.	The learner rarely participates in goal setting.	The learner sets goals that may not be challenging or achievable, and frequently needs guidance.	The learner sets achievable, challenging goals with some guidance.	The learner independently sets achievable, challenging goals.

21st Century Skills Criterion	Beginning 2–3	Approaching 4–5	Meeting 6–7	Succeeding 8–9
Takes initiative with the project, shows evidence of working through problems, and seeks help when appropriate.	The learner relies heavily on teachers for motivation and direction with the project.	The learner relies on teachers for motivation and direction with the project.	The learner takes primary control of project, occasionally needing direction from teachers.	The learner takes full control of the project, works through problems and seeks help when needed.
Monitors his or her own progress and uses time productively.	The learner rarely monitors progress and uses little time for the project.	The learner sometimes monitors progress and inconsistently uses time for the project.	The learner monitors progress and uses time productively.	The learner consistently monitors progress, and provides evidence of using time productively.
COMMUNICATION The learner:				
Uses communication skills to convey message present in the portfolio/product.	The portfolio/product does not include enough evidence to convey a message.	The selection of inappropriate media, a lack of attention to details, and/or disorganization detract from the portfolio's message.	The selection of appropriate media, attention to detail, and organization convey intended message in portfolio.	The selection of a variety of media, rich attention to detail, and organization seamlessly convey intended message in the portfolio.
Uses appropriate format and applicable technology to promote and communicate findings in the portfolio/product.	Findings are not effectively communicated.	Format and/or technology may not be ideally suited to promote and communicate findings.	Uses appropriate format and applicable technology is used to promote and communicate findings.	Format and technology maximize impact of findings.
Shows competence in the application of writing conventions in the portfolio/product.	Poor application of writing conventions in the mechanical aspects of language.	Inconsistent application of writing conventions in the mechanical aspects of language.	Writing conventions show competence in the mechanical aspects of language.	Writing conventions show obvious care in the mechanical aspects of language.
COLLABORATION The learner:				
Shows evidence of seeking expertise in the development of the Capstone project and to answer the essential question.	The learner shows little to no evidence of seeking expertise in the development of the Capstone Project.	The learner shows some evidence of seeking expertise in the development of the Capstone Project.	The learner shows evidence of seeking expertise in the development of the Capstone project.	The learner shows evidence of ongoing consultation and incorporates expert advice and suggestions to improve the project.

APPENDIX 13

High Tech High Project Tuning Protocol

Norms

- Hard on the content, soft on the people
- Be kind, helpful, and specific
- Share the air (or "step up, step back")

Protocol:

1. **Overview** (5 min): Presenter gives an *overview of the work* and explains what *goals* he/she had in mind when designing the project. It may be helpful for the presenter to put the project into the broader context of what is happening in his/her classroom or school. Participants then have an opportunity to *quietly look at "the work"* (e.g., project handout, student work, etc.). Finally, the presenter shares a dilemma by *framing a question* for the critical friends group to address during the discussion.

2. **Clarifying Questions** (5 min): Critical friends ask *clarifying* questions of the presenter. Clarifying questions have brief, factual answers and are intended to help the person asking the question develop a deeper understanding of the dilemma. An example of a clarifying question is "How will groups be chosen for this activity?"

3. **Probing Questions** (5 min): Critical friends ask *probing* questions of the presenter. Probing questions help the presenter expand his/her thinking about the dilemma. However, probing questions should not be "advice in disguise," such as "Have you considered . . . ?" An example of a probing question is "What evidence will you gather to determine the extent to which the goals of your project were met?"

4. **Discussion** (15 min): The presenter reframes the question if necessary and then physically steps back from the group. The group discusses the dilemma and attempts to provide insight on the question raised by the presenter.

   - **Positive feedback:** It is helpful to begin with positive feedback, such as "What strengths do we see in the project design?"
   - **Opportunities for growth:** Next, the group takes a more critical analysis of the work, using the question proposed by the presenter to frame the discussion. For example, "What isn't the presenter considering?" or "I wonder what would happen if . . . ."

   The presenter is not allowed to speak during the discussion but should listen and take notes. It is a good idea for the presenter to physically sit outside of the circle and for the group to close in the circle without the presenter. *Resist the urge to speak directly to the presenter.*

5. **Response** (5 min): The presenter has the opportunity to respond to the discussion. It is not necessary to respond point by point to what others said. The presenter may share what struck him/her and what next steps might be taken as a result of the ideas generated by the discussion.

6. **Debrief** (5 min): The facilitator leads a conversation about the group's observation of the project tuning process. One mark of a good facilitator is his or her ability to lead a good debrief.

Questions posed to the group might include:

- Did we have a good question? How well did we stick to the question?
- To what extent was this process helpful for the presenter? Did our probing questions really push his/her thinking? Did our ideas from the discussion provide insight into possible next steps?
- Was there a moment when the conversation made a turn for the better? Was there any point where we went off track?
- How did we do embodying our norms? (e.g., "hard on the content, soft on the people," "step up/step back," etc.)
- *Resist the urge to turn the debrief back to a discussion of the dilemma.*

Total time: Approximately 30 minutes

Tips for facilitation:

- ***Work with the presenter to frame a good question beforehand.*** Meet beforehand to discuss the dilemma and wordsmith a question that is open ended and not easily solved. Write the question on the whiteboard so that it is visible during the entire conversation.
- ***Stick to the time for each section.*** Use a timer to keep track of time or ask a volunteer to help.
- ***Don't be afraid to keep the group focused on the protocol.*** If a probing question is asked during clarifying questions, gently ask the participant to write it down and wait until you have moved on to that point in the conversation.
- ***Redirect the conversation when necessary*** (*without unnecessarily monopolizing airtime*). If the discussion jumps straight into responding to the dilemma question before sharing positive feedback, make sure to take time to celebrate the thinking or work first.
- ***Resist the urge to skip the debrief.*** The debrief is a crucial way to deconstruct the conversation and improve the quality of our dialogue with colleagues over time. Value this part of the process by honoring the time dedicated to it.
- ***Be courageous and confident.*** Strong facilitation is the key to having successful dialogue about our work and is appreciated by everyone in the group. If it helps to literally read each step to the group, by all means do so. And remember to "cowboy up" or take full ownership of your important role as facilitator!

Index